POLITICS, POSITION, AND POWER

POLITICS, POSITION, AND POWER

From the Positive
to the Regulatory State

FOURTH EDITION

HAROLD SEIDMAN
ROBERT GILMOUR

New York   Oxford
OXFORD UNIVERSITY PRESS
1986

OXFORD UNIVERSITY PRESS

Oxford   New York   Toronto
Delhi   Bombay   Calcutta   Madras   Karachi
Petaling Jaya   Singapore   Hong Kong   Tokyo
Nairobi   Dar es Salaam   Cape Town
Melbourne   Auckland

and associated companies in
Beirut   Berlin   Ibadan   Nicosia

Published by Oxford University Press, Inc.,
200 Madison Avenue, New York, New York 10016

Oxford is a registered trademark of Oxford University Press.

LIBRARY OF CONGRESS CATALOGING-IN-PUBLICATION DATA
Seidman, Harold.
   Politics, position, and power.
   Bibliography: p.
   Includes index.
   1. United States—Politics and government.
I. Gilmour, Robert S. (Robert Scott), 1940-
II. Title.
JK421.S44   1986   353   85-20514
ISBN 0-19-503991-2

Printing (last digit): 9 8 7 6 5 4 3 2

Printed in the United States of America

For our special friends and former students

BARBARA CRAIG, JENNA DORN, AND MARY MC CAFFERY

Preface
to the Fourth Edition

This book was begun more than fifteen years ago as something of a personal memoir by one who had observed the interplay of federal politics, position, and power for nearly a quarter-century as a Washington insider. Since then, though much remains the same, much has changed. Some of the trends just becoming visible in 1970 have continued apace. Directly provided governmental services have continued to decline in importance. Government by proxy and "third parties," directed by contract provisions and regulations and stimulated by transfer payments and tax subsidies—once barely considered important—have become primary means of doing the government's business in the 1980s.

The extension of national governmental power by indirection has changed the traditional understanding of federal organization. A serious treatment of organization issues must now pay closer attention to the results of procedures as well as to those of structural variety. As if to point this up, the Reagan administrative strategy may usher in the most far-reaching organizational changes since Roosevelt's New Deal, yet it is cast in terms of "budgetary controls" and "regulatory relief."

Of crucial importance to these developments have been the changes in and expanded roles of federal courts. Robert Gilmour has been brought into a collaborative effort for this edition to trace the emergence of the judiciary as a prominent participant in the administrative system and to assess its place in the regulatory state. Both authors have reviewed the entire manuscript, which is completely revised.

We are much indebted to those who gave freely of their suggestions for the new manuscript, particularly to our colleague David B. Walker, whose comments were invaluable to a revised look at the rapidly changing world of intergovernmental administration. We also appreciate encouragement and helpful advice from Barbara H. Craig, Mary McCaffery, Nel Minow, Alan B. Morrison, and Ronald C. Moe. We wish to thank Jean Gosselin and Helen Hauschild for typing assistance at a critical moment when the hours were long and time was short. Kara Gilmour put the pages together. Harold Seidman is especially indebted to the Brookings Institution for its warm and helpful hospitality to a "guest scholar."

Washington, D.C.   H.S.
Storrs, Connecticut   R.G.
August 1985

Contents

I

THE POLITICS
OF GOVERNMENT
ORGANIZATION

I

Introduction

ORTHODOX THEORY: CULT OF EFFICIENCY

Reorganization has become almost a religion in Washington. It has its symbol in the organization chart, Old Testament in the Hoover Commission reports, high priesthood in the Office of Management and Budget, and society for the propagation of the faith in sundry groups such as the Citizens Committee for Government Reorganization.[1]

Reorganization is deemed synonymous with reform and reform with progress. Periodic reorganizations are prescribed if for no other purpose than to purify the bureaucratic blood and to prevent stagnation. Opposition to reorganization is evil and attributable, according to Hoover, to the "gang up, log-rolling tactics of the bureaus and their organized pressure groups."[2]

The history of administrative reorganization in the twentieth

1. The name of the Bureau of the Budget was changed by Reorganization Plan No. 2 of 1970 to Office of Management and Budget. The Citizens Committee for Government Reorganization headed by James Roche, board chairman of General Motors, was organized to promote President Nixon's reorganization proposals. It was modeled on the Citizens Committee for the Hoover Report.

2. Herbert C. Hoover, *The Memoirs of Herbert Hoover: The Cabinet and the Presidency, 1920–1933,* The Macmillan Co., 1952, pp. 282–83.

century has been called "a history of rhetoric." Its orthodox credos are closely linked to religious and moral movements.[3]

For the true believer, reorganization can produce miracles. To restore to health an ailing social security system, the National Commission on Social Security Reform prescribes separating the Social Security Administration from the Department of Health and Human Services and establishing it as an independent agency. The President's Commission on Industrial Competitiveness proposes a Department of Trade as one remedy for the United States' growing trade deficit. The myth persists that we can resolve deep-seated and intractable issues of substance by reorganizing. The conviction that the weakness of one organization can be cured by creating another remains a widely held article of faith. Rare indeed is the commission or presidential task force with the self-restraint to forgo recommending an organizational answer to the problems it cannot solve.

Disciples of scientific management are convinced that there is a best way to organize the executive branch, which can be determined by objective analysis. Senate sponsors of legislation to create a new Hoover Commission believe that it is possible "to develop a blueprint for better government in the United States."[4]

The organizational commandments laid down by the first Hoover Commission constitute the hard core of the fundamentalist dogma.[5] The devils to be exorcised are overlapping and duplication, and confused or broken lines of authority and responsibility. Entry into the "nirvana of economy and efficiency" can be obtained only by strict adherence to sound principles of executive branch organization. Of these the most essential are the grouping of executive branch agencies as nearly as possible

3. James G. March and Johan P. Olson, "Organizing Political Life: What Administrative Reorganization Tells Us about Government," *American Political Science Review*, No. 77, 1983. Also see Ronald C. Moe, *The Hoover Commissions Revisited*, Westview Press, 1982.

4. S. 35, 99th Congress, 1st Session, January 3, 1985.

5. The Commission on Organization of the Executive Branch of the Government, "General Management of the Executive Branch," a report to the Congress, February 1949.

by major purposes so that "by placing related functions cheek-by-jowl the overlaps can be eliminated, and of even greater importance coordinated policies can be developed"; and the establishment of a clear line of command and supervision from the president down through department heads to every employee, with no subordinate possessing authority independent of that of a superior.

The commission's report on "General Management of the Executive Branch" represents the most categorical formulation of the orthodox or classic organization doctrine derived largely from business administration and identified with the scientific management movement during the early decades of this century and the writings of Gulick, Urwick, Fayol, and Mooney. Government organization is seen primarily as a technological problem calling for "scientific" analysis and the application of fundamental organizational principles: a single rather than a collegiate executive; limited span of control; unity of command a person cannot serve two masters); a clear distinction between line and staff; and authority commensurate with responsibility.

For Luther Gulick, "work division is the foundation of organization; indeed, the reason for organization."[6] In his view, "the theory of organization, therefore, has to do with the structure of coordination imposed upon the work division units of an enterprise."[7] "Organization as a way of coordination requires the establishment of a system of authority whereby the central purpose or objective of an enterprise is translated into reality through the combined efforts of many specialists, each working in his own field at a particular time and place."[8] Organization structure should be designed to create homogeneous combinations of work units on the basis of major purpose, process, clientele or materiel, or place.

6. Luther Gulick, "Notes on the Theory of Organization" in *Papers on the Science of Administration*, Luther Gulick and L. Urwick, eds., Institute of Public Administration, 1937, p. 3.

7. Ibid.

8. Ibid., pp. 6–7.

Orthodox theory is preoccupied with the anatomy of government organization and is concerned primarily with arrangements
to ensure that (1) each function is assigned to its appropriate
niche within the government structure; (2) component parts of
the executive branch are properly related and articulated; and
(3) authorities and responsibilities are clearly assigned.

The important caveats and qualifications emphasized by Gulick
in his "Notes on the Theory of Organization," particularly coordination "by the dominance of an idea," the futility of seeking
a single most effective system of departmentalism, the need to
recognize that "organization is a living dynamic entity," the limitations of command and the role of leadership, have been largely
ignored by both his critics and his disciples.[9] Such reservations
were not entertained by the Hoover Commission, whose report
echoes, often in identical language, the organization "truths"
first expounded by Herbert Hoover in the 1920s and early
1930s.[10]

Central to the understanding of orthodox theory are certain
basic assumptions about the nature and purpose of organization
and administration. The starting point is a rigid interpretation
of the constitutional doctrine of separation of powers. Public
administration is viewed as being concerned almost exclusively
with the executive branch, "where the work of government is
done,"[11] with only grudging recognition given to the roles of the
legislative and judicial branches in the administrative process.
Preoccupation with the executive branch is coupled with an ill-
concealed distrust of politics and politicians as the natural enemies of efficiency. Politics and administration are regarded as
two heterogeneous functions, "the combination of which cannot
be undertaken within the structure of administration without

9. Ibid., see pp. 6, 31, 37.

10. Library of Congress, *A Compilation of Basic Information on the Reorganization of the Executive Branch of the Government of the United States,
1912–1947*, Washington, D.C., 1947, pp. 1214–23.

11. Luther Gulick, "Science, Values and Public Administration," in *Papers on
the Science of Administration*, Luther Gulick and L. Urwick, eds., Institute of
Public Administration, 1937, p. 191.

producing inefficiency."[12] Execution of policy is a matter for professional, technically trained, nonpartisan career managers, not amateurs. "Efficiency" is held to be the single overriding goal of organization and administration. On this point, Gulick is unequivocal. In his words: "Efficiency is thus axiom number one in the value scale of administration. This brings administration into apparent conflict with the value scale of politics, whether we use that term in its scientific or popular sense."[13]

Since World War II, public administration theologians have become increasingly disenchanted with the orthodox dogmas. Skeptics and agnostics have dismissed the "principles of organization" as mere "proverbs" and exercises in "architectonics." Heretics have challenged the politics-administration dichotomy, notably Paul Appleby, who classified administration as "the eighth political process"[14]; a few have even gone so far as to question whether efficiency and economy are "the ultimate good."[15] Behavioral scientists have attacked the assumptions about human behavior that they believe are implicit in the orthodox theology, namely, that authority flows from the top and employees are inert instruments performing the tasks assigned to them by their superiors. They condemn orthodox organization theory for almost completely ignoring the interplay of individual personality and interpersonal relations, informal groups, interorganization conflict, and the decision process in their conception of formal structure.[16] The literature of dissent is vast and growing.[17]

12. Gulick, "Notes on the Theory of Organization," p. 10.

13. Gulick, "Science, Values and Public Administration," p. 192.

14. Paul H. Appleby, *Policy and Administration,* University of Alabama Press, 1949.

15. Dwight Waldo, *The Administrative State,* The Ronald Press Co., 1948, Chapter 10.

16. William G. Scott, *Organization Theory: A Behavioral Analysis for Management,* Richard D. Irwin, Inc., 1967, p. 109.

17. For critiques of orthodox organization theory, see Warren G. Bennis, *Changing Organizations: Essays on the Development and Evolution of Human Organization,* McGraw-Hill Book Co., 1966; Bertram M. Gross, *The Managing of Organizations: The Administrative Struggle,* Vol. I, The Free

Overlapping and duplication are seen as a positive good rather than an evil by conservative organizations such as the Heritage Foundation. In its *Mandate for Leadership II, Continuing the Conservative Revolution,* the foundation asserts categorically that overlapping and duplication are "necessary" because they create "conflict and competition which in turn produces information which is useful for the political executive in controlling policy implementation."[18]

The Reagan administration condemns the orthodox theories as being too narrowly concerned with structure. Processes and procedures are considered to provide more effective means for establishing presidential control and reorganizing the executive branch.

Some of the criticism represents a form of intellectual exhibitionism, which in its own way is as incomplete and parochial as the orthodox dogmas it condemns. Although the observations on the discrepancies between the orthodox dogmas and the facts of organizational life and behavior are often pertinent and valid, these do not add up to a rational well-articulated set of working hypotheses for dealing with the present and emerging problems of federal organization. It is easy to pick out the flaws in the concepts of unity of command, straight lines of authority and accountability, and organization by major purpose; it is far more difficult to develop acceptable alternatives.

Press of Glencoe, 1964; Daniel Katz and Robert L. Kahn, *The Social Psychology of Organization,* John Wiley & Sons, Inc., 1966; Douglas McGregor, *The Human Side of Enterprise,* McGraw-Hill Book Co., 1960; John D. Millett, *Organization for the Public Service,* D. Van Nostrand Co., Inc., 1966; William G. Scott, *Organization Theory: A Behavioral Analysis for Management,* Richard D. Irwin, Inc., 1967; Herbert A. Simon, *Administrative Behavior,* 2nd ed., The Macmillan Co., 1957; Herbert A. Simon, Donald W. Smithburg, and Victor A. Thompson, *Public Administration,* Alfred A. Knopf, 1950; Dwight Waldo, *The Administrative State,* The Ronald Press Co., 1948; Stephen J. Wayne, *The Legislative Presidency,* Harper & Row, 1978; Herbert Kaufman, "Reflections on Administrative Reorganization," in *Setting National Priorities: The 1978 Budget,* The Brookings Institution, 1977.

18. Stuart M. Butler, Michael Senera, and W. Bruce Weinrod, *Mandate for Leadership II, Continuing the Conservative Revolution,* The Heritage Foundation, 1984, p. 531.

Warren Bennis is one of the few who has had the courage to make the attempt, with his proposal that organizations of the future be "adaptive, rapidly changing temporary systems." These will be organized around problems to be solved. The function of the executive will be to coordinate various project groups. Bennis emphasized that "people will be differentiated not vertically according to rank and role but flexibly according to skill and professional training."[19] But whatever its potential for private institutions or intradepartmental organization, the Bennis approach does not and was not intended to provide a grand design for executive branch structure.

Flawed and imperfect as they may be, the orthodox "principles" remain the only simple, readily understood, and comprehensive set of guidelines available to the president and the Congress for resolving problems of executive branch structure. Individual members of Congress can relate them to their own experience within the Congress or in outside organizations. They have the virtue of clarity, a virtue often scorned by the newer orthodoxies, especially the behavioralists and social psychologists, who tend to write for each other in an arcane language that is unintelligible to the lay public. Dwight Waldo was correct when he concluded that

> . . . not only is the classical theory still today the formal working theory of large numbers of persons technically concerned with administrative-organizational matters, both in the public and private spheres, but I expect it will be around a long, long time. This is not necessarily because it is "true," though I should say it has much truth in it, both descriptively and prescriptively; that is to say, both as a description of organizations as we find them in our society and as a prescription for achieving the goals of these organizations "efficiently." *But in any event a social theory widely held by the actors has a self-confirming tendency and the classical theory is now deeply ingrained in our culture.*[20]

19. Bennis, *Changing Organizations*, p. 12.

20. Italics supplied, Dwight Waldo, "Organization Theory: An Elephantine Problem," *Public Administration Review*, Vol. 21, No. 4, 1961.

Publication of the *Papers on the Science of Administration* in 1937 may have marked the "high noon of orthodoxy in public administration theory in the United States,"[21] but someone apparently stopped the clock.

Herbert Hoover's fundamentalist dogmas were enshrined by the Reorganization Act of 1949 (Chapter 9, Title 5 of the U.S. Code) as the lawful objectives of government reorganization. The president was directed from time to time to "examine the organization of all agencies" and to "determine what changes in such organization are necessary" to carry out the following purposes, which were declared by the Congress to be "the policy of the United States":

> (1) to promote the better execution of the laws, the more effective management of the executive branch of the government and of its agencies and functions, and the expeditious administration of the public business;
>
> (2) to reduce expenditures and promote economy to the fullest extent consistent with the efficient operation of the government;
>
> (3) to increase the efficiency of the operations of the government to the fullest extent practicable;
>
> (4) to group, coordinate, and consolidate agencies and functions of the government, as nearly as may be, according to major purposes;
>
> (5) to reduce the number of agencies by consolidating those having similar functions under a single head, and to abolish such agencies or functions thereof as may not be necessary for the efficient conduct of the government; and
>
> (6) to eliminate overlapping and duplication of effort.

Necessary though it may have been to establish a legal foundation for an extraordinary grant of powers to the president, the long-run effects of freezing the purposes and principles of organization into law have been most unfortunate. They have inhibited creative thinking about federal structure and the development of fresh approaches adapted to the needs of our times. They have

21. Wallace S. Sayre, "Premises of Public Administration: Past and Emerging," *Public Administration Review,* Vol. 18, No. 2, 1958.

sometimes provided the right answers, but often for the wrong reasons. Organizers in the Office of Management and Budget and elsewhere were compelled to develop and justify reorganization proposals within a narrow set of legal constraints. The talents required were more those of a Talmudic scholar than those of a sophisticated political scientist. Witness the tag paragraph found in most reorganization plans to conform with the provision that the president "specify the reduction of expenditure which it is probable will be brought about by the taking effect of the plan" (itemized so far as practicable). A typical example is to be found in the message transmitting Reorganization Plan No. 1 of 1962 to create a Department of Urban Affairs and Housing:

> Although the taking effect of the reorganizations provided for in the reorganization plan will not in itself result in immediate savings, the improvements achieved in administration will in the future allow the performance of necessary services at greater savings than present operations would permit. An itemization of these savings in advance of experience is not practicable.

By its overemphasis on observance of prescribed rituals, the statute has contributed materially to congressional failure, both in hearings and floor debates, to expose to public view the basic political questions posed by reorganization proposals. The more knowledgeable members of the Congress and the executive branch are generally quite well aware what these issues are—and they seldom have anything to do with economy and efficiency. But the real issues are openly discussed, if at all, by indirection and in a language that only insiders can understand. Occasionally these issues do surface, as in the case of Reorganization Plan No. 3 of 1967 to reorganize the government of the District of Columbia, in which the major points of difference were more concerned with the power and prerogatives of the House District Committee than with the strengths and weaknesses of a commission form of government.

Congress has insisted on more, not less, orthodoxy. Congressman John Erlenborn was highly critical of the lack of specificity in presidential reorganization messages concerning which of the purposes of the reorganization statute would be fulfilled by a plan. On Erlenborn's initiative, the House in 1968 adopted an amendment to the statute requiring the president to specify, one by one, which of the enumerated purposes would be accomplished by each plan and to estimate the "aggregate" reduction of expenditures that would result. When the budget director promised, in 1969, that in the future the requested data would be supplied, the House agreed to extend the reorganization authority without including the Erlenborn amendment.[22]

President Carter proposed that the Reorganization Act of 1949 be amended to eliminate the requirement for detailed savings estimates. Instead, the president would provide information on the improvements in management efficiency and delivery of services that would be realized as the result of reorganization. Carter's suggested language was included in the 1977 statute extending presidential reorganization authority, but the Congress retained the requirement that the president "estimate any reduction or increase in expenditures (itemized so far as practicable)."

The theoretical assumptions underlying the orthodox dogmas have been transformed into unassailable eternal verities. Executive branch spokespersons are loath to challenge established "truths" for fear of excommunication. Custom, culture, and role all require OMB officials openly to profess their faith in "economy and efficiency" as the prime goals of organization and reorganization, with emphasis on economy. When Congressman Erlenborn commented that "it would be refreshing sometimes if your messages would say there are no economies," Deputy Budget Director Phillip S. Hughes replied: "It might be refreshing but it might also be disastrous."[23]

22. *Congressional Record*, April 22, 1968, pp. H3057–61, House Report No. 91–80, 91st Congress, 1st Session.

23. Committee on Government Operations, House of Representatives, hearing on H. R. 15688 to extend the reorganization statute, March 13, 1968, p. 13.

Almost every president from Theodore Roosevelt to Ronald Reagan, with the notable exception of Franklin D. Roosevelt, has at one time or another found it necessary to defend reorganization as a means of reducing expenditures. The Nixon administration sought to downplay economy as a major purpose of the president's proposed restructuring of the executive departments, but Roy L. Ash, chairman of Nixon's Advisory Council on Executive Organization, testified that the reorganization to create Departments of Community Development, Economic Affairs, Human Resources and Natural Resources would produce savings of $5 billion.[24] President Reagan estimated that his proposed reorganization of the department of energy would produce savings of $250 million over a three-year period, an estimate challenged by the General Accounting Office.[25]

"We have to get over the notion that the purpose of reorganization is economy," FDR told Louis Brownlow and Luther Gulick in 1936. "I had that out with Al Smith in New York. . . . The reason for reorganization is good management."[26] The overwhelming weight of empirical evidence supports the Roosevelt view that reorganizations do not save money. Indeed, it is now recognized that the measurable and immeasurable costs may be substantial because reorganizations are disruptive and often require transfers and geographical relocation of personnel, physical facilities, and records.[27]

Of the reorganization plans transmitted to the Congress from 1949 through 1980, only six—Reorganization Plan No. 3 of 1952, which would have ended Senate confirmation of postmasters; Reorganization Plan No. 1 of 1965, reorganizing the Bureau of

24. Committee on Governmental Operations, Legislation and Military Operations, Subcommittee, Hearings on Reorganization of Executive Departments (Part I—overview), June and July 1971, p. 239.

25. Comptroller General of the United States, "Analysis of Energy Reorganization Savings Estimates and Plans," August 2, 1982.

26. Richard Polenberg, *Reorganizing Roosevelt's Government,* Harvard University Press, 1966, p. 81.

27. Comptroller General of the United States, "Implementation: The Missing Link in Planning Reorganizations," March 20, 1981.

Customs; Reorganization Plan No. 5 of 1966, abolishing the National Capital Regional Planning Council; Reorganization Plan No. 1 of 1973, abolishing the Office of Science and Technology, the Office of Emergency Preparedness, the National Aeronautics and Space Council, and other components of the Executive Office of the President; Reorganization Plan No. 1 of 1977, reorganizing the Executive Office of the President; and Reorganization Plan No. 3 of 1978, consolidating emergency preparedness functions—were supported by precise dollar estimates of savings. Plan No. 3 of 1952 was disapproved by the Congress. Granted executive branch reluctance to offer savings estimates that can be later used in evidence by the appropriations committees, it is clear that the failure to itemize expenditure reductions reflects the reality that economies are produced by curtailing services and abolishing bureaus, not by reorganizing.

Emphasis is placed more on form than on substance. Frequently, studies of executive branch structure degenerate into sterile box-shuffling and another version of the numbers game. This approach is typified by President Reagan's Private Sector Survey on Cost Control (Grace Commission) citing the following as reasons for reorganization:

> —Both the Office of Management and Budget and the General Services Administration have procurement policy responsibilities.
> —OMB, GSA and the Department of Commerce have government-wide responsibility for automated data processing.
> —The nation's non-military public lands are administered by four agencies in two departments.
> —Federal responsibilities involving water resources development are spread over five different federal entities.[28]

One White House task force on government organization found that if you pushed this approach to its logical conclusion, you would end up with a Department of Foreign Affairs, a Depart-

28. Office of Management and Budget, *Management of the United States Government,* fiscal year 1986, p. 8.

ment of Domestic Affairs, and a Department of Defense, and even then all overlaps would not be eliminated.

Established organization doctrine, with its emphasis on structural mechanics, manifests incomplete understanding of our constitutional system, institutional behavior, and the tactical and strategic uses of organization structure, processes, and procedures as an instrument of politics, position, and power. Orthodox theories applied to the central issues of executive branch organization are not so much wrong as they are largely irrelevant.

Executive branch structure is, in fact, a microcosm of our society. Inevitably it reflects the values, conflicts, and competing forces to be found in a pluralistic society. The ideal of a neatly symmetrical, frictionless organization structure is a dangerous illusion. We would do well to heed Dean Acheson's sage advice that "organization—or reorganization in government, can often be a trap for the unwary. The relationships involved in the division of labor and responsibility are far more subtle and complex than the little boxes which the graph drawers put on paper with their perpendicular and horizontal connecting lines."[29]

EXECUTIVE BRANCH ORGANIZATION: THEORY VS. PRACTICE

Organizational arrangements are not neutral. We do not organize in a vacuum. Organization is one way of expressing national commitment, influencing program direction, and ordering priorities. Organizational arrangements tend to give some interests and perspectives more effective access to those with decision-making authority, whether they be in the Congress or in the executive branch. As Richard Neustadt has pointed out: "In political government, the means can matter quite as much as the ends; they often matter more."[30]

29. Dean Acheson, "Thoughts about Thoughts in High Places," *The New York Times Magazine,* October 11, 1959.

30. Richard E. Neustadt, *Presidential Power—The Politics of Leadership,* John Wiley & Sons, Inc., 1960, p. 47.

Institutional location and environment, administrative arrangements, type of organization, processes, and procedures can raise significant political questions concerning the distribution and balance of power between the executive branch, Congress and the Judiciary; the federal government and state and local governments; states and cities; the federal government and organized interest groups, particularly the principal beneficiaries of federal programs; and finally, among the components of the executive establishment itself, including the president's relationship to the departments and the bureaucracy.

If our democratic system is to be responsive to the needs of *all* our people, organization structure and administrative arrangements need to so balance the competing interests within given program areas that none is immune to public control and capable of excluding less powerful segments of our society from effective participation in the system and an equitable share of its benefits. Failure to maintain this balance has contributed to the present malaise.

President Eisenhower, in his farewell address to the nation, warned against "the acquisition of unwarranted influence, whether sought or unsought, by the military-industrial complex." His warning has gone unheeded and private companies are now in the position of significantly influencing health and energy as well as defense policies. "Privatization" of most public services is an established goal of the Reagan administration.

The political implications of organization structure were recognized as early as 1789, when the states endeavored to control the extension of federal power by limiting the creation of executive departments. In 1849 the bill to establish the Department of Interior was opposed because "it meant the further extension of federal authority to the detriment of the states."[31] Reform and modernization of the army were blocked during the nineteenth century because it was feared that a nationalized army would

31. Lloyd M. Short, *The Development of National Administrative Organization in the United States*, The Johns Hopkins Press, 1923, p. 89.

diminish state power and control of the national guard.[32] President Reagan condemns the Department of Education as a symbol of intrusion into matters that should be left to state and local control.

Application of "economy and efficiency" as the criteria for government organization can produce serious distortions, if political and environmental factors are ignored. It led the first Hoover Commission to proceed from the indisputable finding that the Farmers Home Administration's functions duplicated and overlapped those of the Farm Credit Administration and the Agricultural Extension Service to the seemingly logical conclusion that the Farmers Home Administration ought to be liquidated and its functions divided between its two competitors. The conclusion was obviously faulty to anyone in the least familiar with the histories of the Farm Credit Administration and the Extension Service as creatures of the American Farm Bureau Federation and the most conservative elements in the agricultural community. The Farm Bureau was proud of its role in scuttling the Rural Resettlement Administration and Farm Security Administration, the immediate predecessors of the FHA.[33] If there were ever a case of letting the goats loose in the cabbage patch, this was it. The FHA was created to furnish special assistance to farmers who constitute marginal risks and possess little poliical clout. Commissioners Acheson, Pollock, and Rowe observed in their dissent that "the purpose of the Farmers Home Administration is to make 'good' tenant farmers out of 'poor' tenant farmers, and not to restrict credit to 'good' tenant farmers who can probably obtain credit from other sources."[34]

32. Stephen Skowronek, *Building a New American State,* Cambridge University Press, 1982, Chapter 4.

33. For excellent analyses of the role played by the American Farm Bureau Federations in organizational politics, see Sidney Baldwin, *Poverty and Politics,* University of North Carolina Press, 1968; Philip Selznick, *TVA and the Grass Roots,* University of California Press, 1949.

34. The Commission on Organization of the Executive Branch of the Government, "Federal Business Enterprises," A Report to the Congress, March 1949, p. 102.

Powerful groups in the commercial banking, research, and educational communities favor overlapping and duplication for somewhat different reasons than the Heritage Foundation. Five federal agencies regulate depository institutions—three for commercial banks, one for savings and loans, and one for federal credit unions. The American Bankers Association for the past thirty-five years has successfully blocked efforts to consolidate supervision and examination of commercial banks in a single federal agency. One-time chairman of the federal reserve board, Marriner S. Eccles, described bankers' opposition to reorganization as "based on the old principle of divide and conquer."[35] As noted by the Senate Committee on Governmental Affairs: "the ability of commercial banks to select their bank regulators . . . permits and encourages a regulated bank to select the regulatory agency most inclined toward the type of activity engaged in by the bank."[36]

Overlapping and duplication among federal agencies making research grants do not alarm scientists and educators. On the contrary, diversity in support is held essential to maximize the opportunities for obtaining federal funds and to minimize the dangers of federal control. The Committee on Science and Public Policy of the National Academy of Sciences strongly endorsed a "plural system," which has many roots for its authority "and many alternative administrative means of solving a given problem."[37]

Assignment of administrative jurisdiction can be a key factor in determining program direction and ultimate success or failure. Each agency has its own culture and internal set of loyalties and values that are likely to guide its actions and influence its policies. A number of satellites grow up and around and outside

35. Marriner S. Eccles, *Beckoning Frontiers*, Alfred A. Knopf, 1951, p. 268.

36. Committee on Governmental Affairs, U.S. Senate, *Principal Recommendations and Findings of the Study on Federal Regulation*, Committee Print, 96th Congress, 1st Session, September 1979, p. 50.

37. National Academy of Science, "Federal Support of Basic Research in Institutions of Higher Learning," Washington, D.C., 1964.

the institution and develop a mutual dependence. Private bureaucracies in Washington now almost completely parallel the
public bureaucracies in those program areas in which the federal government contracts for services, regulates private enterprise, or provides some form of financial assistance.

Shared loyalties and outlook knit together the institutional
fabric. They are the foundation of those intangibles that make
for institutional morale and pride. Without them, functions
could not be decentralized and delegated with the confidence
that policies will be administered consistently and uniformly.
But because people believe what they are doing is important and
the way they have been taught to do it right, they are slow to
accept change. Institutional responses are highly predictable,
particularly to new ideas that conflict with institutional values
and may pose a potential threat to organizational power and
survival. Knowledgeable Budget Bureau officials once estimated
that agency position on any major policy issue can be forecast
with nearly 100 percent accuracy, regardless of the administration in power.

There is an ever-present danger that innovative programs that
challenge accepted norms, demand new skills and approaches,
and create conflicts with agency constituencies will be assimilated
into the "system" and their purpose muffled or distorted. One
way to kill a program is to house it in a hostile or unsympathetic
environment.

The Congress tacked a rider to the 1953 RFC Liquidation Act
authorizing the president to designate an agency to make loans
to public bodies for the construction or acquisition of public
facilities.[38] Budget Bureau staff recommended that the Housing
and Home Finance Agency be designated because its mission was
most closely related to urban and community development, but
the then budget director preferred Treasury "because it wouldn't
make the loans." Treasury obviously would be less susceptible
to pressure from state capitols and city halls and could be ex-

38. Reconstruction Finance Corporation Liquidation Act, 1953 (40 U.S.C.
459).

pected to apply strict banking criteria in reviewing loan applications. The final solution was not to make any designation. The
Congress solved the problem by enacting legislation vesting program responsibility in the Housing and Home Finance Agency.

In their zeal to construct neat and uncluttered organization
charts, professional reorganizers and reorganization commissions
tend to downgrade, when they do not wholly ignore, environmental influences. Certainly, the poverty program would have
been different—whether better or worse depends on one's point
of view—if, as many advocated, responsibility at the outset had
been given either to the Department of Health, Education, and
Welfare or to the choice of the big-city mayors, the Department
of Housing and Urban Development. Creation of a new agency
is likely to present fewer problems than reform of an old one
and enables the president and the Congress to finesse competing
jurisdictional claims. Compromise arrangements are possible,
and program seedlings under some circumstances can take root
and grow within established departments if protected during the
developmental period by a self-contained, relatively autonomous
status.

Adherence to the principle of organization according to major
purposes provides no automatic answers. Herbert Hoover would
have resolved the problem by having the Congress define "major
purpose" and then leaving it to the president to reorganize executive agencies in accordance with their purposes as set forth in
law.[39] Granted that Hoover made this proposal in 1924, when
federal programs were simple by today's standards, it is still in-
credibly naïve.

Federal programs are likely to have multiple purposes. Disagreements as to priorities among diverse and sometimes conflicting objectives are a major source of current controversies.
Is the major purpose of the food stamp program to dispose of
surplus agricultural commodities or to feed the poor? Is mass
transportation a transportation or an urban development program? Are school lunches a nutrition or an education function?

39. Library of Congress, *A Compilation of Basic Information*, p. 1216.

Should the federal water pollution control program have health protection as its principal objective, or should it be concerned more broadly with the development of water resources?

Major purposes cannot be ascertained by scientific or economic analysis. Determination of major purpose represents a value judgment, and a transitory one at that. Thus, President Nixon could argue in 1971 that the Department of Transportation "is now organized around methods and not around purposes," although transportation was assumed to be a major purpose when the department was established in 1966.[40] What is the secondary purpose for one, is a major purpose for another. To quote Miles's law: "Where one stands depends on where one sits."[41] Major purposes are not constants but variables shifting with the ebb and tide of our national needs and aspirations.

Debates about organizational type also may mask basic differences over strategy and objectives. Orthodox theory postulates that all federal agencies, with the possible exception of the independent regulatory commissions, be grouped under a limited number of single-headed executive departments and consequently ignores the other possible forms of organization. Except for the regulatory commissions and government corporations, the Hoover Commissions and President's Committee on Administrative Management took little interest in the typology of organization—a disinterest shared by most students of public administration.

The significance of institutional type has been underrated. In Part II we will endeavor to identify and analyze the rich variety of organizational types that have been developed within our constitutional system: executive departments, independent agencies, assorted commissions, boards, councils, authorities, wholly owned corporations, mixed-ownership corporations, "cap-

40. *Papers Relating to the President's Departmental Reorganization Program,* pp. 14–15.

41. Attributed to Rufus Miles, formerly assistant secretary for administration, Department of Health, Education and Welfare.

tive" corporations, institutes, government-sponsored enterprises, foundations, establishments, conferences, intergovernmental bodies, compact agencies, and a wide variety of interagency and advisory committees. The differences among these institutional types are more a matter of convention and tradition than of legal prescriptions. Yet some have acquired a "mystique" that can profoundly influence public attitudes and executive and congressional behavior for good or ill. Institutional type can be crucial in determining who controls—the president, the Congress, or the so-called special interests.

Institutional type, for example, was a major issue when Congress authorized the Marshall Plan. Republicans wanted the plan administered by a government corporation because by definition it would be more "businesslike."[42] A corporation would also make it more difficult for the State Department to meddle in the European recovery program. The compromise was to establish an independent agency outside the State Department and to authorize creation of a corporation, if and when needed.

Scientists devised a new government institution named a "foundation" when existing institutions would not support their postwar grand design of "science governed by scientists and paid for by the public."[43] The ostensible aim was to duplicate within the executive branch a typical university structure. Effective control over the proposed National Science Foundation was to be vested in a twenty-four-member National Science Board to be appointed by the president after giving due consideration to nominations submitted to him by the National Academy of Sciences, the Association of Land Grant Colleges and Universities, the National Association of State Universities, the Association of American Colleges, or other scientific or educational institutions. The board would be required to meet only once a year. It would, in turn, select biennially from among its members

42. House Select Committee on Foreign Aid, "Preliminary Report Eleven—Comparative Analysis of Suggested Plans of Foreign Aid," November 22, 1947.

43. Daniel S. Greenberg, *The Politics of Pure Science,* The New American Library, Inc., 1967, p. 107.

a nine-member executive committee that would meet six times a year and exercise the board's powers. The foundation's full-time executive officer, a director, would be appointed by the executive committee unless the board chose to make the appointment itself.

A bill incorporating the scientists' proposal was enacted by the Congress but drew a strongly worded veto from President Truman.[44] Truman recognized that "the proposed National Science Foundation would be divorced from control by the people to an extent that implies a distinct lack of faith in the democratic process" and would deprive the president "of effective means for discharging his constitutional responsibility." He took particular exception to the provisions insulating the director from the president by two layers of part-time boards and warned that "if the principles of this bill were extended throughout the government, the result would be utter chaos." Truman's views only partially prevailed. The Congress deleted the most objectionable feature by making the foundation director a presidential appointee but retained the basic structure desired by the science establishment.

Institutional advisory bodies often are as much of a potential threat to executive power as the National Science Foundation proposal, but they are far more difficult to combat. Creation of the National Security Council properly could be construed as a ploy by a Republican Congress to circumscribe a Democratic president's powers in areas in which he was constitutionally supreme. Not only did the Congress designate those officials who were to "advise" the president in the exercise of his constitutional powers, but it also included the curious provision that other secretaries and undersecretaries of executive departments could be appointed council members only with the advice and consent of the Senate. Advice is potentially one of the most powerful weapons in the administrative arsenal.

Up to now we have been discussing mainly the strategic implications of executive branch organization. But power relation-

44. Harry S. Truman, Memorandum of Disapproval of the National Foundation Bill (S.526), August 6, 1947.

ships are not always involved in organization decisions. The president, the Congress, and even outside groups may use organizational means to obtain some immediate tactical advantage.

Herbert Hoover himself was not above using organization for tactical purposes. He claimed that he was "a much misunderstood man on this question of committees and commissions." According to Hoover,

> There is no more dangerous citizen than the person with a gift of gab, a crusading complex and a determination "to pass a law" as the antidote for all human ills. The most effective diversion of such an individual to constructive action and the greatest silencer on earth for foolishness is to associate him on research committee with a few persons who have a passion for truth, especially if they pay their own expenses. I can now disclose the secret that I created a dozen committees for that precise purpose.[45]

Presidents have continued to employ committees and commissions to capture and contain the opposition. Committees and commissions can also offer an immediate, visible response in times of national catastrophe, such as the assassinations of President Kennedy and Senator Kennedy or the Watts riot. Study commissions are employed as a kind of tranquilizer to quiet public and congressional agitation about such matters as pesticides, crime, and public scandals. Attention, it is hoped, will be diverted to other issues by the time the commissions report. A poem appearing in *Punch* some years ago put it very well:

> If you're pestered by critics and hounded by faction
> To take some precipitate, positive action,
> The proper procedure, to take my advice, is
> Appoint a commission and stave off the crisis.[46]

Commissions may be employed to defuse sensitive political issues and to compel the opposition to share responsibility for

45. Hoover, *The Memoirs of Herbert Hoover,* p. 281.

46. Geoffrey Parsons, "Royal Commission," *Punch,* August 24, 1955. © *Punch,* London.

unpopular actions. President Reagan has resorted to bipartisan commissions to find the answers to such difficult questions as the funding of the Social Security program, the siting of the MX missile, Latin American policy, and the deficit.

Interagency committees sometimes create an impression of neatness and order within the executive establishments, even when a president cannot or will not resolve the basic differences and jurisdictional conflicts. If differences surface publicly and become embarrassing to the administration, the president's reflex reaction is to appoint another committee or to reorganize existing committees. The pressure is almost overwhelming "to do something" that might do some good and certainly will do no harm. No president can confess that he is stumped by a problem.

Pressure for immediate, tangible answers to highly complex problems may result in reorganizations. President Eisenhower's first response to the national trauma caused by the Soviet Union's successful launching of Sputnik in 1957 was to appoint a special assistant to the president for Science and Technology and to transfer the Science Advisory Committee from the Office of Defense Mobilization to the White House office. Creation of the Department of Energy in 1977 was a response to the energy crisis caused by the 1973 oil embargo.

Reorganization may provide a convenient means to dump an unwanted official, particularly one with strong congressional or constituency ties. The maneuver is not always successful, as was seen with Secretary of State Dean Rusk's abortive plan to abolish the Department's Bureau of Security and Consular Affairs. Abba Schwartz's version of this incident is highly colored, but there is no question that Secretary Rusk's timing was influenced by his desire to shift Schwartz from the bureau directorship to another post. The Bureau of Security and Consular Affairs was the brainchild of Senator Joseph McCarthy, and the Bureau of the Budget had targeted it for reorganization long before Schwartz arrived on the scene.

Use of reorganization to bypass a troublesome committee or

subcommittee chairman in the Congress can also be hazardous when it does not succeed. Transfer of civil defense activities from the Office of Civil and Defense Mobilization to the secretary of defense in 1961 was expected as an incidental benefit to remove the shelter program from the jurisdiction of an unfriendly appropriations subcommittee chairman.[47] Albert Thomas, however, had the power to retain jurisdiction, to the great discomfiture of the civil defense officials.

Organization choices may be motivated almost entirely by a desire to exclude billions in expenditures from budget tabulations. The 1969 budget was the first to include trust funds and mixed-ownership government corporations in the administrative budget. President Eisenhower's 1955 proposal to create a Federal Highway Corporation for financing the construction of the National System of Interstate Highways was deliberately designed to keep the authorized payments of $25 billion out of the budget totals. The proposal was later abandoned when it was found that establishment of a highway trust fund could serve the same purpose. Conversion of the Federal National Mortgage Association from a wholly owned to a mixed-ownership government corporation in 1954 also had as its principal appeal the appearance of a multibillion-dollar budget reduction. When the ground rules were changed with the 1969 budget, legislation was enacted to turn the Federal National Mortgage Association into a "government sponsored private corporation" to keep its expenditures out of the budget.

To escape arbitrary and unrealistic ceilings on civilian personnel, federal agencies have been compelled to utilize so-called nonprofit intermediaries to carry out programs mandated by congressional enactments. The Labor Department's organizational choices were limited when it was allowed forty-nine full-time positions in order to design and implement a complex multimillion-dollar youth employment and training program.[48]

47. Executive Order No. 10952, July 20, 1961.

48. National Academy of Public Administration, *Government Sponsored Non-Profits,* November 1978.

A new name and a new look may be necessary to save a program with little political appeal, particularly one that congressional supporters find difficult to sell to their constituents. At times reorganization supplies the rationale needed by members of Congress to explain their vote. The frequent reorganization and renaming of the foreign aid agency reflect efforts to bolster congressional support and to demonstrate presidential interest rather than to introduce new policies and improve management. There have been no fewer than eight successive foreign aid agencies—from the Economic Cooperation Administration in 1948 to the Agency for International Development in 1961—until 1961 an average of a new agency less than every two years.[49]

For many, organization is a symbol. Federal councils on aging, mental retardation, physical fitness, consumers, and the arts, for example, are more important as evidence of national concern than as molders of federal policies.

Some seek the creation of new federal agencies or reorganizations to enhance their status in the outside community. Their successful demand for an independent National Archives disassociated from the government's "housekeeper," the General Services Administration, in part stemmed from the archivists' desire to improve their standing as a scholarly profession. Several years ago the firemen's association sought Bureau of the Budget support for a Federal Fire Academy. Although the academy was not perceived at the time as fulfilling any identifiable federal need, it would place firemen on a par with policemen, who had a federal "sponsor" in the Federal Bureau of Investigation, and thus strengthen their bargaining position in dealing with mayors and city councils.[50]

The Congress is highly skilled in the tactical uses of organization and reorganization. If you come from a district with a jet airport, establishment of an Office of Noise Abatement in the

49. Michael K. O'Leary, *The Politics of American Foreign Aid*, Atherton Press, 1967, p. 117.

50. A National Academy for Fire Prevention and Control was authorized by the Federal Fire Prevention and Control Act of 1974.

Department of Transportation has tremendous voter appeal. Even though there is doubt that a separate office could do much to reduce noise levels, at least it offers a place where members of Congress can send constituent complaints. While the administration was able to defeat an amendment to the Department of Transportation bill to create such an office on the valid grounds that aircraft noise was a research and development and traffic control problem, Secretary Alan Boyd later found it expedient to create an Office of Noise Abatement by administrative action. Members of Congress are more susceptible to pressures from sectional, economic, and professional interests than is the president, and these often become translated into organizational responses.

Economy and efficiency are demonstrably not the prime purposes of public administration. Even such a single-minded and zealous advocate of "efficiency" and "competency" in government as former President Jimmy Carter has acknowledged that

> Nowhere in the Constitution of the United States, or the Declaration of Independence, or the Bill of Rights, or the Emancipation Proclamation, or the Old Testament or the New Testament, do you find the words "economy" or "efficiency." Not that these words are unimportant. But you discover other words like honesty, integrity, fairness, liberty, justice, patriotism, compassion, love—and many others which describe what human beings ought to be. These are the same words which describe what a government of human beings ought to be.[51]

Supreme Court Justice Louis D. Brandeis emphasized that the "doctrine of separation of powers was adopted, not to promote efficiency but to preclude the exercise of arbitrary power."[52] The basic issues of federal organization and administration relate to power: who shall control it and to what ends?

The questions that now urgently confront us are as old as the

51. Jimmy Carter, *Why Not the Best?* Bantam Books, 1976, p. 132.

52. Cited in Lewis Meriam and Lawrence F. Schmeckebier, *Reorganization of the National Government,* The Brookings Institution, 1939, p. 132.

Republic itself. How can we maintain a government structure and administrative system that reconcile liberty with justice and institutional and personal freedom with the general welfare?

What we are observing today are the strains and tensions inevitably produced by revolutionary changes in the federal government's role and its relationships to other levels of government, institutions of higher learning and other nonprofit institutions, and the private sector. Dividing lines have become increasingly blurred. It is no longer easy to determine where federal responsibilities end and those of state and local governments and private institutions begin. These changes began with the "New Deal" in the 1930s, but the most dramatic developments have occurred since 1961 and have peaked in the 1980s.

The Hoover Commission solution of "placing related functions cheek-by-jowl" so that "the overlaps can be eliminated, and of even greater importance coordinated policies can be developed" it not workable when you must combine the major purpose programs—health, education, manpower, housing—to alleviate the social and economic ills of a specific region, city, or neighborhood. We could regionalize the executive branch, as some have proposed, but members of Congress, governors, and mayors would be unwilling to accept such a concentration of power in any one federal agency. Such modest proposals as those to establish HUD "urban expediters" in key cities are viewed with suspicion. If one official could control the flow of federal funds into a region, that person would be in a position to dictate state and local policies.

Senator Robert Kennedy posed the fundamental question when he asked: "Do the agencies of Government have the will and determination and ability to form and carry out programs which cut across departmental lines, which are tailored to no administrative convenience but the overriding need to get things done?"[53]

Straight lines of authority and accountability cannot be estab-

53. Senate Committee on Government Operations, hearings on "Federal Role in Urban Affairs," 1967, p. 40.

lished in a nonhierarchical system. The federal government is compelled to rely increasingly for accomplishment of its goals on cooperation by nonfederal institutions that are not legally responsible to the president and subject to his direction. Federal powers are limited to those agreed on and enumerated in negotiated contracts. Success of the foreign aid, energy, space and defense research and development programs depends almost as much on performance by contractors as on performance by the government's own employees. About 80 percent of federal expenditures for research and development are made through nonfederal institutions, under either grants or contracts.[54] The government, since 1948, has caused to be organized and wholly financed a host of university- and industry-sponsored research centers and so-called nonprofit corporations for the sole purpose of providing services to the government. Legally, these are private organizations, but many, such as the Institute for Defense Analyses, Aerospace Corporation, Lincoln Laboratory, Public/ Private ventures, and Oak Ridge National Laboratory, have more in common with traditional government agencies than with private institutions. In dealing with such institutions, regulations are the primary instruments of control.

Fundamentalist dogmas were developed for a different universe—for the federal government as it existed in the 1920s and early 1930s. It was a time when Herbert Hoover could be told by one of his predecessors as secretary of commerce that the "job would not require more than two hours of work a day. Indeed that was all the time that former secretaries devoted to it. Putting the fish to bed at night and turning on the lights around the coast were possibly the major concepts of the office."[55] In the 1920s the Department of Commerce was engaged in what were then typical government services: collection and dissemination of statistics, preparation of charts and maps, operation of lighthouses, issuance of patents, and licensing, inspection, and

54. U.S. Bureau of the Budget, "Report to the President on Contracting for Research and Development," April 30, 1962.

55. Hoover, *The Memoirs of Herbert Hoover*, p. 42.

regulation. Except for public works projects, timber, grazing and mineral rights, agricultural loans, and land permits, the federal government had little power to confer or withhold economic benefits. Federal intervention in the economy was indirect through economic regulation, the tariff, fiscal, monetary, and credit policies.

Government and business regarded each other as adversaries, not as potential partners. Theodore Roosevelt argued that establishment of a Department of Commerce would represent "an advance toward dealing with and exercising supervision over the whole subject of the great corporations doing an interstate business."[56] Roosevelt considered that the secretary's first duty would be to regulate commerce and industry, rather than to act as a spokesperson for their interests.

In the years since World War II, the federal table has become crowded with dependents, each clamoring to be fed and demanding the biggest slice of pie. Whereas before the federal government was tolerated as a nuisance or at best a marginal customer, major industries, universities, and other institutions have now come to depend on federal funds for survival.

In contrast with the situation in World War II, and even that during the Korean War, a large share of defense production is performed by highly specialized defense contractors, many of whose products bear little resemblance to civilian items, and who have had little experience outside defense production. For many companies their most important customer is the U.S. government.

In 1983 the General Dynamics Corporation derived 83 percent of its income from sales to the U.S. government. Other federal dependents include Boeing, Grumman, McDonnell Douglas, Northrop, Rockwell International, and United Technologies.[57]

The federal government currently finances almost two thirds of university research and development programs. This money

56. Library of Congress, *A Compilation of Basic Information*, pp. 1205–6.

57. Gordon Adams, *The Politics of Defense Contracting*, Transaction Books, 1982, p. 39.

goes for basic research in such fields as chemistry, physics, biology, astronomy, materials, oceanography, and earth sciences.

States and cities see no solution to their critical financial problems other than more federal money. Federal aid has risen as a proportion of state and local expenditures from 12 percent in 1958 to 21.2 percent in 1984.

Unlike with the regulated industries, it is not enough for these federal dependents to maintain a strong defensive posture. Under our system of checks and balances, it is relatively easy to block action. It is far more difficult to persuade the executive branch and the Congress to do something, particularly when there are strong competing demands for limited resources. Offense demands a new team and a different strategy. Some industries, such as the railroads, have been penalized because they were too slow in getting their defensive team off the field.

Each of the dependents endeavors to manipulate the organization structure, processes, and assignment of program responsibilities so as to maximize its ability to obtain federal funds and to minimize federal interference in the allocation and use of funds. Scientists had these objectives in mind when they developed their original design for the National Science Foundation. Farm organizations were inspired by identical motives when they convinced President Eisenhower to support legislation that provided independent financing for the farm credit system and immunized it to effective federal control. Not all dependents have been as successful as the farm credit organizations in gaining the four freedoms: freedom from financial control by the Congress, freedom from independent audit by the comptroller general, freedom from budget review by the president, and freedom to use federal funds. But for many, these freedoms remain the goals.

The struggle for power and position has contributed to fragmentation of the executive branch structure and the proliferation of categorical programs. With a narrowed constituency, agencies are more susceptible to domination by their clientele groups and congressional committees.[58] Efforts to narrow the

58. For a brilliant analysis of the significance of constituencies, see Grant McConnell, *Private Power and American Democracy*, Alfred A. Knopf, 1967.

constituencies have been accompanied by demands for independent status or autonomy within the departmental structure.

Programs are packaged in such a way as to elicit congressional and clientele support. General programs have far less political appeal than specific programs. Support can be mobilized more readily for federal programs to combat heart disease, blindness, cancer, and mental illness than for such fields as microbiology or for general health programs. For this reason, in 1955, the National Microbiological Institute was renamed the National Institute of Allergy and Infectious Diseases. As was explained at the time, the Institute had been handicapped in making its case to the Appropriations Committees because "no one ever died of microbiology."[59]

It would be a mistake to assume, however, that dependents always have the wisdom to know what is in their own best interests. The maritime unions became so obsessed with the idea that an independent maritime agency would solve all of their problems that they ignored the plain fact that any transportation agency outside the Department of Transportation would be in a very weak competitive position. In 1981 the maritime unions quietly supported legislation to transfer the Maritime Administration from the department of commerce to the department of transportation, thus conceding that a mistake had been made in opposing such a transfer in 1966.

We are faced with the strange paradox that the privilege of access to public funds it believed to carry with it the right to exercise public power, whereas the payment of large amounts in taxes does not. This thesis is expressed in such euphemisms as "decentralization," "grass-roots administration," and "freedom from politics." Thus, Yale alumni were reassured that the university's independence has not been compromised by accepting federal money because "the men who fix the Government's policy in this respect are themselves university and college men. . . ."[60]

59. *The New York Times,* December 14, 1969.
60. *Report of the Treasurer of Yale University for the Fiscal Year Ended June 30, 1967,* p. 18.

The issue of dependence versus subservience is at the heart of our present dilemma. How can we reconcile a growing federal involvement in all aspects of our national life with the maintenance of deeply cherished pluralistic values? The typical answer is that offered by Alan Pifer, president of the Carnegie Corporation.[61] He proposed the creation of a federal center for higher education that would "depend heavily in all its activities on men and women co-opted from the colleges and universities *so that it is as much of higher education itself as it is of government*" (italics supplied).

Few would dispute that federal domination of science and education would be undesirable. Yet grave risks are run when public power is exercised by agricultural, scientific, and educational elites who are more concerned with advancing their own interests and the interests of the institutions they represent than the public interest. Serious disortions and inequities may occur in the allocation of funds among those eligible for assistance. Vested interests are created which are resistant to change and the reordering of priorities to meet new national needs.

As our one elected official, other than the vice president, with a national constituency, the president of the United States stands almost alone as a counterweight to these powerful centrifugal forces. Sometimes the executive branch takes on the appearance of an arena in which the chiefs of major and petty bureaucratic fiefdoms, supported by their auxiliaries in the Congress and their mercenaries in the outside community, are arrayed against the president in deadly combat.

Herbert Emmerich, a highly perceptive student of federal organization, has said: "The Presidency is the focal point of any study of reorganization. . . . The Presidency focuses the general interest as contrasted with the centrifugal forces in the Congress and the departments for the specialized interests of subject matter and of region."[62]

---

61. Alan Pifer, Speech to the Association of American Colleges, January 16, 1968, reprinted in *Congressional Record*, May 1, 1968, p. E.3631.

62. Herbert Emmerich, *Essays on Federal Reorganization*, University of Alabama Press, 1950, p. 7.

It is significant that the lasting contributions of the first Hoover Commission, the President's Committee on Administrative Management, and the earlier Taft Commission on Economy and Efficiency are to be found in their recommendations to strengthen the office of the presidency, not in the long-forgotten proposals for reshuffling agencies and providing more efficient and economical administration.[63] Institutional type and organization structure are important because they can help or hinder the president in performing his pivotal role within our constitutional system.

Reorganization also can be exploited by the president to alter the delicate balance within our constitutional system by eliminating or eroding the checks and balances resulting from the distribution of power within the executive branch as well as among the three branches of government. Watergate and its attendant "horrors" have raised fundamental and disturbing questions about the centralization of power in the White House, the fractionalization of presidential power among assistants to the president, and the division of responsibilities between the White House Office and the statutory agencies within the Executive Office of the President, the executive departments, and independent agencies. It is one thing to support and strengthen the president's capability to perform his pivotal role within the constitutional system. It is quite another to restructure the government so the president, in the words of Assistant to the President Bryce N. Harlow, "is running the whole government from the White House."[64]

There is a growing awareness that we will not make progress by attempting to apply yesterday's solutions to yesterday's problems. The growth of third-party or proxy government raises a different set of issues from those considered by the Brownlow

63. According to Peri Arnold, "it was the supreme political accomplishment of the first Hoover Commission that it masked the managerial presidency with the older value of administrative orthodoxy." Peri Arnold, "The First Hoover Commission and the Managerial Presidency," *Journal of Politics,* Vol. 38, February 1976.

64. Emmet J. Hughes, *The Living Presidency,* Coward, McCann & Geoghegan, Inc., 1973, p. 344.

Committee and the first Hoover Commission. The contest for power and position now focuses as much on processes and procedures as on formal structure. The Senate Committee on Governmental Affairs has identified what it deems to be the most urgent problem facing reorganizers in the 1980s:

> The erosion of accountability in government which stems from the new patterns of administration is possibly the gravest threat to the health of our system. Fragmented authority and ill-defined responsibility fosters the sense that government is out of control. Those responsible for a given issue are difficult to identify and all too often are remote and unresponsive.[65]

65. Senate Report No. 97–179, 97th Congress, 1st Session, August 13, 1981, p. 16.

2

Executive Branch Organization: View from the Congress

One could as well ignore the laws of aerodynamics in designing an aircraft as ignore the laws of congressional dynamics in designing executive branch structure. What may appear to be structural eccentricities and anomalies within the executive branch are often nothing but mirror images of jurisdictional conflicts within the Congress. Congressional organization and executive branch organization are interrelated and constitute two halves of a single system.

Executive branch structure and administrative arrangements are not matters of mere academic interest to members of Congress. Organization or reorganization of executive agencies may influence committee jurisdictions, increase or decrease the "accessibility" of executive branch officials to members of the Congress, and otherwise determine who shall exercise ultimate power in the decision-making processes.

To understand the organization of the executive branch, one must first understand the organization and culture of the Congress and the high degree of congressional involvement in administrative decisions.

It is highly misleading to speak of *the Congress,* as if it were a collective entity. There are, instead, 535 individuals—100 senators and 435 representatives—who form among themselves temporary and shifting coalitions. Conditions have not been altered materially since 1885, when Woodrow Wilson found "power is nowhere concentrated; it is rather deliberately and of set policy scattered amongst many small chiefs."[1]

The structure, procedure, and culture of the Congress tend to obscure the general interest, encourage particularism, and create an environment in which organized interest groups and special pleaders can be assured a sympathetic response. Consequently, dispersion, not integration, has been the dominant organizational thrust imposed on the executive branch.[2] This has created a situation in which, in the words of former White House aide and HEW secretary, Joseph A. Califano, Jr.,

> Congress is eager to establish for each interest its own executive bureau or independent board. . . . The molecular politics of Washington, with power, and often authority and responsibility, fragmented among increasingly narrow, what's-in-it-for-me groups and their responsive counterparts in the executive and legislative branches, has the centrifugal force to tear the national interest to shreds.[3]

Congressional power is divided among 16 major fiefdoms (standing committees) and some 180 petty fiefdoms (standing subcommittees) in the Senate; 22 major fiefdoms and over 138 petty fiefdoms in the House. The Legislative Reorganization Act of 1946 more than cut in half the number of standing committees, but this reduction has been offset by the proliferation of subcommittees. The number of Senate subcommittees has more than doubled in the past forty years, and comparable growth has occurred in the House. The shift from "committee" to "subcommittee" government is one of the most significant developments in the Congress.[4]

1. Woodrow Wilson, *Congressional Government,* Meridian Books, 1956, p. 76.

2. Ronald C. Moe, "To Establish a Commission on More Effective Government: A Background Report and Pro-Con Analysis," Congressional Research Service (Report No. 81–53 Gov.), February 24, 1981, p. 23.

3. Joseph A. Califano, Jr., *Governing America,* A Touchstone Book, 1981, p. 451.

4. See *Congressional Quarterly,* November 8, 1975, p. 2407. Walter Oleszek,

Subcommittees have become independent power centers and function with considerable autonomy. Under the subcommittee "bill of rights" adopted by the House Democratic caucus in 1973, committee chairmen were compelled to yield exclusive power to select subcommittee chairmen and to define subcommittee jurisdictions. This power is now exercised by all Democrats on a committee. Each subcommittee is guaranteed staff and an adequate budget. A chairman is required to refer most measures to subcommittees within two weeks.

Subcommittee reform has enabled more junior members of the Congress to assume posts of leadership and power. The impetus for reform came from what Congressman Thomas S. Foley called a "generational conflict."[5] But reform has been gained at the cost of further fractionalization of power and jurisdictions within the Congress.

Generalizations about congressional committees should be approached with caution. Each committee and subcommittee has its own culture, mode of operations, and set of relationships to executive agencies subject to its oversight, depending on its constituency, its own peculiar tradition, the nature of its legislative jurisdiction, its administrative and legislative processes, and the role and attitude of its chairman. Richard F. Fenno, Jr.'s, analysis reveals significant differences among House committees with respect to member goals, environmental constraints, strategic premises, decision-making processes, and conclusions.[6] Committees have only two things in common. First, power within a committee is earned by specialization. A new member is advised that "to make a great name for himself in the Congress a man must be a specialist."[7] Second, jurisdictional prerogatives are zealously

Congressional Procedures and Policy Process, Congressional Quarterly Press, 1978, pp. 42, 60, 64.

5. *Congressional Quarterly,* ibid., p. 2409.

6. Richard F. Fenno, Jr., *Congressmen in Committees,* Little, Brown and Company, 1973.

7. Neil MacNeil, *Forge of Democracy—The House of Representatives,* David McKay Co., Inc., 1963, p. 130.

guarded and raids by other fiefdoms are resisted with a jealous frenzy.

Growth of a congressional bureaucracy and institutionaliza-tion of committees and subcommittees have deepened the moats dividing the fiefdoms and accentuated the innate disposition of the Congress to concentrate on administrative details rather than basic issues of public policy. Professional staffing for all congressional committees became established only in 1946 with the passage of the Legislative Reorganization Act. Committee staff now exceed 3000. Approximately 11,000 persons are em-ployed on the personal staffs of senators and representatives.[8]

According to Samuel C. Patterson, "committee staff members tend to adopt the goal orientations dominant among the mem-bers of the committee for whom they work." He has found that there is minimal communication among the professional staffs of the different congressional committees, even when they have overlapping jurisdictions, and that staff appear "to be very much isolated from one another."[9]

Staff develop alliances with the executive branch bureaucracy and the bureaucracies representing interest groups. Most are highly capable, but some develop narrow interests in particular programs, are highly parochial in outlooks, and provide a rally-ing point for those fighting reorganizations that upset committee jurisdictions. Roger H. Davidson and Walter J. Oleszek acknowl-edge that the House Select Committee on Committees seriously underestimated the ability of staff to mobilize outside allies to protect their domains.[10] Those who hope further expansion of the congressional bureaucracy will make it possible for the Con-gress to look at the big picture and regain legislative leadership

8. Norman Ornstein, Thomas Mann, Michael Malbin, Allen Schick and John Bibby, *Vital Statistics of Congress 1984–85*, American Enterprise Institute, 1984, p. 120.

9. Samuel G. Patterson, "Staffing House Committees," in working papers, House Select Committee on Committees, June 1973.

10. Roger H. Davidson and Walter J. Oleszek, *Congress Against Itself*, In-diana University Press, 1977, p. 263.

are pursuing a will-o'-the-wisp. On the contrary, few would dissent from James L. Sundquist's observation that "as members become managers of professional staffs, the chambers disintegrate as 'deliberative bodies' in the traditional sense of legislators engaged in direct interchange of views leading to a group decision. . . . With each passing year, the House and Senate appear less as collective institutions and more as collections of institutions—individual member-staff groups organized as offices and subcommittees."[11]

Standing committees and subcommittees, like the major executive departments, tend to be composed of individuals who share much the same background, interests, and values. Members seek assignments that will best enable them to advance the interests of their constituents. Those from agricultural states or districts want to be on the agriculture committees, and preferably on the subcommittee concerned with the dominant crop produced in their area. House members from port or shipbuilding districts seek seats on the Merchant Marine and Fisheries Committee. Representatives from western states control almost a majority on the House Interior Committee, which has jurisdiction over reclamation projects, grazing, timber and mineral rights—issues of primary interest to voters in those states.[12]

Reform proposals have focused mainly on distribution of power within the Congress, staffing, procedures, and processes. Efforts to reorganize the committee structure in the House failed. The Temporary Select Committee to study the Senate Committee System, chaired by Senator Adlai E. Stevenson III, was more successful than its House counterpart, because senators serve on several committees and have less to lose through committee restructuring than House members. Although the number of Senate committees has been reduced, according to one informed observer, the realignment has left "jurisdictional lines

11. James L. Sundquist, *The Decline and Resurgence of Congress*, The Brookings Institution, 1981, p. 411.

12. Steven S. Smith and Christopher J. Deering, *Committees in Congress*, CQ Press, 1984, p. 106.

pretty much untouched, concentrating instead on consolidating several obsolete committees." He concludes that "neither the House nor the Senate has succeeded in recasting its work groups in conformity with the altered shape of public problems."[13]

The Commission on Operation of the Senate found that "the legislative process as it presently operates appears to be organized primarily for incremental decision making rather than addressing major problems in a comprehensive manner."[14] In vital areas, such as energy, programs that have been reorganized or are effectively coordinated at the executive level remain fragmented in the Congress. Hoped-for benefits are lost when comprehensive and well-integrated plans developed by the executive must be broken up and considered in separate pieces by the Congress.

The cochairman of the select committee to study the senate committee system, Senator Adlai E. Stevenson, came to the following conclusion:

> We are compartmentalists; we have sliced our daily routines into superficial fragments, and we have divided and subdivided problems into a host of committee cubbyholes. It is no wonder that there is little consistency or coherence to what we do hear. Do we have anything that could be fairly called a "policy" in such fields as energy conservation, environmental protection, or healthcare?[15]

The Budget and Impoundment Control Act of 1974 did provide an institutional structure for coordinating congressional actions on budget and fiscal policy. But except for budget and fiscal policy, there remains no place short of the floor of the Congress where important programs that cut across established agency and committee jurisdictions can be considered in their totality.

13. Roger H. Davidson, "Our Changing Congress: The Inside (and Outside) Story," paper delivered at the Conference on Congress and the Presidency, Lyndon Baines Johnson Library, Austin, Texas, November 14–17, 1977.

14. Senate Document No. 94–278, December 1976, p. 42.

15. *Congressional Record*, September 30, 1976, p. 34018.

Diffusion of responsibility provides opportunities to divide and conquer by playing off one committee against another.

Committee jurisdictions are overlapping and cannot be neatly delineated. Although one of the smaller executive departments, the Department of Housing and Urban Development is subject to oversight by no less than forty committees and subcommittees.[16] Turf problems among committees exercising jurisdiction over the Treasury and Justice departments are admitted to be one of the obstacles to eliminating the double clearance of travelers entering the country by the customs service and the immigration service.[17] Efforts to simplify administration of private pension regulation, currently divided among the Treasury and Labor departments and the Pension Benefit Guaranty Corporation, are complicated by the competing jurisdictional claims of the tax and labor committees.[18] A jurisdictional dispute between the Senate Labor and Human Resources Committee and Commerce, Science and Transportation Committee prevented enactment of annual authorizing legislation for the National Science Foundation.[19]

Inability to resolve competing jurisdictional claims among the House committees on Government Operations, Armed Services, Ways and Means, Education and Labor, Banking and Currency, and Judiciary led to creation of a Commission on Government Procurement to evaluate the effectiveness of present statutes affecting government procurement. It was acknowledged that "a Commission on Government Procurement would be able to do what the congressional committees cannot readily do—examine

16. Comptroller General of the United States, "Increasing the Department of Housing and Urban Development's Effectiveness Through Improved Management," January 10, 1984, p. 3.

17. *The New York Times*, May 7, 1984. A rider to a continuing resolution in Public Law 98–473 prohibited reduction of the regions, districts, or entry processing locations by the U.S. Customs Service.

18. Michael S. Gordon, "Reflections on Selected Issues of Private Pension Regulation," *National Journal*, August 11, 1984.

19. Richard Corrigan, "Heading Back into the Future," *National Journal*, November 5, 1983.

in a concerted and comprehensive way many important procurement problems in their multiple interrelationships and in terms of their impact on public policy and the national economy."[20]

Folklore has it that the camel is an animal conceived by an interagency committee. The camel is a perfectly fashioned animal compared with some spawned out of the maelstrom of conflicting committee jurisdictions. When jurisdictional problems could not be resolved, the Congress in 1966 created two agencies—the National Highway Safety Agency and the National Traffic Agency—to administer the highway safety program. The president was authorized to designate a single individual to head both agencies. All that was gained by creating two agencies, where only one was needed, was to give two Senate committees a voice in the confirmation of the agency head.

Organizational arrangements may be skewed to establish or maintain committee jurisdictions. A Senate bill authorizing the National Science Foundation to provide financial assistance to academic institutions for training, research, and advisory services to exploit marine resources was in normal course referred to the House Education and Labor Committee. To gain jurisdiction over the sea grant college program, the House Merchant Marine and Fisheries Committee introduced its own bill, which was subsequently enacted, to bring the program under the general policy guidance of the National Council on Marine Resources and Engineering Development. Thus, in one of its grant and contract programs assisting educational institutions, NSF policy-making responsibility was not centered in the National Science Board but was shared with an outside agency. The program was transferred from the National Science Foundation to the National Oceanic and Atmospheric Administration, Department of Commerce, in 1970.

In 1978 seabed mining legislation was held up by a dispute between the House Merchant Marine Committee and the Interior Committee. Each committee insisted that the program be

20. House of Representatives, 90th Congress, 1st Session, Report No. 890.

administered by the executive agency subject to its oversight. The Merchant Marine Committee proposed that jurisdiction be vested in the Department of Commerce; the Interior Committee favored the Department of the Interior.[21]

Reorganization proposals repeatedly have foundered on the shoals of competing committee jurisdictions. Chairman Chet Holifield of the House Committee on Government Operations warned proponents of President Nixon's 1971 proposals to create Departments of Community Development, Natural Resources, Human Resources and Economic Affairs:

> If by this reorganization you affect in a major way the powers of the various committees in the Congress, you may as well forget it. The only way I know to get one or more of these departments through is to allow the committees that now have the programs within their jurisdiction to follow their programs, just as they are followed now, and authorize these programs wherever they are distributed.[22]

A bill to establish a Department of Community Development reported favorably by Holifield's committee in 1972, was blocked in the Rules Committee by the opposition of the chairmen of the Interior, Public Works, Banking and Currency, Education and Labor, Agriculture, and Appropriations committees.

Congresswoman Shirley Chisholm argued against President Carter's legislation to establish a Department of Education because creation of such a department might encourage renewed efforts to split the House Education and Labor Committee. "As members of Congress," Rep. Chisholm testified before the House Government Operations Committee, "we must also take note of the impact the reorganization of HEW and Federal education programs would probably have on the committee structure in the House of Representatives. Although my distinguished colleague, Chairman Perkins from the Education and Labor Committee,

21. *Congressional Quarterly*, February 25, 1978, p. 525.

22. House Committee on Government Operations, Legislation and Military Operation Subcommittee, hearing on "Reorganization of Executive Departments," Part I, June–July 1971, p. 324.

has denied the likelihood of committee division, others may decide to spearhead a drive to divide this committee."[23]

Objections by appropriations subcommittees sometimes can be safely ignored, but presidents run grave risks when they threaten the jurisdiction of the major legislative committees. Legislative committee chairmen have what amounts to a veto. Interior Committee objections killed a plan to consolidate weather modification functions in the Environmental Science Services Administration, even though in this instance the three agencies administering weather modification programs—Interior, National Science Foundation, and Commerce—agreed that reorganization was desirable. Interior Committee disapproval also brought to a halt plans for consolidating general purpose cartographic activities in the Department of Commerce. The committee feared that transfer of the Topographic Mapping Division from Geological Survey to Commerce might result in the eventual transfer of the Geological Survey itself. The Agriculture Committees forestalled efforts to transfer responsibility from the Department of Agriculture to the Agency for International Development for foreign assistance programs involving surplus agricultural commodities. On the other hand, the Agriculture committees persuaded the Congress to enact legislation requiring that the president's budget classify expenditures for such programs "as expenditures for international affairs and finance rather than for agriculture and agricultural resources."[24]

Organizational arrangements for the conduct of federal water resource programs violate each of the organizational commandments handed down by Herbert Hoover. Almost every objective observer has confirmed the Hoover Commission's findings that the existing sharing of water resource responsibilities among Interior, Agriculture, and the U.S. Army Corps of Engineers has resulted in poor planning, working at cross purposes, and waste-

23. Hearings before a subcommittee of the House Committee on Governmental Operations, on H.R. 13343, to establish a Department of Education, July–August 1978, p. 380.

24. 7 U.S.C. 1703.

ful competition. Entrenched interests within the bureaucracy and outside community constitute major obstacles to needed reorganization. But these obstacles would not be insuperable, if the schism in the executive branch did not have its counterpart in the Congress. As conceded by Robert A. Roe, chairman of the House Public Works and Transportation Subcommittee on Water Resources: "There ought to be, in the interests of the nation, just one committee that has total jurisdiction over water resources. But that's not going to happen. The political structure won't allow it."[25]

Congressional organization and executive branch organization with respect to water resources are so closely interlinked that they cannot be considered separately. Control over project authorizations and funding are the essence of congressional power. Jurisdictional rivalries within the executive branch pale by comparison with those among congressional committees. The Senate Energy and Natural Resources Committee and the House Interior Committee exercise jurisdiction over the Bureau of Reclamation and the Senate Environment and Public Works Committee, the House Public Works and Transportation Committee over the Corps of Engineers, and the Agriculture Committees over the Soil Conservation Service.

The current organization of federal water resources functions results from a series of laws each of which was directed toward a single objective, such as improvement of rivers and harbors, flood control, irrigation, and watershed protection. Given the original limited missions, the logic of assigning rivers and harbors and flood control functions to the Corps of Engineers, reclamation to Interior, and watershed protection to Agriculture could not be reasonably disputed. West Point was our first engineering school, and the Corps alone among federal agencies at the time possessed adequate engineering competence. The lands to be reclaimed were mostly arid western lands under Interior's jurisdiction. Agriculture pioneered a watershed improvement program that extended to the major watersheds of the Mississippi and its tributary, the Missouri.

In contrast with the early laws directed toward a single objective, the Federal Power Act of 1920 expressed a multipurpose concept of river basin planning and development. Clientele groups and congressional committees who had come to identify their interests with those of the Corps, Interior, and Agriculture did not object to the new concept—provided that it was carried out on their terms and by "their" agency. Instead of awarding custody to a single agency or dividing the baby into three parts, the decision was to produce triplets. Initially the three factions, the secretaries of agriculture, interior, and war, constituted the Federal Power Commission.

Since 1920 the Corps, Interior, and Agriculture have obtained parallel and, in some respects, identical authorities for multipurpose development of water resources, although Interior's jurisdiction is limited to the western states and Alaska and Agriculture's authority under the 1954 act is limited in terms of the size of the structure for watershed improvement.

Except when all parties are agreed on the dominant project objective, the decision as to which agency will undertake a particular multipurpose project requires a time-consuming, complex, and often bitter bargaining process. At some point the president must make a determination, but it is seldom final and can be upset by appeal to the Congress. Even the "peace treaties" negotiated by the Corps and Reclamation, under which one assumed responsibility for construction and the other responsibility for operation and maintenance of certain projects, have been negated by subsequent congressional actions.

The Kings River project in California is often cited as a classic illustration of the inherent weakness of federal resource management.[26] More significantly, this case history shows the linkages between organization and legislative policy. The Bureau of Reclamation and the Corps of Engineers were in agreement on

26. See Arthur Maass, *Muddy Waters—The Army Engineers and the Nation's Rivers,* Harvard University Press, 1951.

the design of the project. The differences resulted from the conflicting water use philosophies developed by the two agencies in keeping with their individual legislative mandates. Reclamation emphasized water conservation and maximum water use, and the Corps emphasized local flood protection. This was not solely a bureaucratic contest for power. Economy and efficiency were not the issues. The significant disagreements centered on the policy issues raised by the choice among administrative agencies. These included differences over repayments and distribution of benefits, restrictions on acreage and speculation, operation of irrigation facilities, power development, and method of congressional authorization. Such issues cannot be resolved by reorganization, and regardless of who makes the initial decision, the president and the Congress will be the final arbiters.

Former congressman and TVA director Frank Smith concluded as follows:

> Ideally, the old concept of one single department of conservation and resource development, responsible for all Federal planning and action in the field, might still work if it could be achieved by waving a magic wand. It simply cannot be achieved, however, without a bloody, bone shattering fight, which would leave the landscape so scarred that the conservation cause would be lost in the critical years immediately ahead.[27]

President Reagan was unwilling to undertake such a bloody, bone-shattering fight and gave short shrift to Budget Director David Stockman's plan to create a single water resource development agency.

The boldest congressional advocates of a Department of Natural Resources have been exceedingly timid in facing up to problems of congressional organization. Senator Edward Kennedy reassured the Congress that the sponsors of a bill to establish a Department of Natural Resources had no intention of

27. Frank E. Smith, *The Politics of Conservation*, Pantheon Books, 1966, p. 306.

upsetting the status quo and that, because of the special expertise acquired by the committees and their staffs, "legislative authority should remain where it is, relying upon effective administration of the programs to provide essential coordination."[28]

The natural allies for many agencies are the legislative committees. Herbert Kaufman found, in his case studies of federal bureau chiefs, that "the more responsive a bureau and its chief are to the wishes of a committee, and the better their reputations, the more ardent the committee's defense of the bureau against attacks will be."[29] Complaints about unelected bureaucrats generally are directed by congressmen against bureaus under the jurisdiction of committees other than their own.[30] As explained by one witness before the House Select Committee on Committees, "If you leave the same jurisdiction year after year, with the same bureaucrats appearing for 20 years, the same committee members for 20 years, and the same staff members, soon there isn't much to disagree about because everyone understands how they think their little piece of the world ought to be run."[31]

A close affinity often exists between a committee chairman and the senior career staff of the departments and agencies under his jurisdiction. The chairmen and ranking committee members probably know more about the details of an agency's program and are better acquainted with the senior career staff than most agency heads who serve for relatively brief periods. New secretaries quickly find that some officials whom they want to reassign are "untouchables." Others whom they may want to keep must be replaced because they have been declared *persona non grata* by the chairman of the legislative committee or appropriations subcommittee. Even so revered a figure as Wilbur K. Carr, who

28. Senate Committee on Government Operations, Subcommittee on Executive Reorganizations, hearing on S.886 to establish a Department of Natural Resources, October 17, 19, and 20, 1967, p. 36.

29. Herbert Kaufman, *The Administrative Behavior of Federal Bureau Chiefs*, The Brookings Institution, 1981, p. 170.

30. Ibid., p. 169.

31. Randall Ripley, House Select Committee on Committees, Panel Discussions, Vol. 2 of 3, Part 1 of 3, June 1973, p. 52.

served for forty-seven years in the State Department, much of the time as its principal executive officer, was packed off as Minister to Czechoslovakia when a new appropriations subcommittee chairman refused to do business with him.[32] Probably more executive branch officials have been fired or reassigned as a result of pressure from the Congress than from the president.[33]

An executive agency's ability to withstand legislative committee pressures, assuming that it desires to do so, depends on many factors. Most vulnerable are the agencies that are required to do one or a combination of the following: renew their legislative charters at specific time intervals; obtain authorizing legislation before appropriations can be made; obtain congressional directives to undertake surveys and legislative authorization for individual projects; and keep committees "fully and currently informed" of pending action and supply copies of all correspondence. Single-headed agencies are more resistant to pressure than are boards and commissions, and Cabinet departments have greater immunity than do independent agencies.

The annual authorizing bill has been seized upon by the legislative committees as a means for obtaining leverage over executive agencies and counteracting Appropriations Committee influence over administration. Until 1948 most programs, with the exception of the civil works program of the Army Corps of Engineers, were either authorized on a permanent basis or for multiyear periods. In 1948 the foreign aid program was made subject to annual authorization, and since then the requirement has been extended to programs constituting almost one third of the federal budget.[34] Programs requiring both periodic authorizing legislation and annual appropriations include foreign aid, defense construction and procurement, space, maritime, intelli-

32. Incident recounted in Katherine Crane, *Mr. Carr of State—Forty-seven Years in the Department of State,* St. Martin's Press, 1960, pp. 328–29.

33. For discussion of congressional influence on appointments and removals see Louis Fisher, "Congress and Removal Power," *Congress and the Presidency,* Vol. 10, No. 1, Spring 1983.

34. U.S. General Accounting Office, "Observations on Oversight Reform," PAD81–17, 1981, p. 5.

gence, Department of Energy, Department of Justice, Coast Guard, National Science Foundation, Panama Canal Commission, Environmental Protection Agency (research and development), Bureau of Mint, U.S. Trade Representative, Federal Election Commission, and Travel and Tourism Administration.

The Congress would do well to subject the system of annual authorizations to a rigorous cost-benefit analysis. The costs are high and can be measured in public confusion and dissatisfaction (the average citizen does not recognize the subtle distinction between an authorization and an appropriation), program uncertainties and delays, late appropriations, and diversion of committees and executive branch officials from perhaps more productive endeavors. Long-range planning is not possible with one-year authorizations. When the process degenerates into a form of "gamesmanship" between the legislative and appropriations committee, it is not calculated to enhance the public image of Congress. The requirement ought to be employed selectively and only for those programs for which the need for annual review and legislative authorization can be clearly demonstrated.

As allies, the executive agencies and legislative committees make common cause against the "third house of the Congress"— the Appropriations Committees. Lords of the executive establishment generally enjoy the cozy atmosphere of legislative committee hearings, where they are received with courtesy and the deference due their office. They shun, wherever possible, meetings with appropriations subcommittees, whose chairman on occasion may accord them about the same amount of deference as a hard-boiled district attorney shows to a prisoner in the dock. Before the House Appropriations Committee obtained new quarters, it was not uncommon for high officials to stand hat-in-hand for up to an hour in the corridors of the Capitol basement waiting to be summoned by their appropriations subcommittee.

Actions by the appropriations committees may override presidential directives or nullify laws enacted by the Congress itself.[35]

35. Michael W. Kirst, *Government Without Passing Laws*, The University of North Carolina Press, 1969.

The appropriations "rider" is frequently employed for this purpose. Provisos attached to appropriations acts reversed administration regualtions and policies on school busing and abortion. Riders have also controlled such administrative details as proposed reductions in the time period for Marine Corps basic training, the consolidation of training programs for Navy helicopter pilots, and exemptions from environmental impact statements.[36]

Riders, at least theoretically, are subject to review by the Congress as whole and sometimes can be eliminated on a "point of order" as legislation in an appropriation act. There is no effective way, however, for the Congress to review or amend the directives contained in Appropriations Committee reports that may tell an agency what to do, when to do it, where to do it, and how to do it. Reports do not have the force and effect of law, but agencies ignore such directives at their peril. A committee report was used to rescind one of the most important sections of the District of Columbia Reorganization Plan only a few months after the Congress had allowed the plan to go into effect. The plan conferred upon the D.C. commissioner authority to reorganize the district government and to establish so many agencies and offices, with such names or titles as he shall from time to time determine. The committee directed that the commissioner obtain its "prior approval" before exercising his statutory authority, thus restoring an unsatisfactory arrangement that the plan was intended to eliminate. Modernization of the D.C. government had been estopped for fifteen years by the requirement that the Congress approve each transfer, no matter how minor. Senator Mike Mansfield attempted to soften the committee report by having Senator Robert C. Byrd (West Virginia) agree on the Senate floor that he wanted merely to be informed of "major changes in organization or financing plans." Senator Byrd would have none of it and made the following statement:

> . . . I want to emphasize that I for one do not want to bind the Appropriations Committee by a colloquy which leaves only

36. Sundquist, *The Decline and Resurgence of Congress,* pp. 358–59.

so-called major changes subject to congressional approval
when there can be wide variations of interpretations as to
what constitutes major changes. I do not mean to be evasive,
nor do I want to appear to be unyielding or difficult. I want
the Appropriations Committee to be informed of all such
transactions, as they have been in the past. And, as far as I
am concerned, this is what the language means.[37]

Committee jurisdictions are the most important single factor
influencing program assignments among executive agencies. Congressional dynamics can be equally significant in molding and
shaping the choice of administrative instruments, advisory arrangements, delegations, and field structure.

Institutional types are judged by their relative accessibility to
members of Congress, not by juridical concepts or abstract principles of organization. For members of Congress, the executive
branch is divided among the "president's men"—White House
staff, heads of executive office units, and Cabinet secretaries—and
"agencies of the Congress"—independent boards and commissions
and the Army Corps of Engineers. Administrators of independent agencies, such as the General Services Administration and
Small Business Administration, sit uncomfortably in a no-man's
land between the "president's men" and "agencies of the Congress" and are considered fair game for both sides. These distinctions are based not on law, except possibly for the independent regulatory commissions, in which the Supreme Court has
limited the president's power, but on "understandings" tacitly
accepted by the president and the Congress.

Least accessible to the Congress are members of the White
House staff. As a matter of long-standing practice, White House
staff do not testify before congressional committees. To his later
regret, President Kennedy departed from this custom in allowing
James Landis in 1961 to present a series of reorganization plans
related to the regulatory commissions. When four of the seven
plans were disapproved, it was construed as a personal rebuff to

37. *Congressional Record,* November 8, 1967, p. S16080.

the president. Sherman Adams did testify, but in a personal capacity to explain charges that had been made against him, as did Wallace H. Graham, Harry Vaughan, Donald Dawson, Peter Flanigan, and Edwin Meese III.

Congress was particularly frustrated by its inability to obtain information and testimony from the president's special assistant for science and technology. Senator John McClellan complained that "Unless legislative action is taken by the Congress to establish some medium through which reliable information and supporting technical data is made available to Congress by officials who are responsive to its needs, the committees of the Congress will continue to be denied information necessary to the legislative process in establishing policies in the fields of science and technology."[38] The reorganization creating the Office of Science and Technology in 1962 was, in part, the president's response to congressional demands for better access to his principal science adviser.

Presidents ask for trouble when they co-opt a congressional agent as a White House aide. The Congress regards such "two-hatted" arrangements as a violation of the rules of the game. Atomic Energy Commission Chairman Lewis Strauss invoked his position as a special adviser to the president on atomic energy affairs in flatly refusing to answer questions asked by the Joint Committee.[39] Lingering resentment from this incident was one of the factors that led the Senate to reject Strauss's nomination as secretary of commerce.

President Nixon's designation of the secretary of the treasury and the director of the Office of Management and Budget as assistants to the president, and the secretaries of HEW, HUD, and agriculture as presidential counselors, was seen by some members of the Congress as a device for limiting congressional access to

38. Senate Committee on Government Operations, Report No. 1828 on S. 2771 to establish a Commission on Science and Technology, 87th Congress, 2nd Session, p. 9.

39. Morgan Thomas and Robert M. Northrop, *Atomic Energy and Congress*, University of Michigan Press, 1956, p. 174.

these officials. The director of the OMB, the heads of other executive office units, and the Cabinet secretaries spend much of their time meeting with members of Congress and testifying before committees. But Congress recognizes that it is subject to certain restraints when dealing with these officials. These restraints were noted by Senator J. William Fulbright in opposing the 1950 reorganization plan to transfer the Reconstruction Finance Corporation to the Department of Commerce:

> Under the accepted principles of our government, the Secretary of Commerce is a member of the Executive family. He looks primarily to the President for his policy and his influence. We all know he is removable at the discretion of the President. It is customary also, whenever a Cabinet nomination comes up here, whether we like him or not, it is generally understood that we confirm him, in contrast to some of the other agencies, the Federal Reserve or one of the others which we look upon more as a congressional agency. I think the Cabinet is in a little different position in relationship with the Congress than the heads of these independent agencies.[40]

Senator Fulbright acknowledged, "We rarely, if ever, call up the Secretaries of any of the major departments and question them and examine them like we do the heads of agencies."[41] He contended that the reorganization would tend to insulate the RFC from the committee's supervision and place "between us and the RFC a member of the President's Cabinet who is given supervision and policy guidance over that Board. I think the tendency would be to look upon it as not our responsibility anymore."[42] Senator Fulbright's views were confirmed by the committee in its report recommending disapproval of the reorganization plan. The report observed the following:

> This proprietary attitude of the Congress toward the Reconstruction Finance Corporation was emphasized time after time

40. Senate Committee on Expenditures in Executive Departments, hearing on Reorganization Plan No. 24 of 1950, June 14 and 15, 1950, p. 8.

41. Ibid., p. 39.

42. Ibid., p. 15.

during the course of the hearings, invariably coupled with the fear that, were the corporation to be placed within the framework of an executive department, the affinity between the corporation and the Congress would increasingly become a thing of the past.[43]

The Congress does not concede, however, that a secretary's right to reign over a department necessarily carries with it the power to rule. Herbert Hoover discovered as secretary of commerce that the Congress "while giving us generous support for our new activities . . . refused to add to my personal staff."[44] Secretary Hoover employed two secretaries and three assistants at his own expense.

Limitations on congressional access to Cabinet members do not extend to their principal bureau chiefs. At one time, many bureau chiefs, for all practical purposes, were immune to secretarial authority. These chiefs were appointed by the president subject to Senate confirmation, often for fixed terms of office, and statutory powers were vested in them, not in the secretary. The first Hoover Commission found that "statutory powers often have been vested in subordinate officers in such a way as to deny authority to the President or a department head."[45] Since 1949, the number of autonomous bureaus has been reduced by a series of reorganization plans, but by no means wholly eliminated. The plans transferred the statutory functions of all subordinates to the department head.

Even the Executive Office of the President has not been wholly immune from infiltration by the Congress. What some in Congress have termed a "congressional agency," the Office of Federal Procurement Policy (OFPP) was established within the Office of Management and Budget in 1974. The OFPP administrator is

43. Senate Committee on Expenditures in Executive Departments, Senate Report No. 1868, 81st Congress, 2nd Session, June 26, 1950, p. 10.

44. Herbert C. Hoover, *The Memoirs of Herbert C. Hoover, The Cabinet and the Presidency, 1920–1933*, The Macmillan Co., 1952, p. 43.

45. Commission on Organization of the Executive Branch of the Government, "General Management of the Executive Branch," a report to the Congress, February 1949, p. 4.

appointed by the president, by and with the advice and consent of the Senate, and the office's functions are vested in him, not in the OMB director. The administrator is required to keep the Congress and its committees "fully and currently informed" and to transmit, at least 30 days prior to the effective date, proposed policies and regulations to the Government Operations Committees of the House and Senate. The bill's Senate sponsor, Senator Lawton Chiles, emphasized that the law made the administrator independently responsible for carrying out the office's duties and keeping the Congress informed.[46]

Congress has been somewhat less successful in its attempts to exert its influence by limiting the president's power to appoint and remove federal officers, other than by indirect means. The Tenure of Office Act of 1867 provided that certain civil officers, appointed by and with the advice and consent of the Senate, should hold office during the term of the president who appointed them and one month thereafter. This act was declared unconstitutional.[47] Congress provided that members of the Tennessee Valley Authority Board could "be removed from office at any time by concurrent resolution of the Senate and House of Representatives," but this power has never been exercised and is of doubtful constitutionality. Congress has gone so far as to vest removal power exclusively in the hands of an agency, thus presumably taking it away from the president. Board members of the Legal Services Corporation may be removed "by a vote of seven members" for specified causes.[48]

Executive power also may be offset by specifying terms of office coterminous with or exceeding that of the appointing official. Such was the congressional intent when it specified nine-year overlapping terms for members of the Postal Service Board of Governors.

46. Judith H. Parris, "The Office of Management and Budget: Background Responsibilities, Recent Issues," Congressional Research Service, July 27, 1978.

47. *Meyers* v. *United States,* 272 U.S. 52 (1926).

48. 42 U.S.C. 2996c (E).

Efforts by the Congress to assume the appointing power have been rebuffed by the Supreme Court. The Court held unconstitutional a 1974 statute authorizing the Congress to appoint four members of the Federal Elections Commission. All six voting Commission members (including two to be nominated by the president) were to be confirmed by both Houses of the Congress. The Court ruled that administrative functions had to be carried out by "officers of the United States" appointed in the manner prescribed by the Constitution.[49]

Congress may bypass the established chain of command either by providing independent lines of communication to the Congress or by subjecting specified executive actions to veto by a congressional committee or by one or both houses of the Congress. Examples of dual reporting requirements are those applicable to inspectors general and certain regulatory commissions. The Inspector General Act of 1978 requires inspectors general to keep both their administrative superiors and the Congress fully and currently informed about any deficiencies detected by their offices. The Commodity Futures Trading Commission and the Consumer Product Safety Commission are directed by law to transmit concurrently to the Congress copies of budget estimates and any legislative recommendations submitted to the president.

Congressional determination to influence or control administrative decisions was illustrated most dramatically by the proliferation of statutory provisions requiring the president or his subordinates to submit proposed orders, regulations, and plans to the Congress for review and potential veto. In effect, by this device the Congress was giving itself the power to preaudit executive branch proposals. Since 1932, about 210 laws containing some 320 separate veto provisions were enacted, most since 1970.[50] The Supreme Court, in its historic Chadha decision of June 23, 1983, in one stroke invalidated as unconstitutional virtually every variety of congressional veto enacted in the last 50 years.

49. *Buckley* v. *Valeo*, 424 U.S. 1 (1976).

50. *Congressional Research Service Review*, Fall 1983, p. 5.

Congress is now exploring constitutional alternatives to the legislative veto. These include *report-and-wait* provisions requiring that proposed regulations or actions be reported to Congress for a specified period prior to implementation; joint resolutions of approval or disapproval that would have to be adopted by a majority of both Houses and submitted to the president for his approval; and nonbinding concurrent resolutions expressing the views of the Congress on pending matters.[51]

Statutory interdepartmental committees are condemned by James Rowe, Jr., as another device "striking directly at the jugular of Presidential responsibility."[52] These and statutory advisory committees can be used to limit presidential and secretarial discretion by controlling their sources of advice. Rowe correctly concludes that once an interdepartmental committee or advisory body "is given a statutory floor with defined powers and a separate staff, it too begins to look toward its creator, the Congress, for sustenance." Our foreign assistance programs have been profoundly influenced by the lead role given to the secretary of the treasury as chairman of the National Advisory Council on International Monetary and Financial Problems. Congress intended, and with some success, to ensure that a tough-minded money man would have the decisive voice in passing on foreign loans and in coordinating international monetary transactions, although the authority to make loans was lodged elsewhere. Reorganization Plan No. 4 of 1965 abolished nine statutory committees, including the NAC, but the president reestablished the NAC by executive order with somewhat more limited powers.

51. For pros and cons of legislative veto and discussion of post-Chadha alternatives, see Robert S. Gilmour and Barbara H. Craig, "After the Congressional Veto: Assessing Alternatives," *Journal of Policy Analysis and Management*, Vol. 3, No. 3, 1984; Frederick M. Kaiser, "Congressional Control of Executive Actions in the Aftermath of the Chadha Decision," *Administrative Law Review*, Vol. 36, Summer 1984; Louis Fisher, *The Politics of Shared Power*, Congressional Quarterly Press, 1981, pp. 92–103; Sundquist, *The Decline and Resurgence of Congress*, Chapter XII; Barbara H. Craig, *The Legislative Veto: Congressional Control of Regulation*, Westview Press, 1983.

52. James Rowe, Jr., "Cooperation or Conflict: The President's Relation with an Opposition Congress," Georgetown Law Journal, Vol. 36, 1947.

In the same year, the Congress created the Water Resources Council by law.

Multiheaded agencies are classified indiscriminately by the Congress as "agencies of the Congress" without regard to nice distinctions between executive functions and quasi-judicial and quasi-legislative functions. Boards and commissions are unloved by everyone but the Congress. Plural executives may be inefficient administrators, but the Congress is more concerned with responsiveness than efficiency. Congress has gone along somewhat reluctantly with strong chairman plans for most commissions. It was once feared that a chairman designated by the president and with control over a commission's budget and personnel might open the door to presidential influence.

Reorganizations to replace boards and commissions with single administrators are opposed out of fear of disturbing the delicate balance of power between the executive and the Congress. It is too easy for a single administrator to become a "president's man." President Eisenhower was able to put through a reorganization plan in 1953 abolishing the board of directors of the Export-Import Bank, but the Congress in 1954 reestablished the board. In objecting to the substitution of one commissioner for the three-member board of commissioners of the District of Columbia, Chairman John McMillan of the House District Committee did not argue about public administration theory. He put it bluntly:

> There are not many members of Congress here of the old school whom I have not helped somewhere along the line since I have been serving as chairman of the committee. I imagine that from now on if this plan is adopted, members of Congress will be required to get District of Columbia automobile tags, as you will no longer have the kind of reciprocity that you have now as a member of Congress from every state in the Union.[53]

Despite growing criticism, the commission form of government in the District of Columbia endured unchanged from 1874 to

53. *Congressional Record*, August 9, 1967, p. H10190.

1967. The situation had deteriorated by then to the point that reform could no longer by postponed. Chairman McMillan's objections did not prevail.

Almost every member of Congress feels obliged at times to rise above principle. The urge is overwhelming when the issues involve the location or relocation of federal field offices or delegations of decision-making authority to the field.

Wrangling over proposed locations of Customs' regional headquarters came close to defeating Reorganization Plan No. 1 of 1965 abolishing the offices of collector of customs, comptroller of customs, surveyor of customs, and appraisers of merchandise.[54] The plan itself did not specify regional headquarters locations, but an independent study by a group of management experts had recommended Boston, New York, Miami, New Orleans, San Francisco, and Chicago. To salvage the plan, Treasury bowed to congressional pressures and added regional offices in Baltimore, Houston, and Los Angeles—districts represented by influential members of the Committee on Government Operations and Appropriations Committee. The Government Operations Committee has jurisdiction over reorganization plans.

Decentralization makes an excellent theme for campaign speeches, but those who take campaign promises seriously run the risk of incurring congressional displeasure. Governors and mayors are competitors of senators and representatives. Once decisions are made outside the nation's capital, local officials can deal directly with federal field staff, and members of Congress are excluded from a key role in the decision-making processes. Constituents do not have to come to their senator or representative for assistance. What is worse, a local official may announce a federal project or grant before the member of Congress can issue a press release.

Franklin Roosevelt became painfully aware of senatorial jealousy of governors when he bypassed the Senate delegations and

54. Dominic Del Guidice, "Reorganization of the Bureau of Customs: A Struggle for Status," in *Reorganization by Presidential Plan: Three Case Studies,* National Academy of Public Administration, 1971.

dealt directly with his former colleagues in the Governors' Conference. He told Frances Perkins, "Every governor, particularly in states where the governor's salary is about $3,000 looks forward to being a United States Senator. No United States Senator, even if he belongs to the same party, likes to be ousted by the superior prestige and patronage which the expenditure of federal money may get for the governor. Well, *that* is something to remember."[55]

The House Committee on Appropriations in 1967 warned "against overemphasis on regionalization." In the committee's view, "Many people fear that the regional offices will, to a great extent, become one more administrative layer that important matters must clear, since there will always be the right of appeal to headquarters, and with regard to many decisions, headquarters will have to give final approval in the absence of an appeal. The committee feels that there is valid reason for this apprehension."[56] The committee denied requested increases to finance strengthening of HEW field staffs and decentralization of the office of education. In barring further regionalization, the committee was reflecting not only the traditional congressional bias but also lobbying by state education agencies that preferred to deal directly with Washington rather than with their own state houses.

If we persist in treating separately those things that are inseparable, we will seek in vain the improvements in government structure and processes that must be accomplished to maintain the effective functioning of our democratic system. More studies of executive branch organization in isolation from the Congress are likely to be unproductive. These interrelationships are beginning to be recognized. The Senate Committee on Governmental Affairs, in its report recommending enactment of legislation to establish a Commission on More Effective Government,

55. Frances Perkins, *The Roosevelt I Knew*, The Viking Press, 1946, p. 172.

56. House Committee on Appropriations, Departments of Labor and Health, Education, and Welfare Appropriations Bill, 1968, Report No. 271, 90th Congress, 1st Session, p. 4.

made clear that the proposed Commission's mandate would include executive–legislative relations. It cautioned, however, that the Commission would not have a roving charter "for the study of congressional organization and operations per se."[57]

In proposing regorganization of the congressional committee structure the Senate and House Select Committees on Committees largely ignored interrelationships with executive organization. Roger H. Davidson and Walter Oleszek, who served on the staff of the House Select Committee, report that the committee "though not adverse to promoting better legislative–executive relationships, never gave the matter high priority."[58] The members of the House Committee deliberately rejected the concept of developing a structure parallel to that of the executive branch. Committee structure was viewed by both committees as something almost exclusively concerned with distribution of power within the Congress.

Admittedly, reform of congressional organization presents a unique complex of difficult issues that are not raised by executive reorganization. Every member of the Congress constitutes an independent sovereign entity subject to no authority other than the Congress as a whole or the voters in his or her constituency. Congressional structure must be capable of reconciling the needs of members and the needs of the Congress as an institution.

Existing arrangements result from compromises and historical accidents, not from conscious organizational philosophy or planning to achieve identified purposes. Committee jurisdictions reflect a series of pragmatic decisions designed mainly to provide an acceptable division of the workload and to secure committee assignments that enhance an individual member's ability to represent and serve his or her constituency. Inadequate attention has been given to the implications of these decisions for government policies, program-administration, and relationships with the executive branch.

57. Senate Report 97–179, 97th Congress, 1st Session, p. 8.

58. Davidson and Oleszek, *Congress Against Itself*, p. 9.

In determining committee jurisdictions, the Congress should be aware that the kind of constituency that is being created can significantly influence policy outcomes and encourage or discourage alliances with executive agencies and interest groups. Constituencies can be established in such a way that a committee will be uninterested in or actually hostile to certain program objectives. If, for example, members seek assignments on the House Education and Labor Committee principally because of their interest in labor legislation, then education is certain to be a matter of secondary concern. Care must be taken to ensure that committees have reasonably consistent sets of program responsibilities and that no single function is so dominant that it will determine committee membership and outlook.

Committee assignments should be viewed as something more than a means for distributing power within the Congress. If the government is to function effectively, congressional organization also must be compatible with that of the executive branch. Speaker Carl Albert was of the view that "up to a point" legislative committee jurisdictions should reflect the organization within the executive branch.[59] This does not imply that executive and legislative organization structures must be identical. A legislative body has different requirements from the executive.

Obviously any committee structure that fails to serve the needs of individual members and their constituents will be unacceptable. But compensating features should be built into the present system to balance the strong centrifugal forces representing the particular interests of professional and economic groups and regions. Such urgent problems as energy, rural poverty, and urban transportation should not be permitted to fall within the cracks of the present committee and subcommittee structure. If the Congress is to be something more than a representative and advocate of the diverse interests in our society, it must be capable of examining problems from a national perspective and reviewing and appraising the results of executive operations.

59. House Select Committee on Committees, Vol. 1 of 3. Part 1 of 2, May 1973, p. 15.

Sooner or later the Congress will be compelled to grasp the nettle. The existing status quo breeds frustration in the Congress, ineffectiveness in the executive branch, and rising dissatisfaction among the citizenry.

3

Executive Branch Organization: View from the White House

Andrew Jackson saw it as the president's "especial duty to protect the liberties and rights of the people and the integrity of the Constitution against the Senate, or the House of Representatives, or both together."[1] As the elected representative of *all* the American people, the president alone has the power and the responsibility to balance the national interest against the strong centrifugal forces in the Congress for the special interests of subject matter or region. His effectiveness in performing this pivotal role within our constitutional system depends in no small measure on his instinctive grasp of the political and strategic uses of organization type and structure.

Such insight is not likely to be gained within the halls of the Congress or in the military service. Perspectives, attitudes, and behavior patterns developed on Capitol Hill or in the Pentagon become a way of life. They are the key to understanding the style, values, and administrative habits of Presidents Truman, Eisenhower, Kennedy, Johnson, and Ford.

Five of our last eight presidents earned their public reputations in the Congress. Whatever its other virtues as a breeding ground for presidents, the Congress is a poor school for execu-

1. Quoted in Clinton Rossiter, *The American Presidency*, The New American Library, Inc., 1956, p. 92.

tives and managers. The emphasis in a legislative body is on individuals, not institutions or organizations. Legislators do not think in institutional terms, except when some immediate constituency interest is threatened. The skills needed are those of the tactician, not the long-range strategist. Congress cannot respond to problems, other than with speeches, press releases, investigations, and, ultimately, enactment of laws and appropriation of money.

Some senators are critical of what John Gardner calls "the vending-machine concept of social change. Put a coin in the machine and out comes a piece of candy. If there is a social problem, pass a law and out comes a solution."[2] Senator Abraham Ribicoff acknowledged that "because we rely so heavily on the programmatic approach—passing a program whenever we discover a problem or a part of the problem—and rely so little on a systematic approach that would treat our major problems in a comprehensive manner—our efforts often are marked by confusion, frustration, and delay."[3] But the critics are unable to offer clear alternatives. The diffusion of power within the Congress and the inherent constraints of the legislative process do not foster concentration on long-range goals or allow anything other than a piecemeal approach to problem solving.

Within the Congress, words are sometimes equated with deeds. Votes represent final acts. There is concern with administration, but it is focused principally on those elements that directly affect constituency interests or committee jurisdictions. Legislative proposals are seldom debated from the viewpoint of their administrative feasibility. Grubby details of planning, organizing, staffing, and developing the administrative system to translate laws into working programs are for someone else to worry about. It is assumed that the executive branch or, in the case of grants-in-aid, state and local governments have or can obtain the neces-

2. John W. Gardner, *No Easy Victories,* Harper & Row, 1968, p. 28.

3. Senate Committee on Government Operations, Subcommittee on Executive Reorganization, hearings on Modernizing the Federal Government, January–May 1968, p. 2.

sary competence to devise and install efficient delivery systems. If things go wrong, failure can always be attributed to the incompetence or stupidity of the administrators.

Congress is weak on follow-through, even though it has been devoting increasing attention to legislative oversight. Laws on the statute books are not news, except when investigations disclose scandals or serious abuses in their administration. The political payoffs from measures to improve administrative efficiency or to promote administrative reform are minimal. To capture the headlines, studies must be launched into problems of the moment and new legislative proposals thrown into the hopper. An ambitious senator with an eye on the White House has an insatiable appetite for "ideas" that will keep him on the front pages and contribute to his national image.

For a president, long service in the Senate or House carries with it special disabilities. President Johnson saw the outside world through the eyes of the Congress, particularly the Senate. Congressional reaction on major issues was, for him, the most accurate and reliable expression of the national will. As a result, his sensitivity to evolving trends in public opinion and national concerns was markedly reduced.

The Johnson "system," which functioned admirably in the Senate, had fundamental weaknesses when installed in the White House. The essence of the Johnson system was a network of loyal henchmen who could be counted on to furnish timely information and help when needed, bilateral negotiations, and meticulous head counts before action. You moved when you had the votes, not before. Effective operation of the system placed a premium on secrecy. Premature disclosure of the majority leader's position would seriously impair his ability to harmonize the contending forces and arrive at a consensus.

Presidential leadership demands something more than the talents of an expert congressional power broker. People want to know where the president stands and what he stands for. Secrecy cuts off the communication flow within the executive branch and blurs the president's public image. Presidential greatness is not measured by his legislative batting average or his standing in the public opinion polls. A true gauge is his capacity for leadership—his ability to anticipate and articulate the nation's needs, hopes, fears, and aspirations. In the words of the first president: "For the more combined and distant things are seen, the more likely they are to be turned to advantage."[4]

Introduction of the congressional style and culture into the White House was in part an inevitable by-product of growing dependence by the Congress on the president for leadership and initiative in developing major legislative proposals and in setting the legislative timetable. This trend was visible before President Johnson, but, because he did nothing on a small scale, it was magnified and brought into sharper focus during his administration. President Johnson instructed his 1964 task forces that he wanted to be an activist president, "not a caretaker of past gains." So far as his domestic program was concerned, he conceived of activism primarily in terms of bold, innovative legislative proposals.

Activist presidents necessarily will continue to think in these terms, even those who have not graduated from the Congress. Major White House emphasis will and should be given to development of the legislative program; indeed, the Congress will insist on it. Difficulties occur when the approach is not systematic and selective, and the enactment of administration bills in wholesale lots becomes the overriding objective.

Unlike a legislator, a president should view the passage of a law as a beginning, not an end. His responsibility does not cease when he has decided *what* to do. The less politically rewarding and often more complex task of determining *how* to do it must be undertaken by the executive, if programs are to produce results. Training in the Congress does not equip a president to deal with the *how* to, and he is predisposed to downgrade its importance. The tendency has been, as noted by Louis Brownlow, "to elevate the political consideration, the *what* to do, above the

4. Quoted in Douglass Cater, *Power in Washington*, Vintage Books, 1964, p. 253.

administrative consideration of how to do it," and "even on the rare occasions when administrative questions do rise to a level where they are subject to general and popular discussion, very frequently that discussion will go off at a tangent whose direction is determined by some political, even some partisan or pressure group, interest."[5]

Brownlow made this observation some thirty years ago. In the interim, the strengthening of the staff resources available to the president has not noticeably enhanced White House appreciation or understanding of administrative management. If anything, the growing preoccupation with the legislative program and legislative and political tactics reinforce the disposition to dismiss administrative and organization problems as annoying trivia.

Presidents would do well to heed the advice of Joseph A. Califano, Jr., who came to the following conclusion as the result of his experience as a senior presidential assistant and cabinet secretary:

> Those who try to govern must be tenacious and pragmatic. The task is not for anyone who thinks that deciding an issue, signing a memorandum, or ordering that something be done is the end of the matter. It is only the first step in an arduous journey of thousands of bureaucratic miles.[6]

Responsibility for reminding the president and his immediate staff of the importance of the "how to" was assigned to the Bureau of the Budget. But the Bureau's effectiveness as the advocate of management planning declined as budget directors became more preoccupied with fiscal and economic policy.

Reorganization Plan No. 2 of 1970 was designed to reemphasize the management role of the Office of Management and Budget (the successor to the Bureau of the Budget) and provide the president with substantially enhanced institutional staff capability in

5. Louis Brownlow, *The President and the Presidency,* Public Administration Service, 1949, p. 91.

6. Joseph A. Califano, Jr., *Governing America,* A Touchstone Book, 1981, p. 449.

areas of executive management other than the budget—"particularly in program evaluation and coordination, improvement of executive branch organization, information and management systems, and development of executive talent."[7] Whatever its intentions, the reorganization plan has not restored the Office of Management and Budget, as an organization, to its position as the "President's principal arm for the exercise of his managerial function." The office has not reestablished the monopoly the Bureau of the Budget once exercised as the "unique supplier of presidential services" and adviser on legislation and government organization.[8]

In the first year of the Reagan administration, the OMB displayed almost a total lack of interest in management issues, except for controls over travel, audiovisuals, and motor vehicles. Finally, in September 1982 the OMB lost even nominal management leadership with the creation of the Cabinet Council on Management and Administration, chaired by Edwin Meese III.

As now structured, the OMB cannot serve effectively as the president's "management conscience" and organization strategist. What Chester A. Newland calls the "politicization and deinstitutionalization of the Executive Office of the President" has eliminated the "neutral competence" that enabled the Bureau of the Budget ably to serve both Democratic and Republican presidents.[9] Hugh Heclo is correct in noting that neutral competence "entails not just following orders but having the practical knowledge of government and the broker's skills of the governmental

7. Message of the President of the United States transmitting Reorganization Plan No. 2 of 1970, House Document No. 91–275, 91st Congress, 2nd Session.

8. For analysis of the change in the Bureau of the Budget's role, see Allen Schick, "The Budget Bureau That Was: Thoughts on the Rise, Decline and Future of a Presidential Agency," *Law and Contemporary Problems,* School of Law, Duke University, Vol. 35, Summer 1970.

9. Chester A. Newland, "Executive Office Policy Apparatus: Enforcing the Reagan Agenda," in Lester M. Salamon and Michael S. Lund, eds., *The Reagan Presidency and the Governing of America,* The Urban Institute, 1985, p. 167.

marketplace that makes one's advice worthy of attention. Thus neutral competence is a strange amalgam of loyalty that argues back, partisanship that shifts with the changing partisans, independence that depends on others."[10]

The distinction between institutional staff in the Executive Office of the President serving the presidency and the White House staff serving the president has been seriously eroded. OMB's director functions more as an assistant to the president than the head of an independent office. At its senior levels, the OMB has been almost completely politicized and career staff rarely have direct access to the principal policymakers in the OMB and the White House.

These developments have led nonpartisan organizations such as the National Academy of Public Administration to find that "OMB no longer has the talent base nor the recognized capacity for leadership" to sustain the Reagan administration's widely publicized Reform '88 project to improve, consolidate, and streamline the federal government's management systems. The Academy has urged that responsibility for management reform be transferred from the OMB to a new Office of Federal Management in the Executive Office of the President.[11] The Grace Commission also recommended establishing an Office of Federal Management, but it would be more akin to a department of administration with jurisdiction over personnel and procurement functions as well as budget and administrative management.[12]

President Roosevelt recognized that the White House staff is not immune to a virulent species of Parkinson's disease. Work will expand in proportion to the number of people available to do it. The president needs help, but he does not need helpers

---

10. Hugh Heclo, "OMB and the Presidency—The Problem of 'Neutral Competence,' " *The Public Interest*, No. 38, Winter 1975.

11. National Academy of Public Administration, "Revitalizing Federal Management: Managers and Their Overburdened Systems," November 1983, p. 12.

12. Presidents Private-Sector Survey on Cost Control, *Task Force Report on Federal Management Systems*, June 13, 1983.

who monopolize his time and try to interpose themselves between him and his department heads. President Ford was estimated to have spent 50 percent of his time with White House staff, even though he desired to maintain an open office.[13] When James H. Rowe, Jr., one of the original assistants with a "passion for anonymity," asked President Roosevelt for an assistant, his request was politely but firmly denied. Roosevelt told him that if he was unable to do his job without assistance, he was not doing what the president wanted him to do.

Rowe was impressed by Roosevelt's deep understanding of government organization and "what in it was good for Presidents," and his insistence that "the White House not do everything." He pushed as much on the departments as he could and wanted only vital matters to come to him and then only for a last quick look.[14]

Roosevelt drew a sharp distinction between staff who served him as president and those whose first duty was to the presidency. Rowe was assigned responsibility to assist in the process of reviewing and developing recommendations on enrolled bills, but with precise instructions that his job "was to look after the President," and the Budget Bureau's job was to protect the interests of the presidency.[15] The personal, political interests of an incumbent president and the interests of the presidency as an institution are by no means identical, although it may be hard at times for White House staff to see the difference. Continuity is essential for protection of the institution, and this is something no White House staff can provide.

Roosevelt emphasized that his administrative assistants were to be "personal aides to the President and shall have no authority over anyone in any department or agency, including the Executive Office of the President." Executive Order No. 8248, September 8, 1939, establishing the divisions of the Executive

13. Stephen J. Wayne, *The Legislative Presidency,* Harper & Row, 1978, pp. 54–55.
14. Letter to the author from James H. Rowe, Jr., dated February 17, 1969.
15. Ibid.

Office of the President, directed: "In no event shall the administrative assistants be interposed between the President and the
head of any department or agency or between the President and
any one of the divisions in the Executive Office of the President."
The executive order reflected the President's Committee on Administrative Management's view that assistants to the president
"would not be Assistant Presidents in any sense" and should remain in the background, "issue no orders, make no decision,
emit no public statements."[16]

President Nixon did not rescind or modify Executive Order
No. 8248. Shortly after his inauguration he explained that his
personal staff would function exclusively as "information gather-
ers," not as major policy advisers or "freewheeling" operators.[17]

The contrast between the White House office prescribed by
executive order and envisaged by President Nixon in 1969 and
that described by H. R. Haldeman, John Ehrlichman, John
Dean, and other witnesses before the Senate Select Committee
on Presidential Campaign Activities could not be more dramatic. From analysis of the testimony and evidence, it would
appear that President Nixon's principal assistants acted on the
following assumptions:

—The president's constitutional powers, including his inherent
  powers, are delegable and may be legitimately exercised by
  his principal assistants acting in his name.
—The president must operate on the basis that staff come to
  him only when called.
—As surrogates of the president, the principal assistants must
  be "self-starters" because "in the Nixon White House there
  is no one else who is going to have the time to supervise,
  make assignments, decide what should be looked into. It
  would be impossible for the President, or any one person in

16. Report of the President's Committee on Administrative Management,
U.S. Government Printing Office, 1939, p. 5.

17. See column of Rowland Evans and Robert Novak, *Washington Post*, January 16, 1969.

his behalf, to keep informed of everything being done by the staff, even in areas of major current interest or concern."

—Department and agency heads must obey orders from the White House even in those areas in which statutory powers are vested in them and they are legally accountable for the actions taken. Agency heads should understand that when a request comes from the White House, they must accomplish it without being told how to do it.[18]

No development in the past quarter of a century has been more striking or significant than the growth in the size and power of the president's personal household. The 1984 budget provided for a White House complement of 443 permanent positions. Thomas E. Cronin, among others, has noted that "the Presidency has become a large bureaucracy itself, rapidly acquiring many dubious characteristics of large bureaucracies in the process: layering, overspecialization, communication gaps, inadequate coordination, and an impulse to become consumed with short-term operational concerns at the expense of thinking systematically about the consequences of varying sets of policies and priorities and important long-range problems."[19]

Tensions between political "dilettantes" and civil service "experts" are inevitable, as Max Weber observed in his classic essay on bureauracy, but these tensions are heightened when the competing White House bureauracy is staffed with inexperienced outsiders with little knowledge of the federal government. Ronald Reagan initially surrounded himself with cronies from California—Edwin Meese III and Michael K. Deaver, James A. Baker III, whose ties were to vice president elect George Bush and President Ford, and survivors from the Nixon White House, including Martin C. Anderson and Richard V. Allan. The Reagan staff was considerably more knowledgeable about Washington mores than that of Jimmy Carter, but the primary qualifica-

18. Senate Select Committee on Presidential Campaign Activities, hearings May–August 1973, pp. 1682, 2514–17, 2599.

19. Thomas E. Cronin, "The Swelling of the Presidency," *Saturday Review*, February 1973.

tion for selection appears to have been personal association with Reagan and service in the political campaign.

What has come into being is a presidential court with all the trappings and intrigues associated with an ancient monarchy. The Johnson court is vividly characterized in George Reedy's book, *The Twilight of the Presidency,* as a "mass of intrigue, posturing, strutting, cringing and pious commitment to irrelevant windbaggery."[20] Members of the White House staff possess no power in their own right and depend for status, prestige, and influence on the favor of the president. Consequently, staff compete with each other, other units in the Executive Office of the President, and Cabinet secretaries for information and presidential access.

No one will quarrel with the need for some growth in the size of the White House staff. The world of Ronald Reagan is not the world of Franklin D. Roosevelt. Some would argue that the centralization of power in the White House is a necessary and inevitable response to the incompatible and contradictory demands made on the government, the consequences of the technological revolution, the increasing number of federal programs cutting across established jurisdictional lines and the frequency of jurisdictional disputes, the need to control departmental and bureau satrapies that are responsive only to their constituencies, the decline of the Cabinet as an institution, and the supineness of the Congress.

But there are dangers. One of the prime lessons of Watergate is that large "do-it-yourself" staffs can isolate the president and, if they mirror his personality too closely, accentuate rather than compensate for his weaknesses. Most important, a large, ambitious, and able staff can create for the president an illusion of self-sufficiency where none exists. Congressman Morris K. Udall summed it up well in the following words:

> Certainly no loyal American would begrudge any President
> the expertise or manpower needed to cope with the pressing

20. George E. Reedy, *The Twilight of the Presidency,* The New American Library, Inc., 1970, p. xii.

problems of the nation and the world. But a serious problem
does arise when the White House staff begins to replace both
the functions of the Cabinet and the career civil service.[21]

Few studies of the presidency have failed to quote with ap-
probation Charles G. Dawes's statement that "Cabinet members
are the natural enemies of the President." They rarely, however,
quote the first budget director in full. What Dawes said was that
"Cabinet members are vice presidents in charge of spending, and
as such they are the natural enemies of the President."[22] Dawes
obviously was speaking from the perspective of budget director.
Cabinet members may be the natural enemies of the budget director, or White House staff, but they are the president's natural
allies. A president may not like his Cabinet members; he may
disagree with them and suspect their loyalty; but he cannot destroy their power without seriously undermining his own.

Sudden awareness of his dependency on the executive establishment and the bureaucracy can produce severe cultural shock
in a president fresh from the Congress or, for that matter, from
the Pentagon or a state house. A president is not self-sufficient.
The Congress can perform its constitutional functions without
the executive establishment and the bureaucracy. A president
cannot.

It is the agency heads, not the president, who have the men,
money, materiel, and legal powers. With a few exceptions, such
as foreign assistance, disaster relief, and economic stabilization
activities, funds are appropriated to the agencies and authority
to execute the programs is vested by law in agency heads. As a
general rule, the president cannot enter into a contract, make
a loan or grant, initiate a public works project, or hire and fire
federal employees other than those appointed by him. The president's authority to approve or modify regulations issued by agencies has been challenged on the grounds that such power has not

21. House Committee on Post Office and Civil Service, Committee Print No.
20, April 24, 1971, pp. 2–3.

22. Kermit Gordon, *Reflections on Spending*, The Brookings Institution,
1967, p. 15.

been expressly granted to him by law.[23] To work his will in the Congress and outside community, a president must have at his disposal the trade goods controlled by the agencies and be able to enlist the support of their constituencies.

The occupant of the "most powerful office on earth" quickly learns the harsh truth. His executive power has a very frail constitutional foundation—the power to appoint officers of the United States. Appointing authority may be so hedged about with restrictions as to limit severely his discretion. He can fire officers performing administrative duties, but here again his power is limited. Dismissal of a high official is a measure of last resort, which can be utilized only under extreme provocation.

A president does not enforce his will by dictate. His instructions are not obeyed automatically. Jesse Jones admitted that when the president "asked me to do something which in my opinion we could not or should not do—and that happened only a few times—we just did not do it."[24] Harry Truman believed that the principal power possessed by a president was "to bring people in and try to persuade them to do what they ought to do without persuasion. That's what I spend most of my time doing. That's what the powers of the President amount to."[25]

An alliance—which is what the executive branch really is—is by definition a confederation of sovereigns joined together in pursuit of some common goal. Some members may be more powerful than others, but they are nonetheless mutually interdependent. Individual purposes and goals are subordinated only to the extent necessary to hold the alliance intact. Each member will find it necessary at times to act contrary to the interests of the alliance when compelled to do so to protect his own vital interests. Unless a president is able to convince his departmental allies that they need him as much as he needs them, they will inevitably gravitate to another power base.

23. Committee on Energy and Commerce, "Presidential Control of Agency Rulemaking," Committee Print 97-0, 97th Congress, 1st Session.

24. Jesse H. Jones, *Fifty Billion Dollars: My Thirteen Years with the RFC (1932–1945)*, The Macmillan Co., 1951, p. 262.

25. Rossiter, *The American Presidency*, p. 149.

The executive branch is no more a monolith than the Congress. There are multiple power centers, and the president must employ all of the authority and ingenuity at his command "to evoke the prime loyalty of the divers parts of the great governmental machine, each part being also animated by loyalty to its particular purpose."[26]

Intellectually, presidents recognize that their own power is not entirely separable from that of their department heads. President Reagan was echoing the words of Jimmy Carter and Richard M. Nixon when he pledged to have the Cabinet rather than the White House staff take the lead in helping him formulate policy.[27] A plan to have Cabinet secretaries take offices in the Executive Office Building next to the White House was seriously considered but later abandoned.

But presidents operate under rigid time restraints. What they want, they want now. They are impatient with solutions that go beyond the next congressional election, and their maximum time span is four years. They say they welcome disagreement and dissent, but cannot understand why Cabinet members do not share the presidential perspective. The fiefdoms are fractious, and the machinery of government moves too slowly to suit their purposes. Their experience in the Congress has given them neither the knowledge nor the aptitude to energize the executive establishment, so as far as possible they attempt to bypass and neutralize it.

Executive departments and the bureaucracy are called on to behave in a way that is contrary to their very nature. McGeorge Bundy reflected a typical White House view when he said, "Cabinet officers are special pleaders" and "should run their part of the government for the Administration—not run to the Administration for the interests of their part of the government."[28] One might as well repeat Professor Henry Higgins's plaint in *My Fair*

26. Brownlow, *The President and the Presidency,* p. 64.

27. *The New York Times,* February 15, 1981.

28. Senate Committee on Government Operations, p. 282.

Lady, "Why can't a woman be more like a man?" as ask "Why can't Cabinet members act more like presidents?" Those who accept the differences can enjoy them and put them to proper use.

The bureaucracy is damned as "uncreative" because it is unable to satisfy the White House appetite for immediate solutions to complex social and economic problems and dramatic imaginative proposals for the legislative program. "Slow moving," "unresponsive," "disloyal" are among the milder epithets used to describe the bureaucracy. Bundy is dismayed because "the contest between the President and the bureaucracy is as real today as ever, and there has been no significant weakening in the network of triangular alliances which unite all sorts of interest groups with their agents in the Congress and their agents in the bureaucracy."[29]

As an entity, the bureaucracy is no better equipped to manufacture grand designs for government programs than carpenters, electricians, and plumbers are to be architects. But if an architect attempted to build a house, the results might well be disastrous. What the White House identifies as bureaucracy's inherent deficiencies are often its strengths. Effective functioning of the governmental machine requires a high degree of stability, uniformity, and awareness of the impact of new policies, regulations, and procedures on the affected public.

The bureaucracy all too frequently is not asked for its advice on the "how to," for which it does have the knowledge and experience to make a contribution. Senior career managers attribute the government's "loss of credibility" to the "gap between federal policies and their implementation." In their judgment, "better means are needed to draw the experienced program manager into the processes of drafting legislation or developing administration policy so that practical problems of implementation are faced as a regular part of those processes."[30]

29. Ibid., p. 281.

30. U.S. Office of Personnel Management, Federal Executive Institute, "Management Improvement Agenda for the Eighties," June 30–July 2, 1980, p. 2.

Although the White House may not consider a Cabinet member's participation in the development of a legislative proposal essential, the president will hold him to account for ensuring its enactment by the Congress. As far as the president is concerned, a Cabinet member's primary responsibility is to mobilize support both within and outside the Congress for presidential measures and to act as a legislative tactician. Major questions of policy and legislative strategy are reserved, however, for decision by the White House staff.

To perform in this role, a department head must maintain the loyalty of his subordinates and strengthen his alliances with congressional committees and interest groups, which in turn raises questions about his allegiance to the president and confirms White House distrust. John Ehrlichman complained that Cabinet officers "go off and marry the natives."[31] Senior Carter staff maintained that Cabinet secretaries were given too much leeway at the start of the administration and had to be put on notice that "we expect them to work with the President in a positive way."[32] "Loyalty" and "ability to work with White House staff" were the primary tests employed by President Carter in determining who would be retained in his Cabinet. The net result was that more and more, those responsible for carrying out policies were excluded as "special pleaders" from the development of the policies they were to administer. The ill-concealed unhappiness of several Carter Cabinet members was not surprising.

Joseph W. Bartlett, former undersecretary of commerce, noted the difficulties posed for Cabinet officers by the "baffling ambivalent" White House attitude. White House staff demand "unquestioning obedience" to orders, but the president expects secretaries to maintain "at least the public image of independence" and the capability to enlist their constituencies in support of presidential proposals. Bartlett observed: "In short, a Cabinet officer who is loyal to the President and his deputies but feels con-

31. *Washington Post,* August 24, 1972.

32. Dom Bonafede, "Carter Sounds Retreat from 'Cabinet Government,'" *National Journal,* July 17, 1976.

strained to retain some independence must anticipate trouble in carrying water on both shoulders."[33]

No president can afford to allow his Cabinet, the Congress, or outside constituencies to restrict his choice of counselors or the devices he employs to obtain advice. He must be no less zealous in preventing his own staff from doing so.

Each component of the governmental system has its own special function. Each has its strengths and each its weaknesses. The White House staff is no exception. The most critical and difficult job facing a president is to learn the system and to ensure that each component is properly utilized and exploited to its full potential.

Perhaps a president's most important lesson is to learn the strengths and limitations of his personal staff. There are many things the White House staff cannot do or will do poorly. They do not have technical competence and do not have the time to acquire it. Errors may occur when staff usurp the functions of technicians. These errors can be embarrassing.

Authorship of a proposal necessarily narrows the staff's vision and judgment. The advice they give the president and their evaluation of conflicting opinions will inevitably be colored by their own biases. They are disposed to discount objections and to exaggerate potential benefits. The president cannot rely on them to report accurately and promptly on their projects that go sour. A president has too many advisers who are protagonists of special interests; he does not need them in his own household.

Members of the staff do not have to explain or justify their proposals before the Congress. White House staff do not testify. The fact that one ultimately has to undergo cross-examination by the Congress is a healthy tempering influence and compels an official to anticipate the questions that are going to be asked. It is too easy for a staffer to gloss over the unanswered questions.

Unless decisions are fed into the institutional machinery, there

33. Joseph W. Bartlett and Douglas N. Jones, "Managing a Cabinet Agency: Problems of Performance at Commerce," *Public Administration Review*, Vol. 34, No. 1, January–February 1974.

will be no effective follow-through. President Johnson's senior aide, Joseph Califano, conceded, "We are not equipped to maintain day-to-day relationship with only one program—no matter how important."[34] If a White House aide picks up the ball and runs with it, no one will be around to retrieve the ball when it is dropped.

Bill Moyers is right when he observes that power is the president's greatest resource and "is not something that he is likely to invest in people whose first allegiance is not to him."[35] Moyers does not seem to appreciate, however, that a president can conserve his power by delegating decision-making *authority* to agency heads. The distinction between power and authority is vital. When authority is delegated, the president can employ his power selectively and let others absorb the heat of the initial contact.

Presidential power is a precious commodity and is not inexhaustible. It retains its potency only as long as it is applied to issues of immediate presidential importance. White House staff have no power of their own, and whenever they exercise power they drain the president's limited resources. The Watergate record graphically demonstrates the consequences of allowing the presidency to speak with many voices. Furthermore, the president cannot disavow acts by White House aides even when they are acting on their own. All their mistakes become the president's mistakes.

According to John Ehrlichman, "jurisdictional conflicts between Cabinet officers and departments, levels of government all now find their way to the White House by some law of governmental gravity."[36] The assumption, however, that "White House clout" is always necessary to settle such disputes is questionable. If the White House enters a dispute prematurely, there is no appeal mechanism short of the president himself. It is far preferable to use the Office of Management and Budget, or some other executive office agency, to sort out the issues and act as a shock

34. Bernard J. Frieden and Marshall Kaplan, *The Politics of Neglect*, The MIT Press, 1975, p. 112.

35. *Washington Monthly*, February 1969.

36. Senate Select Committee on Presidential Campaign Activities, p. 2516.

absorber. When the differences are crystallized, the White House is in a better strategic position to step in and pronounce final judgment on the unresolved issues.

The answer does not lie in having the presidency secede from the executive branch and constituting it as an independent branch of the government. The Nixon administration moved in this direction by attempting to run the whole government from the White House. The bureaucratization and institutionalization of the White House as a separate branch has continued under Ronald Reagan.

What the president *does not do* may be as important as what he does do. It has been Reagan's strategy to avoid the mistakes of his immediate predecessors by limiting the subjects with which the president becomes personally identified. Overcentralization of decision making in the White House inevitably encourages buck passing and stifles initiative.

White House involvement inevitably produces a chain reaction that has repercussions throughout the executive establishment. Decisions are sucked up to the top, with the result that department heads may be compelled to deal with matters that might best be left to their bureau chiefs, and Washington bureau chiefs with matters that ought to be delegated to the field. Cabinet members are reluctant to delegate authority when their actions are subject to close White House scrutiny.

A president should carefully pick and choose the issues that merit his personal participation in the give and take of policy formulation. This does not imply that he should allow himself to become the captive of completed staff work to the point that his only option is to say yes or no. It does imply a need for a keen sense of timing as to when presidential participation will not cut off debate at too early a stage and discrimination to avoid overexposure and dilution of presidential influence.

President Truman deliberately limited his attendance at National Security Council meetings because he believed that his presence would inhibit frank and open discussion.[37] If a presi-

37. Sidney W. Souers, "Policy Formulation for National Security," *The American Political Science Review*, June 1949.

dent says at a council meeting, "I think thus and so," the others will take their cue from him.

A president's most important challenge is to harness the energy produced by diversity in support of the national good, not to try to eliminate it. The bureaucratic bastion cannot be reduced by bombarding it with a fusillade of White House directives ordering it to be more creative and more efficient. The perspectives of the president's chief lieutenants cannot be broadened or redirected by concentrating more and more power in the president's own household. More effective means for meeting the challenge are at a president's disposal, if he has the knowledge to use them and is willing to pay the cost.

A president should be as alert to safeguarding the powers and prestige of his department heads as to safeguarding those of his own office. To the extent that any department head's status and authority are downgraded, he is less able to resist the pressures brought on him by his constituencies, congressional committees, and the bureaucracy.

Kermit Gordon has cited instances in which the Budget Bureau "sometimes works in quiet collusion with an agency head who wants to make a sound but unpopular decision which would strain his relations with a bureau chief or the agency's clientele; the Bureau, exploiting its more secure sanctuary, will make no denial when word is passed to the protesting parties that the objectionable action was pressed on the agency by the Bureau of the Budget."[38] The White House and the Executive Office should not be permitted to become refuges for timid administrators. Yet confidence that in a crunch they can count on White House support fosters department heads' loyalty to the president and gives them the courage to take unpopular actions. Proposed reorganizations almost always require this kind of support. The secretary of the treasury, for example, cannot publicly advocate transfer of the Coast Guard to a Department of Transportation without jeopardizing his future relationships to the Coast Guard by mak-

38. Gordon, *Reflections on Spending*, p. 16.

ing it feel "unwanted." Whatever his personal views, he is obliged to protest for the record, even though he is quite prepared to be overruled.

Frontal assaults on the bureaucracy and entrenched constituencies can yield, at best, temporary gains, and the cost may well be excessive. A president is not powerless to bring about significant transformations in the bureaucracy and in the balance of power among constituencies, but his approach must be indirect. To secure lasting results, a president has to take positive action to alter the bases of bureaucratic and constituency power—administrative systems and organization structure—so as to adapt them to the nation's long-range goals and requirements. The task is fraught with hazards, but it can be done if the president exercises leadership and exploits fully the powers at his command. The likelihood of success is enhanced if actions are planned within the context of a well-conceived and realistic organization strategy. It is in the development of a sound and realistic organization strategy that recent presidents have failed most conspicuously.

In the words of Morton H. Halperin: "Every President needs to know how bureaucratic interests interact, in order to be the master rather than the prisoner of his organization, and also in order to mold the rational interests of the bureaucracies into the national interest as he sees it."[39]

Personnel systems are the nerve center of bureaucracy. It is idle for presidents to complain that the State Department is a "bowl of jelly," and then do nothing to reform the Foreign Service system, which makes the State Department what it is. The Department's career professionals have condemned the recruitment and promotion system for stifling "the creative dissent and responsible questioning of alternatives which could have helped the organization adapt to changing times."[40]

39. Morton H. Halperin, "Why Bureaucrats Play Games," *Foreign Policy*, No. 2, Spring 1971.

40. *Diplomacy for the 70's: A Program of Management Reform for the Department of State*, U.S. Government Printing Office, 1970, p. 306.

Control of the nonfederal agents on whom the government increasingly relies for service delivery demands a different strategy and set of tactics. Federal influence over these third parties—state and local governments and various private entities—is exercised mainly through the regulatory process. President Reagan was perhaps the first to recognize the need for procedures to ensure that regulations accord with administration policies.

Organization and reorganization can be used to change program emphasis and to modify the power balance among constituencies. But as Hugh Heclo has observed, "Reorganization plans or techniques like management by objectives and zero-based budgeting are all executive proclamations that presume rather than create changes in subordinates' behavior. Instituting new management techniques and making them part of the bureaucracy's standard operating procedure lie at the end of state-craft, not the beginning."[41] If he is to be successful in promoting desired change, a president must have an organization strategy. A miscellaneous collection of reorganization proposals, which may by design or otherwise include some of tremendous strategic significance, does not add up to an organization strategy.

James Webb demonstrated in the National Aeronautics and Space Administration what could be done with organizational restructuring as an "element of leadership."[42] In his efforts to maintain management initiative and drive, Webb "deliberately employed fairly frequent organizational restructuring. . . ."

Reorganization and restructuring are important, but they can be overemphasized. Califano exaggerates the difficulties when he asserts that "Any President may have one or two shots at it in his career, but that's all, maybe one that's already under way when he comes in and one he gets up himself."[43] There is no

41. Hugh Heclo, *A Government of Strangers: Executive Politics in Washington,* The Brookings Institution, 1977, p. 220.

42. Foreword to *Preliminary History of the National Aeronautic and Space Administration During the Administration of Lyndon B. Johnson,* National Aeronautics and Space Administration, January 15, 1969.

43. Meg Greenfield, "Joe Califano: Lessons of Experience on Decentralization," *Washington Post,* December 16, 1968.

contesting the fact, however, that major reorganizations do call for a heavy investment of presidential capital. The same results can sometimes be achieved at considerably less cost by building sound organizational concepts into the design of new programs. It is here that the lack of organizational strategy has hurt the most. Without agreed upon organizational concepts and goals, policies will be related solely to short-term tactical objectives.

At times the White House may give the impression of dashing off simultaneously in several different and conflicting directions. The Reagan White House has had particular difficulty in making up its mind whether the Department of Commerce should absorb most of the Department of Energy or be converted to a Department of Trade and Industry. It was unclear whether the administration supported either or both proposals.

When Franklin D. Roosevelt was president, he had a personal organization strategy. Roosevelt played with federal agencies as if they were pawns in a chess game, moving them wherever it would best strengthen his strategic position. He delighted in violating the organizational commandments laid down by the orthodox theorists. Organization for him was "fun," something that could not be said of any of his successors. Only Roosevelt could have written to his budget director:

> I agree with the Secretary of the Interior. Please have it carried out so that fur-bearing animals remain in the Department of the Interior.
>
> You might find out if any Alaska bears are still supervised by (a) War Department (b) Department of Agriculture (c) Department of Commerce. They have all had jurisdiction over Alaska bears in the past and many embarrassing situations have been created by the mating of a bear belonging to one Department with a bear belonging to another Department.
>
> F.D.R.
>
> P.S. I don't think the Navy is involved but it may be. Check the Coast Guard. You never can tell![44]

44. Memorandum for the Director of the Bureau of the Budget, July 20, 1939.

Roosevelt relied heavily on competition among agencies and checks and balances to keep final authority in his own hands.[45] Innovative programs were cultivated with care so they could grow strong roots before being transferred to old-line agencies that might stunt their development. Staff for the New Deal agencies was recruited from outside the civil service. At the same time, Roosevelt knew how to use his department heads and encouraged rather than deplored their dedication to departmental programs.

In fostering competition, Roosevelt was not organizing to produce conflict. Competition and conflict are not the same thing. One is constructive; the other is destructive. This difference is misunderstood by those who believe incorrectly that Roosevelt was promoting conflict for its own sake.

Roosevelt's organization strategy was formulated before he entered the White House. As assistant secretary of the Navy, he advocated strongly a national budget system under the president's direction and urged that department heads should be given complete authority in all matters over bureau chiefs. Rexford G. Tugwell cited this Roosevelt statement as providing

> something of a preview of his sophistication, as he entered the Presidency, in such matters. . . . As many still living can testify, one of the most obsessive preoccupations of Roosevelt as President was to be reorganization of the government. . . .[46]

Roosevelt knew in general terms what he wanted from his Committee on Administrative Management. The committee's primary focus was to be on "what gives the President more effective managerial control," rather than on the traditional goals of economy and efficiency.[47] Roosevelt instructed the committee to

45. For a description of the Roosevelt mode of operations, see Louis W. Koenig, *The Chief Executive*, Harcourt, Brace & World, Inc., 1964, pp. 166–68.

46. Quoted in A. J. Wann, "Franklin D. Roosevelt and the Bureau of the Budget," *Business and Government Review*, University of Missouri, March–April 1968.

47. Richard Polenberg, *Reorganizing Roosevelt's Government*, Harvard University Press, 1966, p. 17.

"not get lost in detail" and waste its time on constructing a neat and orderly organization chart. When Brownlow and Gulick discussed the committee's draft report with the president, they found that their recommendations were in accord with Roosevelt's own thinking. The president's Committee on Administrative Management performed an indispensable service, but its contribution consisted mainly in providing a conceptual framework for the president's organization strategy. Unless a president has an organization strategy, he runs a considerable risk in establishing an outside commission on federal organization that may devise its own strategy without regard for the president's interests and objectives.

President Truman had an organization strategy, but it was that supplied to him by the first Hoover Commission. The Hoover Commission reports provided a conceptual framework for the organizational philosophy developed by Herbert Hoover during his years as president and secretary of commerce, and did not stem from Truman's own thinking. There is no evidence, however, that the return to orthodoxy symbolized by many of the commission's recommendations was in conflict with Truman's views.

Of the forty-one reorganization plans transmitted by President Truman under the Reorganization Act of 1949, nine dealt with relatively minor matters and had little if any strategic significance. Most of the others did have a unifying theme—a theme that tied together the recommendations of the first Hoover Commission and made them a consistent whole. Though expressed in terms of the orthodox dogmas, they complemented the recommendations of the President's Committee on Administrative Management and were Rooseveltian in their concepts of presidential power. The fourteen reorganization plans vesting in department heads the functions previously vested in subordinate officers, and transferring "executive functions" to regulatory commission chairmen designated by the president were calculated to eliminate some of the impediments to the effective exercise of presidential and secretarial power. The Congress reacted by disapproving the plans reorganizing the Treasury Department, Interstate Commerce Commission, Federal Trade Commission, and Federal Communications Commission.

Truman did accomplish the first restructuring of executive departments since 1913. At his initiative, steps were taken toward unification of the armed services, and this led to formation of the National Military Establishment in 1949. The powers of the new secretary of defense as head of the establishment were compromised seriously in order to accommodate the deep-seated and often bitter differences among the Army, Navy, and Air Force. Truman twice failed in attempts to elevate the Federal Security Agency to Cabinet rank. The idea for a Department of Welfare or Department of Health, Education, and Security did not originate with Truman but with the president's Committee on Administrative Management.

Truman was not given to theorizing about organization, but, as in other areas, his intuitive responses exhibited a keen understanding of the issues. He was quick to sense threats to the powers of the presidency. His adroit maneuvers scotched the schemes of those who wanted to assure Defense domination of the National Security Council by housing the Council in the Pentagon, where office space already had been prepared, and by designating the secretary of defense as chairman in the president's absence.[48] Truman's forthright veto of the bill creating the National Science Foundation took courage and his veto message forecast the problems that would result if public powers were yielded to private institutions.

President Eisenhower shared Truman's orthodoxy, but not his intuition or convictions about the powers of the presidency. A President's Committee on Government Organization, composed of Nelson Rockefeller, Milton Eisenhower, and Arthur Flemming, was organized prior to the inauguration and remained more or less active throughout the Eisenhower administration. Neither Eisenhower nor the committee produced a coherent organization doctrine.

48. Senate Committee on Government Operations, Subcommittee on National Policy Machinery, "Organizing for National Security," Vol. 2, Studies and Background Materials, p. 421, and footnote, p. 422.

Except for the 1953 reorganization of the Department of Defense and the establishment of the Department of Health, Education, and Welfare, Eisenhower's fourteen reorganization plans either represented follow-up on Hoover Commission recommendations or dealt with minor items. President Eisenhower passed on the most controversial proposals coming from his Advisory Committee—a First Secretary of Government, an Office of Executive Management, a Department of Transportation, and transfer of the Army Corps of Engineer's civil functions to the Department of the Interior—as a legacy to President Kennedy.

President Eisenhower was willing to say the right things, but he was less willing to act. Draft veto messages occasionally became signing statements, as is evidenced by signing statements deploring legislation requiring executive agencies "to come into agreement" with congressional committees, or circumventing the president's veto authority.[49] He did veto a few of these so-called encroachment bills. President Eisenhower hailed the Farm Credit Act of 1953, which for all practical purposes made the farm credit system independent of the president, as "another milestone in our march toward an agriculture which is productive, profitable, responsible and free from excessive regulation."[50] He had some second thoughts when the board later defied his instructions, but, nonetheless, approved "despite some misgivings" the Farm Credit Act of 1956, which relaxed the few remaining controls over the farm credit institutions.[51]

President Eisenhower warned about the growing influence of the military-industrial complex, but apparently he did not recognize the role of institutional arrangements in fostering that influence. In any event, he did nothing to curb the power of the industry advisory committees that flourished and multiplied during his administration and sometimes arrogated to themselves effective decision-making authority.

49. See, for example, the signing statements of the 1956 Defense Appropriation Act and the Small Reclamation Act of 1966.

50. Statement of President Eisenhower on signature of H.R. 4353, August 6, 1953.

51. Statement of President on H.R. 10285, July 26, 1956.

President Kennedy evinced little interest in organization structure and administration; his orientation was almost entirely toward individuals and programs. He appointed a panel of advisers on government organization but never used them collectively, and rarely as individuals, except for Neustadt. The main thesis of Sorensen's book, *Decision-Making in the White House,* which stems from his experience in the Kennedy administration, is that there is too much preoccupation with "form and structure" and too little with "the more dynamic and fluid forces on which Presidential decisions are based."[52]

Kennedy was unwilling to send forward a reorganization plan unless he was assured that it was noncontroversial. His reaction to the letter from the Atomic Energy commissioners proposing their own demise was that he would support a bill if introduced by the chairman of the Joint Committee. President Kennedy chastised the Budget Bureau when a 1963 amendment to the Reorganization Act prohibiting the use of reorganization plans to create executive departments was construed as a defeat for the president and advised the bureau in no uncertain terms that *he* had never asked for extension of the act. The reorganization authority was allowed to lapse and was not restored until Lyndon Johnson took office.

Kennedy sent forward ten reorganization proposals, four of which relating to regulatory commissions were disapproved. None were designed to strengthen the president's powers, and the creation of the Office of Science and Technology was in the main a response to pressures from the Congress for access to the president's science adviser. His one major reorganization effort, establishment of a Department of Urban Affairs and Housing, met with a crushing defeat.

Lyndon Johnson's all-encompassing concern with every aspect of government policies, programs, and operations included government organization and reorganization along with everything else. For him, important reorganization measures—such as those

52. Theodore C. Sorensen, *Decision-Making in the White House: The Olive Branch and the Arrows,* Columbia University Press, 1963, p. 3.

establishing the Department of Transportation and the Department of Housing and Urban Development, and reorganizing the District of Columbia government—were trophies to be hung on his wall next to the other landmark bills enacted during his administration. Johnson could react boldly to attempts by the Congress to encroach on the president's constitutional powers and did not shrink from direct confrontations over such issues. His position on provisions requiring committee consent to executive actions or bypassing the president's veto authority was unequivocal, and he was less inclined to compromise than any of his predecessors.

President Johnson's thinking about government organization was traditional. His messages invariably made proper obeisance to the gods of "economy and efficiency" and overlapping and duplication. He stressed that he would take steps to "modernize and streamline" the government with the objective of ensuring that federal programs are "administered effectively and at minimum cost to the taxpayer."[53]

Johnson's reorganization program and decisions on organization issues reflected little if any unity of purpose. His approach was episodic and pragmatic, and sometimes gave the appearance of being improvised on the spur of the moment.

Emmette S. Redford's and Marlin Blissett's in-depth analysis of President Johnson's efforts to reorganize the executive branch found that "the president's actions—though measured for political effectiveness—did not reflect an overall organizational strategy. In the main they were piece meal and reactive."[54] Lyndon Johnson was a master legislative tactician, not a strategist. To facilitate passage of an administration measure in the Congress, he was quite prepared to rise above organizational principles and was not disturbed in the least by inconsistencies.

53. Memorandum from Joseph A. Califano, Jr., to the heads of executive departments on reorganization proposals, January 15, 1966.

54. Emmette S. Redford and Marlin Blissett, *Organizing the Executive Branch: The Johnson Presidency*, The University of Chicago Press, 1981, p. 220.

Several Johnson reorganizations did have a significant strategic impact. The transfer of water pollution control responsibilities from Health, Education, and Welfare to Interior was motivated by a desire to obtain a change in program emphasis and to wean Interior away from its narrow western orientation. The reorganization of the District of Columbia made its government somewhat less susceptible to domination by the House and Senate District committees. The plans relating to the Public Health Service, customs, locomotive inspection, statutory interagency committees, mass transit, and narcotics accomplished subtle alterations in the balance of power with respect to the affected programs and afforded an opportunity to reexamine and reorient program objectives.

Opportunism can be self-defeating, as shown by Johnson's controversial proposal to merge the Commerce and Labor departments—probably his worst fiasco. A combination of circumstances, the impending resignation of Secretary of Commerce Connor, White House irritation with both the Commerce and Labor departments, and, perhaps most of all, the search for a "surprise" to liven up the 1967 State of the Union Message inspired the idea. White House staff had unearthed the 1964 task force recommendation for a Department of Economic Development, which would absorb the Department of Commerce, Office of Economic Opportunity, Small Business Administration, and at a later date, the Department of Labor. The president agreed to the merger, but not the rationale. By recommending simply the consolidation of the two departments and preserving the words "Labor" and "Commerce" in the title, the president hoped to avoid alienating the two constituencies involved.[55] The Budget Bureau was told that it could not refer to economic development or economic planning and had to develop a new justification out of whole cloth *after* the recommendation had gone to the Congress.

Neither the justification nor the details had been thought through prior to the State of the Union Message. Labor and

55. *Washington Monthly,* February 1969.

business opposition probably would have been sufficient by itself to doom the proposal. Defeat was guaranteed by an indis-
criminate dragnet operation to identify functions that could be
transferred to the Commerce and Labor Department. This trig-
gered immediately the powerful defensive mechanisms within
the departments and the bureaucracy.

Consolidation of the Labor and Commerce departments had
a superficial logic, but not much more. Absent an intention to
create a Department of Economic Development, the arguments
for the reorganization were strained indeed. It is certainly open
to doubt that merger of his organized labor and business constituencies would have been to the president's advantage. Interlock-
ing arrangements between organized labor and organized business have rarely been in the public interest. Some within the
administration feared that the proposed merger represented a
step toward a new mercantilism.

At the very time when government programs increasingly
called for a high degree of teamwork and unity in program
design and execution, the Johnson administration did not oppose and sometimes supported measures that stimulated the powerful centrifugal forces working within the federal structure. Its
principal institutional innovation was the twilight zone agencies—the Urban Institute, the private Federal National Mortgage
Association, and the National Housing Partnerships—which are
insulated against effective public control and diminish the president's powers.

President Johnson devoted more personal time and attention
to government organization than any president since Roosevelt.
Measured by customary standards, his accomplishments were
fantastic—two new executive departments and the first reorganization of the District of Columbia in almost a century, all
within the space of two years. The times, however, called for
strategy adapted to a radically different mix of organizational
problems, and this Lyndon Johnson was unable to provide.

4

Nixon's New American Revolution

For Richard M. Nixon the major cause of ineffectiveness of government was not a matter of men or money. It was "principally a matter of machinery."[1] Government reorganization was to be the means for bringing about "a new American Revolution." President Nixon's concept of government as a machine was at odds with that of Franklin D. Roosevelt, who stressed that "reorganization is not a mechanical task, because government is not a machine, but a living organism."[2]

President Nixon apparently did not believe that accomplishment of the "new American Revolution" called for the development of revolutionary doctrines. The forging of "new institutions to serve a new America" was to be achieved by strict application of the orthodox dogmas. As in the case of the "New Federalism," the new, in fact, represented a return to the old.

What President Nixon described as "the most comprehensive and carefully planned . . . reorganization since the executive was first constituted in George Washington's administration 183 years ago"[3] professed to be a nonpartisan measure without political implications and to contain nothing that would offend the fundamentalists. In his several reorganization messages, Presi-

1. President's Message on Reorganization, March 25, 1971.
2. President's Message on Administrative Organization, January 12, 1937.
3. President's Message on Reorganization, March 29, 1972.

dent Nixon repeatedly reaffirmed his faith in the orthodox doctrines: economy and efficiency as the objective of organization and administration; organization around major goals or purposes; policy administration dichotomy; rigid separation of powers; limited span of control; and straight lines of authority and accountability with each subordinate expected to obey the orders of his superior.

President Nixon argued that the organizational principles he advocated had been "endorsed" by the Brownlow and Hoover commissions, but the underlying philosophy has its roots in Max Weber's ideas about bureaucracy and power relationships. Weber is concerned with the special type of power relationship he calls domination. As explained by Nicos P. Mouzelis, "domination refers to a power relationship in which the ruler, the person who imposes his will on others, believes that he has a right to the exercise of power; and the ruled consider it their duty to obey his orders. . . . Domination, when exercised over a large number of people, necessitates an administrative staff which will execute commands and which will serve as a bridge between the ruler and the ruled."[4]

It is with respect to the career civil service or the bureaucracy, to use Nixon's code word, that Nixon parted company with Brownlow. The President's Committee on Administrative Management recommended that "the merit system be extended upward, outward and downward to include all positions in the Executive Branch of Government except those which are policy-determining in character."[5] President Nixon considered that President Eisenhower had committed a major error in failing to clean out the "Democrat-infested" federal bureaucracy. He was resolved to replace Democratic civil servants with Republican civil servants.[6] Nixon's viewpoint is reflected in an internal White House memorandum, which complains that "the lack of key Re-

4. Nicos P. Mouzelis, *Organization and Bureaucracy*, Aldine Publishing Co., 1968, pp. 15–16.

5. Report of the President's Committee on Administrative Management, 1937.

6. Rowland Evans, Jr., and Robert D. Novak, *Nixon in the White House*, Random House, 1971, p. 12.

publican bureaucrats at high levels precludes the initiation of policies which would be proper and politically advantageous."[7]

Distrust of the bureaucracy was a recurring theme in almost all of Nixon's public statements. "Ossified" and "obstructive" are typical of the adjectives applied to the civil service. When he signed the legislation establishing the Special Action Office for Drug Abuse, the president threatened that "heads would roll" if "petty bureaucrats" thwarted the efforts of the office director.[8] John Ehrlichman was not exaggerating when he described relationships with the bureaucracy as "guerrilla warfare."[9] As it ultimately evolved, the major objective of Nixon's organization strategy was to contain and neutralize the bureaucracy. This became clear in his March 1972 reorganization message, which stated the following:

> Notwithstanding the famous sign on President Truman's desk —"the buck stops here"—there will be no stopping of the buck, no ultimate clarification of blame and credit, and no assurance that voters will get what they contracted for in electing Presidents, Senators, and Congressmen until the present convoluted and compartmentalized Washington bureaucracy can be formed anew and harnessed more directly to the people's purposes.

President Nixon did not come into office with a preconceived organization strategy. He did not see in organizational and procedural reform—reorganization, decentralization, and revenue sharing—a vehicle for achieving his political goals. Government reorganization was something that could be left to businessmen who would solve the government's management problems by applying sound business techniques. In 1969 he established an Advisory Council on Executive Organization, chaired by Roy L.

7. Senate Select Committee on Presidential Campaign Activities, June–July 1973, Book 4, p. 1683.

8. Douglas M. Fox, "The President's Proposals for Executive Reorganization: A Critique," *Public Administration Review*, Vol. 33, No. 5, September–October 1973.

9. Senate Select Committee on Presidential Campaign Activities, Book 6, p. 2518.

Ash, then president of Litton Industries, to study and recommend reform of the government structure. All the council members, except former Texas governor John B. Connally, were businessmen without significant government experience. Evans and Novak reported that the president's eyes would glaze during the council's periodic reports. Only a strong protest from Ash gained an appointment with the president to discuss the council's proposals for reorganization of the Executive Office of the President.[10]

Management of domestic affairs was something that Nixon at first thought could be left to the Cabinet. He told an interviewer: "All you need is a competent Cabinet to run the country at home. You need a President for foreign policy; no Secretary of State is really important; the President makes foreign policy."[11] There was to be no Sherman Adams or Joe Califano in the Nixon White House. All the president had to do was put the right people in charge and let them do the job.[12]

The initial reorganization plans transmitted to the Congress by President Nixon broke no new ground and were relatively noncontroversial. Reorganization Plan No. 1 of 1969 provided for a strong chairman designated by the president for the Interstate Commerce Commission—thus applying to the ICC the pattern of organization adopted for all other major regulatory commissions. Reorganization Plan No. 1 of 1970 created an Office of Telecommunications Policy in the Executive Office of the President, as recommended by the Jackson Subcommittee and the House Committee on Government Operations.

Reorganization Plan No. 2 of 1970, which changed the name of the Bureau of the Budget to the Office of Management and Budget and established the Domestic Council, reflected the thinking of the Ash Council and Haldeman and Ehrlichman, not that of the president. Ehrlichman reacted negatively to the Ash

10. Evans and Novak, *Nixon in the White House,* pp. 238–240.

11. Ibid., p. 11.

12. *Washington Post,* January 20, 1969.

Council draft, but changed his mind after he secured modifications designed to enhance his power.[13] The Ash Council intended that the Domestic Council be a small agency with a highly qualified professional staff that would (1) help define national goals and objectives; (2) synthesize policy alternatives into consistent domestic programs; (3) provide policy advice on pressing domestic issues; and (4) consider policy implications on ongoing programs. To avoid the necessity of Senate confirmation, it was recommended that the council's executive director be an assistant to the president, but it was expected that the designated assistant would testify before congressional committees in his capacity as executive director.

John Ehrlichman wanted the Domestic Council to be a part of his personal apparatus, a power base comparable to Henry Kissinger's National Security Council staff. He insisted that (1) the plan be revised to eliminate the provision for staff appointments within the career civil service and (2) the Congress be advised that under no circumstances would the executive director be available for questioning. The latter qualification came close to defeating the plan.

Congressman Chet Holifield objected bitterly to the "90-man faceless, formless group" made up of "a group of people that apparently are political appointees, they have not been confirmed, and they can do many things and can remain hidden in the things that they do."[14] The House Committee on Government Operations voted against approval of the reorganization because, among other objections, the executive director of the Domestic Council and his staff would not be accountable to the Congress and would be "beyond the power of the Congress to question."[15] The plan survived on a close House vote. Reorganization Plan No. 2 of 1970 is significant mainly because it marks the begin-

13. Evans and Novak, *Nixon in the White House*, p. 240.

14. House Committee on Government Operations, Subcommittee on Legislation and Military Operations, Reorganization of Executive Departments (Overview), June–July 1971, p. 226.

15. House Report No. 91–1066.

ning of the trend toward formalizing the transfer of power to the president's personal staff. The director of the OMB also was given a status comparable to that of Ehrlichman when he was housed in the White House and designated as assistant to the president.

With the 1971 State of the Union Message, structural reform moved from the wings to center stage. In defining his "six great goals," President Nixon stated: "I shall ask not simply for more new programs in the old framework, but to change the framework itself—to reform the entire structure of American government so we can make it again fully responsive to the needs and wishes of the American people." Included among the major goals were revenue sharing and a bold plan, modified from the blueprint prepared by the Ash Council, for abolishing the constituency- and clientele-oriented departments of Agriculture, Commerce, Labor, and Transportation and distributing their functions among four "goal-oriented" super departments of Community Development, Economic Affairs, Human Resources, and Natural Resources.

Herbert Roback, staff director of the House Committee on Government Operations, explained the shift in emphasis from substantive programs to structural reform as the logical outgrowth of fiscal conservatism. According to Roback, "reorganization fits nicely with fiscal conservatism since it requires no significant budgetary outlays. In that sense, reorganization is policy on the cheap, an inexpensive commitment to progress."[16]

A desire to promote "progress" without significant budgetary costs obviously made the reorganization plan attractive. But the strategic objectives of the proposal were far more subtle and aimed at nothing less than a fundamental change in the balance of power within the federal system. It is something of a measure of Nixon's and his advisers' naïveté and administrative inexperience that they assumed initially that Cabinet officers were mere

16. Herbert Roback, "Problems and Prospects in Government Reorganization," *Selected Papers of the National Academy of Public Administration*, No. 1, January 1973.

extensions of the presidency and had no competing loyalties. Discovery of the triangular alliance among departments, congressional committees, and clientele groups, known to any reasonably sophisticated observer of the Washington scene, came as a rude and nasty shock. Obscured within the sixteen pages of full-blown rhetoric and theoretical justification contained in the March 25, 1971, reorganization message is the following key sentence: "When any department or agency begins to represent a parochial interest, then its advice and support inevitably become less useful to the man who must serve *all* of the people as their President." Administration spokesmen conceded privately that a major purpose was to break "the linkages of professional groups and bureaucracies."

Even such an astute analyst as *New York Times* columnist Tom Wicker failed to grasp the full import of the Nixon plan. Wicker characterized the reorganization proposal as "the most brilliant stroke of Mr. Nixon's administration" and "squarely in line with the President's campaign pledges and the managerial tradition on which Republicans pride themselves."[17] Political scientists and public administration experts were somewhat more cautious but generally supported the proposed departments of Community Development and Natural Resources as constructive measures to achieve long overdue reforms.[18] Enthusiasm was considerably more restrained in the Congress and among constituencies that would be deprived of their bases within the executive branch.

Given the political difficulties of enacting any single departmental reorganization, the very dimensions of the Nixon plan raised serious problems of credibility.[19] Some congressmen viewed it as a "grandstand play," which was not to be taken seriously. Nixon's legislative tacticians miscalculated in thinking it "easier to win large wars than small ones." By uniting in opposition

17. *The New York Times*, January 24, 1971.

18. See House Committee on Government Operations (Overview).

19. Herbert Roback, "The Congress and Super Departments," *The Bureaucrat*, Spring 1972.

such unlikely allies as farmers, labor unions, highway contractors, poor people's organizations, and congressional committee chairmen fearing loss of jurisdictions, the "New American Revolution" faced almost overwhelming odds.

Compromises had been incorporated in the Nixon grand design in an effort to placate the U.S. Army Corps of Engineers and the protectors of the pork barrel. Presidents Harding, Hoover, and Eisenhower and the Hoover Commission Task Force recommended that the civil functions of the Corps of Engineers be transferred as an integral unit to the Department of the Interior.[20] On the pretext of retaining an essential training capability in the Corps, an argument disputed by President Eisenhower among others, Nixon provided for only a partial transfer to the proposed Department of Natural Resources. He recommended that the Corps retain responsibility for project construction, operation, and maintenance.[21] Further concessions to the Corps and the Department of Agriculture incorporated in the 1973 proposal for a Department of Energy and Natural Resources cannot be reconciled with President Nixon's stated purpose of establishing "a center of responsibility for natural resources, energy and water policies" and "a single key official" on whom the president could rely to carry out natural resource policies and programs.[22] The Corps and the Soil Conservation Service would retain responsibility for preparation of feasibility reports, project design, construction, operation, and maintenance, but the secretary of energy and natural resources would be made responsible for project approval, budget requests, and justifications. The proposed reorganization did not eliminate but perpetuated fragmentation of executive responsibilities for energy and natural resource programs.

The solicitude shown for pork barrel programs did not extend to the social and economic programs identified with the

20. Papers Relating to the President's Departmental Reorganization, March 1971, pp. 160–61.

21. Ibid., p. 168.

22. Ibid., p. 162.

New and Fair deals and President Johnson's "Great Society." If the bureaucracy was the primary target of the "New American Revolution," certainly the "Great Society" programs and comparable measures designed to assist and provide access for the disadvantaged were a secondary target. The poverty agency, the Office of Economic Opportunity, was to be retained as a symbol but stripped of its major programs, which would be transferred to the departments of Community Development, Economic Affairs, and Human Resources. The Small Business Administration was to be abolished and responsibility for loans to small businesses and minorities lodged, along with services to big business, in an Administration for Business Development in the Department of Economic Affairs. Also to be abolished was the Farmers Home Administration, whose programs to assist small farmers were to be split up among the departments of Community Development, Natural Resources, and Economic Affairs.

The House Committee on Government Operations conceded a need for executive branch reorganization but expressed doubts about the feasibility of super departments modeled on corporate conglomerates. It noted that the organizing principle for conglomerates is profitability, not functional similarity or common goals.[23] In the committee's view the attempt to organize around "basic goals" presented serious difficulties because: "Such goals, characteristically, are broad, overlapping and open-ended. Furthermore, they can be formulated in different ways, so that alternative or additional organizational patterns could be readily devised."[24]

Administration witnesses were hard pressed to identify the basic goals for the disparate programs (business loans, labor–management relations, transportation, etc.) to be lodged in the Department of Economic Affairs. The Department looked like a last-minute creation to accommodate the pieces left over from

23. House Committee on Government Operations, "Executive Reorganization: A Summary Analysis," House Report No. 92–922, March 1972, p. 26.

24. Ibid., p. 25.

the other reorganizations. George P. Shultz, then OMB director, acknowledged that "to a certain extent it is true that everything is related to everything else. . . . So some sort of breakdown within the total picture is necessary, and the problem is to design a reasonably small number of packages and to find dividing lines that make sense in terms of their effectiveness in generating policy in managing the results of the legislative process."[25]

The ultimate defeat of the "New American Revolution" could not be blamed entirely on its enemies, powerful as they were. Administration support was at best lukewarm. On the very day that the Undersecretary of Agriculture J. Phil Campbell was dutifully testifying before the House Committee that the Department of Agriculture ought to be abolished as a constituency and clientele-oriented department, the president, disturbed by the political repercussions of declining farm prices, announced that the plan had been abandoned and that the Department of Agriculture would be retained as the representative for farmers. The position that what was good for farmers was not good for organized labor or other interest groups could not be logically sustained. The president's failure to veto the Rural Development Act of 1972 placed the supporters of the bill to create a Department of Community Development in an awkward position and made it easier for the Rules Committee to kill the legislation.

Enthusiasm may have cooled because of growing awareness that the sources of bureaucratic power would not be reduced significantly by rearranging the big boxes on the organization chart. The real power centers in the federal structure are the bureaus. Breaking up the constituency-oriented departments might make the secretaries more responsive to the White House, but not necessarily the bureaus. Most secretaries today have difficulty in managing and controlling their departments, and without a strong, relatively cohesive constituency their power would be reduced further.

Even if it had succeeded, the "New American Revolution"

25. House Committee on Government Operations (Overview), p. 154.

never would have amounted to more than a paper revolution. This could not be said of the new Cabinet and White House staff relationships established by President Nixon on January 5, 1973, "to revitalize and streamline the Federal Government in preparation for America's third century." As a panel of the National Academy of Public Administration reported to the Senate Select Committee on Presidential Campaign Activities, if it were not for the accidental discovery of the Watergate break-in, the American state might well have been transformed into "Max Weber's ideal type of monocracy, ruled from the top through a strictly disciplined hierarchical system" with impeachment the only means of holding a president accountable.[26]

By White House press release, the president created a corporate type of structure with a rigid hierarchy in which

—Access to the president was limited to five assistants to the president (a more accurate description would be assistant presidents).

—Four assistants to the president would act as presidential surrogates with responsibility "to integrate and unify policies and operations" in the following areas: domestic affairs (Ehrlichman); foreign affairs (Kissinger); executive management (Ash); and economic affairs (Shultz).

—Access to the assistants to the president would be limited with some exceptions, to three counselors (to be housed in the Executive Office Building) for human resources (secretary of HEW), natural resources (secretary of agriculture), and community development (secretary of HUD). An anonymous "think-piece" supplied by the administration to the Senate Committee on Government Operations indicated that within his assigned area a counselor would be informed and make judgments on budget matters; control key personnel positions and manpower strength; provide policy direction on legislation and legislative strategy; and review speeches, testimony, press releases, and internal policy statements.

26. Frederick C. Mosher et al., *Watergate: Its Implications for Responsible Government*, Basic Books, 1974, p.11.

In effect, the president had converted the executive branch into a three-tiered structure with the assistants to the president at the top and department and agency heads (other than those designated as counselors) at the bottom. The clear intent was to transfer to the president's immediate staff effective control over executive branch policies and programs and to reduce Cabinet officers to an essentially ministerial role. In the words of John Ehrlichman: "There shouldn't be a lot of leeway in following the President's policies. It should be like a corporation, where the executive vice presidents (the Cabinet officers) are tied closely to the chief executive, or to put it in extreme terms, when he says jump, they only ask how high."[27]

White House control over the departments would be maintained directly through key deputies appointed by and reporting to assistants to the president. The *Washington Post* disclosed that over a hundred people formerly employed by the White House, Office of Management and Budget, and Committee to Re-elect the President had been reassigned to departments and occupied such strategic positions as undersecretary (HEW, Interior, Transportation), deputy director of OMB, Federal Aviation administrator, and director of the National Parks Service.[28] Politically endorsed appointees recruited by the deputy director of OMB and operating under his general supervision replaced the departmental assistant secretaries for administration, most of whom had been career civil servants. Assistant secretaries for administration, with their control of budgets, management services, and personnel, were regarded as potentially powerful instruments of control—"an instant bush telegraph into the jungle."[29] President Ford's transition advisers, headed by Secretary of the Interior Rogers C. B. Morton, were highly critical of the OMB role and recommended that steps be taken to prevent the OMB from boring holes "below the waterline in the departments."[30]

27. *Washington Post*, August 24, 1972.

28. *Washington Post*, July 19, 1973.

29. *The New York Times*, December 23, 1972.

30. *Washington Post*, August 23, 1974.

No doubt as a result of the Watergate disclosures and the resignation of top White House aides, the press was advised in a very low key announcement on May 10, 1973, that the president was reinstituting "a direct line of communication with the Cabinet" and discontinuing the "experiment" with counselors, except on an informal basis.[31]

President Nixon's organization strategy stemmed from certain ideological biases and his unique interpretation of the president's role within our constitutional system. Although he never precisely articulated his philosophy of government, if one puts the bits and pieces together certain basic premises emerge:

—As "the President of all the people," the president does and should occupy a superior position to that of the Congress, which represents narrow parochial interests.

—As the sole definer and protector of the "national interest," the president has the implied constitutional authority and moral obligation to take such actions as he deems necessary to carry out his responsibilities.

—Protection of the national interests, as defined by the president, requires undivided loyalty to the president and unquestioning obedience to his orders.

—Department and agency heads function as presidential delegates and powers vested in them by law are, in fact, powers stemming from the president as chief executive.

—Loyalty to the office of the presidency and loyalty to the incumbent are indivisible.

—The bureaucracy or civil service represents the principal threat to presidential power. Members of the civil service cannot be trusted because they are either disloyal or have divided loyalties.

Richard M. Nixon was a self-proclaimed Gaullist. Aaron Wildavsky pointed out that Nixon shared with de Gaulle "a plebiscitary view of the Presidency," one in which the presidency exists wholly apart from other institutions and is at one

31. *Weekly Compilation of Presidential Documents*, May 11, 1973, pp. 662–63.

with the people.[32] This plebiscitary view was reinforced by the "mandate" of November 1972.

The organization strategy developed after the 1972 election was aimed squarely at the vitals of bureaucratic power. Political appointees too narrowly identified with programmatic and constituency interests, or with an independent power base, were purged. The transition between the first and second terms was as extreme as most transitions from one political party to another.[33] The bureaucracy was neutralized and isolated by (1) leaving major departments "headless" by co-opting the secretaries as assistants to the president and White House counselors, thus preventing "capture" by the natives; (2) depriving it of resources through revenue sharing and impoundment; and (3) cutting lines of communication by interposing regional councils under White House and OMB control between departments and their agents in the field. The departments were to be allowed to wither away, with the White House assuming direct operational responsibility.

The testimony and evidence presented to the Senate Select Committee on Presidential Campaign Activities underscore the serious and disturbing constitutional questions raised by the centralization of power in the White House, the fractionalization of presidential power among assistants to the president, and the assumption that statutory powers of executive agencies automatically vest in the president and his principal assistants.

The Nixon strategy reflected a profound misunderstanding of the executive establishment and its culture and personality. Emmet J. Hughes observed most perceptively: "And the President who dreads this legion of careerists, as a conspiracy bent on his embarrassment or frustration, fails to perceive the realities as completely as the President who wastes dreams on a vision of mobilizing them in an army eager to do battle for his own political success."[34]

32. Aaron Wildavsky, "Government and the People," *Commentary*, August 1973.

33. Mosher et al., *Watergate*, pp. 8–9.

34. Emmet J. Hughes, *The Living Presidency*, Coward, McCann & Geoghegan, 1973, p. 186.

5

Carter's "Bottom-Up" Reorganization

If nothing else, President Jimmy Carter shared with Richard M. Nixon a profound distrust of the bureaucracy and faith that bureaucrats can be brought to heel through structural change. As used by President Carter, reorganization appeared to be a code word symbolizing citizens' hostility toward intrusive government and frustration with the bureaucratic system. President Carter again stressed this antibureaucracy theme in his 1979 State of the Union message in which he stated, "With the support of the Congress, we have begun to reorganize and get control of the bureaucracy."

Jimmy Carter ran for president on a platform of government reorganization. He promised that he would duplicate the success he had had in Georgia by drastically reducing the number of agencies and by making the bureaucrats more efficient and responsive. He told the Democratic Platform Committee: "Our government in Washington now is a horrible bureaucratic mess. . . . We must give top priority to a drastic and thorough reorganization of the Federal bureaucracy, to its budgeting system and to the procedures for analyzing the effectiveness of its services."[1] In New Hampshire he advised voters: "Don't vote

1. *Congressional Quarterly*, October 16, 1976, p. 3009.

for me unless you want to see the executive branch of government completely reorganized."[2]

Outsider Jimmy Carter was at a serious disadvantage in debating fundamental issues of foreign and domestic policy with his more experienced rivals for the Democratic nomination. Government reorganization was a safe issue, as long as he avoided specifics, and it was an advantage not to be identified too closely with the existing "bureaucratic mess."

Except for one lapse when he pledged to reduce 1900 federal agencies to 200, Carter refused to go into the details of his reorganization proposals. Jules Witcover, who covered Carter's primary campaign, concluded that "he was unable or unwilling to be more specific."[3] The 1900 figure remained an unexplained mystery for some time and apparently included 1189 advisory committees.

Jimmy Carter as a candidate appeared to recognize that he ran grave political risks by talking about reorganization in other than general terms. As Vice President Walter F. Mondale said at a later date: "Organizing the government is very much like cutting the Federal budget. Everyone is for it in principle, but the difficulties and controversies arise when you get specific."[4]

If candidate Jimmy Carter had a well-articulated organization strategy and precise reorganization objectives, these were never revealed by President Jimmy Carter. In his book *Why Not the Best?* Carter argues against an incremental approach and concluded that reorganization proposals are doomed unless "they are bold and comprehensive."[5] President Carter's approach to government reorganization was not bold or comprehensive. Instead, the President's Reorganization Project adopted "an incre-

2. Quoted in John R. Dempsey "Carter Reorganization: A Midterm Appraisal" *Public Administration Review,* Vol. 39, No. 1, January–February 1979.

3. Jules Witcover, *Marathon,* The New American Library, Inc., 1978, p. 221.

4. Rochelle Stanfield, "The Reorganization Staff Is Big Loser in Latest Shuffle," *National Journal,* March 10, 1979.

5. Jimmy Carter, *Why Not the Best?,* Bantam Books, 1976, p. 172.

mental, people-centered, bottom-up approach."[6] The "bottom-up approach" was proclaimed as an innovative method of analyzing organization structure as it affects people directly, and not looking at it from the top down, as was done in previous reorganization studies.[7]

The reorganizers appeared to assume that the people would be able to tell them what should be reorganized, or at least give them clues on the trouble spots. In a letter on June 24, 1977, Richard A. Pettigrew, assistant to the president for reorganization, invited citizens to submit comments on reorganization issues to "assist both in guiding initial studies and in identifying additional reorganization priorities." Approximately 2000 replies were received. According to staff, none was useful and a number were typical crank letters. Few citizens are concerned with or directly affected by the structure of federal agencies or the subtleties of bureaucratic politics.

Jimmy Carter was called, perhaps unfairly, "the first process President."[8] But the President's Reorganization Project clearly emphasized the *how* above the *what* and *why*. Innovations were limited to the methods and tactics of conducting reorganization studies.

No unifying theme or set of innovative organizational principles can be discerned from analysis of Carter's proposals for Departments of Energy, and Education, as well as for civil service reform and consumer protection. The same can be said for his reorganization plans for the Executive Office of the President, International Communication Agency, Equal Employment Opportunity Commission, Federal Emergency Management Agency, and Employment Retirement Income Security Act. Ex-

6. Statement by Richard A. Pettigrew, assistant to the president for reorganization, at meeting of the American Society for Public Administration on "Reorganizing the Federal Establishment," Washington, D.C., December 1–2, 1977.

7. Richard A. Pettigrew, "Improving Government Competence," *Publius*, Vol. 8, No. 2, Spring 1978.

8. Thomas E. Cronin, "The Carter Presidency," *National Journal*, Reprint Series, "The Carter Presidency: The White House at Mid-Term," 1978–79.

cept for civil service reform, none can be related specifically to Carter's goal of energizing and controlling the bureaucracy.

Overall reorganization objectives were described in almost meaningless generalities—streamlining the government and making it more competent to serve the people. Specific proposals were justified mainly by reference to orthodox doctrines: elimination of overlapping and duplication, consolidation of related functions, improved economy and efficiency, and more effective planning and coordination.

Absence of organization "principles" was regarded as a virtue, not a vice, by the Carter reorganizers. Harrison Wellford, executive associate director of the Office of Management and Budget for reorganization and management, emphasized, "We're not operating under the assumption that the government is so simple that it can be reorganized according to one or two basic principles."[9] The pragmatic and *ad hoc* approach to reorganization was explained by OMB Director James T. McIntyre, Jr., as (1) concentrating on solving problems, (2) looking for the least disruptive remedies to identified problems, and (3) following a process committed to openness and public and congressional involvement.[10]

Congressmen John W. Wydler, Thomas N. Kindness, and Arlan Strangeland were highly critical of the absence of a "defensible administrative theory" in objecting to President Carter's first reorganization plan restructuring the Executive Office of the President.[11] In their dissent they wrote, "Aside from this highly dubious 'shell game' of showing more or fewer employees in any particular part of an organization chart, a reader will search in vain for any indication of a basic premise underlying the plan. This is one of its most serious shortcomings."

9. Jean Conley and Joel Havemann, "Reorganization—Two Plans, One Department Down, Much More to Come," *National Journal*, December 3, 1977.

10. Senate Committee on Governmental Affairs, hearing on nomination of James T. McIntyre, Jr., to be director of the Office of Management and Budget, March 16, 1978, p. 39.

11. House Report No. 95–661, 95th Congress, 1st Session, p. 60.

Without a well-conceived presidential organization strategy and agreed upon organization concepts, reorganization proposals are highly vulnerable to attack on political grounds. Reorganizations attract many enemies and almost no friends. A major mistake of Carter was to deal with reorganization as if it were a purpose in itself, divorced from policy and program development.

The comprehensive plans developed over two years by the President's Reorganization Project to consolidate into four Cabinet departments fragmented programs in four areas—economic and community development, natural resources, food and nutrition, and trade—were shot down in whole or in part by the White House staff. The proposals were written off as politically naïve. Senior White House aides "raised serious questions about the wisdom of advancing such controversial proposals at a time when the Administration will be battling with the Congress on many other fronts."[12]

Peter S. Szanton, who was responsible for the Carter reorganization studies, reported that the "President's predilections to reorganize were steadily resisted by the officials closest to him, especially his domestic policy adviser and Vice President Mondale. The result was that although great effort and substantial time were expended at high levels in the planning of ambitious change, the only substantial reorganizations proposed by the Carter Administration were those made unavoidable by either explicit campaign commitments or powerful congressional pressure."[13]

The plans for a Department of Development Assistance, a Food and Nutrition Department, and a Trade Department were dropped altogether. The plan for a Department of Natural Resources emerged in an emasculated form, without the water resource functions, and it finally was abandoned because of strong opposition by key members of the Congress.

12. Rochelle Stanfield, "The Best Laid Reorganization Plans Sometimes Go Astray," *National Journal,* January 20, 1979.

13. Peter S. Szanton, ed., *Federal Reorganization: What Have We Learned?* Chatham House Publishers, 1981, p. 5.

In the light of the political heat generated by congressional committees, clientele groups, and others whose turf was threatened by proposed reorganizations, President Carter was advised "to point to civil service reform, declare victory in reorganization and withdraw from the field."[14]

Organizational errors made in the initial program design can be undone by subsequent reorganizations only rarely or at considerable cost. Presumably, the expertise developed by the President's Reorganization Project would have been useful to the White House staff concerned with program development, but it was seldom utilized. As in past administrations, decisions were dictated by political expediency. HEW Secretary Joseph A. Califano, Jr., admitted that when he served in the Johnson White House "often we didn't know where to put a program . . . and we didn't particularly care where it went; we just wanted to make sure it got enacted. That's one reason why the government is disorganized now."[15]

The Carter administration's credibility as experts in government organization was shaken when the president could not decide whether the secretary of HUD, commerce, or treasury should be given control of a proposed National Development Bank. A compromise vesting administration of the bank in a triumvirate consisting of the three secretaries obviously carried within it the seeds of future organization problems. The bank proposal subsequently was dropped.

The incremental, people-centered, bottom-up approach to reorganization implied an absence of presidential direction and leadership. For President Carter reorganization appeared primarily to represent fulfillment of a campaign commitment, not an opportunity to alter the distribution of power within the government in ways that would support accomplishment of his long-range programmatic goals and strengthen the institution of the presidency.

The President's Reorganization Project was a project, or series

14. Stanfield, "The Best Laid Reorganization Plans."

15. Timothy B. Clark, "The Power Vacuum Outside the Oval Office," *National Journal,* February 24, 1979.

of projects, not a program. Project teams were organized to undertake organization studies in discrete functional areas such as border law enforcement, disaster preparedness, education, economic analysis, food and nutrition, and small agency reduction. None was assigned responsibility for examining the total government system and identifying problems cutting across functional lines or common to all agencies. Consequently, critical issues were ignored by the project staff. The implications of the drift toward third-party government with the increasing reliance on nonfederal instrumentalities for service delivery were neither seen nor understood. The piecemeal incremental approach inevitably yielded piecemeal results.

Measured against President Carter's expressed goal of energizing and controlling the bureaucracy and making a substantive change in the government's behavior and outlook, his reorganization program must be judged a failure. Four years of intensive and highly publicized efforts, in the opinion of Ronald C. Moe, specialist in American National Government, Congressional Research Service, "resulted in more, not fewer departments and agencies and in more agencies and programs being considered outside of direct accountability to the president. To his critics, therefore, the net effect of this reorganization exercise has been to further undermine the president's managerial authority and influence over the administrative instrumentalities of the federal goverement."[16] President Carter's own evaluation of his reorganization program is perhaps indicated by the fact that he devotes fewer than 3 pages of his 596-page memoirs to a discussion of his much-vaunted campaign promise.[17]

16. U.S. Senate Committee on Governmental Affairs, "The Federal Executive Establishment: Evolution and Trends," Committee Print, 96th Congress, 2nd Session, May 1980, p. 20.

17. Jimmy Carter, *Keeping Faith*, Bantam Books, 1982, pp. 69–71.

6

Reagan: From the Positive to the Regulatory State

If Franklin Roosevelt's "New Deal" marks the birth of the positive state, Ronald Reagan's "revolution" symbolizes its end. The evolution from the positive to the regulatory state commenced in the 1960s, but President Reagan was the first to redefine the federal government's role as limited, wherever possible, to providing services without producing them.[1] This theme is echoed in the 1984 Republican platform, which proclaims the following:

> To benefit all Americans, we support the privatization of government services whenever possible. This maximizes consumer freedom and choice. It reduces the size and cost of government, thus lessening the burden on the taxpayers. It creates jobs. It demonstrates the primacy of individual action which, within a free market economy, can address human needs most effectively.

In its embrace of privatization, the Reagan doctrine represented not so much the beginning as the culmination of a trend in federal administration and management of domestic programs. As noted by Lester M. Salamon, "While political rhetoric and a considerable body of academic research continue to picture

1. See Report of the President's Private Sector Survey on Cost Control (Grace Commission), Vol. II of II, VIII, 1984, p. 92.

the federal government as a rapidly expanding behemoth growing disproportionally in both scope and size relative to the rest
of society in order to handle a steadily growing range of responsibilities, in fact something considerably more complex has been
underway."[2] Except for programs such as social security, there
has been a shift from direct to what Salamon calls "indirect or
'third party' government," with responsibility for service delivery
delegated to quasi-government or nonfederal entities such as government-sponsored enterprises, nonprofit corporations, states,
cities, counties, special districts, and a wide variety of private
businesses. The preferred means for carrying out federal programs are grants-in-aid to states and local governments, contracts, loan guarantees, tax subsidies, and regulation.

The change in the way the federal government conducts its
business is clearly evident from the statistics of federal civilian
employment:

—From 1970 to 1980 the size of the civilian executive branch
  workforce decreased by 120,000 employees, as total federal
  expenditures increased about 195 percent. In the same period expenditures for service contracts increased 28 percent.
—From 1954 to 1984 federal employment per 1000 population
  decreased from 14.6 to 12.0.
—The budgets of Defense, Health and Human Services, and
  Education support four indirect workers for every person on
  the federal payroll.[3]

Grants-in-aid to state and local governments as a means of accomplishing federal objectives were not invented by Presidents
Kennedy and Johnson. But it was in their administrations that
grants became the chosen instrument for administering a wide

2. Lester M. Salamon, "Rethinking Public Management: Third-Party Government and the Changing Forms of Government Action," *Public Policy*,
Vol. 29, No. 3, Summer 1981.

3. Alice Mosher, "The Relationship Between Personnel Ceilings and Contracting Out," Congressional Research Service, August 5, 1980, p. 12.

diversity of federal social and economic programs. The fifty
states, some 26,000 cities, and a variety of nonprofit corporations
were to be the administrators of federally funded "Great Society" programs in economic opportunity, education, health, employment, community development, transportation, law enforcement, and justice. Grant outlays nearly doubled between 1960
and 1969.

Employment of contractors to manage and operate government facilities and "captive" corporations such as Rand and
Aerospace to provide analytical services commenced shortly after
World War II, but use was confined to the defense and atomic
energy programs. The 1960s and 1970s witnessed not only an increasing reliance on contractors to manage and operate government facilities and programs but also a proliferation of agencies
outside the normal executive branch framework such as the Legal Services Corporation, Corporation for Public Broadcasting,
and Synthetic Fuels Corporation.

Federal assistance for housing, agriculture, exports, students,
veterans, and small businesses is provided through private financial institutions, although some or all of the risk is assumed by
the federal government, which guarantees the loans. The guaranteed loan has the same economic effects as a government direct
loan, but it is the private lenders who negotiate the terms and
conditions. Commitments for guaranteed loans are estimated at
$406.9 billion for 1985.

The reasons for bypassing the established government apparatus and utilizing third parties to administer federal programs are
complex. The trend, in part, reflects a widespread antigovern-
ment and antibureaucratic bias. Typical is President Reagan's
statement in his first inaugural address: "Government does not
solve problems, it is the problem." Most recent presidents have
considered growth in the number of federal civilian employees
to be a major political liability.

Perhaps more important, the trend reflects political expediency because third-party arrangements permit the president and
the Congress to take credit for acting without assuming respon-

sibility for program design, administration, and results. For example, if the law enforcement assistance program does not curb crime, the feds can blame the state and local program administrators for the failure. New York City Mayor Edward Koch argues that "nonaccountability" motivated Mayor John Lindsay to turn over administration of the city hospitals to a third party. According to Koch, Lindsay formed the Health and Hospitals Corporation so that he could say, "Don't blame me. I don't have anything to do with hospitals."[4] Politicians are also by no means unaware of the political payoffs for obtaining federal grants and contracts for constituents—what has sometimes been described as the "social pork barrel."

It has reached the point that distinguished scholars such as Bruce L. R. Smith believe distinctions between the "public" and "private" sectors have "ceased to be an operational way of understanding reality."[5] Peter Drucker goes so far as to contend that governing has become "incompatible with doing" and that "any attempt to combine governing with 'doing' on a large scale paralyzes the decisionmaking capacity."[6]

Whatever other reasons may be cited, the primary, and often the determining factor in resorting to third parties or proxy agencies is the need to escape controls that government has imposed on itself. Implicit in the arguments advanced by proponents of privatization is an assumption that it is no longer possible to design and staff government institutions that can function with flexibility, speed, and independence. Existing controls, whether rational or irrational, are accepted as fixed and immutable.

The General Accounting Office has criticized the Departments of Defense and Energy for contracting out basic management functions that should be performed by government personnel, including the determination of national energy policies and development of plans and organizational responsibilities in the

4. Edward L. Koch, *Mayor,* Warner Books, 1985, p. 58.

5. Bruce L. R. Smith, "Changing Public-Private Sector Relations: A Look at the United States," *Annals, AAPSS,* Vol. 466, March 1983.

6. Peter F. Drucker, *The Age of Discontinuity,* Harper & Row, 1969, p. 233.

event of mobilization.[7] Military officers are hired by private contractors to do the same thing they did when directly employed by government. Some of the defense contractors are organized and staffed by retired military personnel.[8] Personnel ceilings and personnel freezes have made it impossible for these agencies to obtain staff necessary to perform essential tasks mandated by the president and the Congress and funded in the budget.

Federal managers complain that their capacity to manage has been significantly reduced by "the growing complexity, time delays and hassling which burden our management systems."[9] Managers are expected to find their way through a maze of 8814 pages of personnel regulations and 6300 pages of central and agency procurement regulations, not to mention the myriad requirements for impact statements and reports to the central control agencies and the Congress on everything down to relatively minor details of administrative actions. Personnel must be diverted from carrying out the agency's mission to doing the paperwork.

In 1981 senior career civil servants urged the Office of Management and Budget to initiate a project to deregulate the government and to reduce red tape, which now constrains federal managers. Fifteen departments and agencies sponsored a National Academy of Public Administration project on "Revitalizing Federal Management." The Academy report came to the following conclusion: "Federal managers are captives of a series of internal management systems which they do not control. These systems have tended to become so rigid, stultifying, and burdened with red tape that . . . managers' capacity to serve the public on a responsive and low cost basis is seriously undermined."[10]

7. Comptroller General of the United States, report to Congress on "Civil Servants and Contract Employees: Who Should Do What for the Federal Government?" June 19, 1981.

8. *Washington Post,* March 2, 1985.

9. U.S. Office of Personnel Management, Federal Executive Institute, "Management Improvement Agenda for the Eighties," June 30–July 2, 1980, p. 1.

10. National Academy of Public Administration, *Revitalizing Federal Management: Managers and Their Overburdened Systems,* November 1983, p. vii.

The Reagan administration has acknowledged that current management systems "are becoming obsolete or falling into disrepair faster than we know how to fix them" and "should be given urgent attention."[11] It is doubtful, however, that an administration committed to reducing the government's size and privatizing government services will accord high priority to measures to free federal managers from burdensome constraints. Those who believe that government is inherently inefficient and incapable of "doing" are not disposed to invest political capital and resources in programs to improve its effectiveness and thereby disprove their thesis.

Few practitioners or scholars have attempted to analyze the causes or the consequences of the massive shift from direct to indirect government. Frederick C. Mosher was one of the first to recognize that the fundamental change in the role and responsibilities of the federal government and the way it conducts its business called for rethinking of orthodox theories and development of new strategies and approaches to public administration.[12] We have yet to develop a theory or theories that reflect the rise of grant and contract administrators, regulation writers, and auditors as the new generation of public administrators. Today, management inevitably tends to be identified with control of the third parties who provide the goods and services rather than with responsibility and accountability for service delivery.

Lester M. Salamon accurately described the "reshaped landscape of federal operations" when he wrote the following:

> What is involved here, moreover, is not simply the contracting out of well-defined functions or the purchase of goods and services from outside suppliers. The characteristic feature of many of these new, or newly expanded tools of action is that they involve the sharing of a far more basic governmental

11. Office of Management and Budget, *Management of the United States Government*, Fiscal year 1986, p. 9.

12. Frederick C. Mosher, "The Changing Responsibilities and Tactics of the Federal Government," *Public Administration Review*, November–December 1980.

> function: the exercise of discretion over the spending of fed-
> eral funds and the use of federal authority. They thus con-
> tinually place federal officials in the uncomfortable position
> of being held responsible for the programs they do not really
> control. . . . Instead of a hierarchical relationship between
> the federal government and its agents, therefore, what exists
> in practice is a far more complex bargaining relationship in
> which the federal agency often has the weaker hand.[13]

Theories positing the establishment of clear lines of authority
and accountability from the president down through department
heads to every employee with no subordinates possessing authority independent from their superiors are no longer relevant for
many federal programs. A strategy that assumes presidential primacy within the system can be maintained by manipulating the
boxes on the organization chart is certain to be unproductive.
Although the outer executive branch structure retains symbolic
importance and may influence policy positions and allocation of
resources, in most instances altering the structure is not calculated to enhance the president's ability to direct the third parties
who administer federal programs.

In many respects Ronald Reagan is unique among recent presidents. His agenda is highly selective and was established before
he was inaugurated. His goal is to reverse the federal government's direction by cutting domestic programs and spending, reducing taxes, and limiting federal regulations. To gain control
of the vast federal establishment and harness it to his purposes,
he has had to devise a new approach and a radically different organization strategy.

Reagan learned from the mistakes made by Jimmy Carter. Organizational change in the traditional sense of departmental
restructuring ranked at the bottom of his priorities and was
regarded as something concerned with mere housekeeping and
not with matters of fundamental importance.[14] Attempts by

13. Salamon, "Rethinking Public Management."

14. See testimony of OMB Deputy Director Edwin L. Harper before the Committee on Governmental Affairs, U.S. Senate, on S.893, May 6, 1981.

prior administrations to reform government management were criticized because they "dealt more with structure than with process."[15] Congress in November 1984 extended the president's reorganization authority until the end of the year, which did not allow the president sufficient time to submit reorganization plans before the Reorganization Act expired, even if he had desired to do so.

Reagan made gestures toward old-style reorganization, but there was little if any follow-through. As promised during his campaign, he proposed dismantling the departments of Energy and Education. The very existence of these departments was considered to symbolize "the progressive intrusion of the federal government into the educational system" and federal intervention with the workings of the free market, which should determine energy development. Claims that abolition of the Department of Energy would produce $250 million in savings over a three-year period were found to be without substance by the General Accounting Office.[16] Faced with strong congressional opposition to the reorganizations, President Reagan made no effort to push his proposals. At the beginning of his second term, President Reagan informed the Congress that he had "no intention of recommending abolition of the Department of Education at this time,"[17] and plans for combining the Interior and Energy departments never emerged from the discussion stage. Members of Congress were permitted to take the lead in pressing for establishment of a Department of Trade and Industry with somewhat lukewarm support from the administration. Several controversial reorganizations recommended by the Office of Management and Budget, including transfer of the Bureau of Reclamation to the Department of Defense and the Forest Service to the Department of Interior, died aborning.

Though not indulging in old-style reorganization, the Reagan

15. Office of Management and Budget, *Management of the United States Government*, p. 1.

16. Comptroller General of the United States, *Analysis of Energy Reorganization Estimates and Plans*, August 2, 1982.

17. *Washington Post*, January 1, 1985.

administration devised a strategy for centralizing unprecedented decision-making power in the White House and reorganizing the executive branch without a significant change in the organization chart. It was a strategy focused on command relationships and processes rather than on formal structure; it was a strategy that, for the most part, could be implemented administratively and that was not dependent for success on enacting legislation.

The Reagan strategy consisted of four main elements: (1) centralization of the budgetary process, (2) centralization of the appointments process, (3) centralization of decision making, and (4) centralized control of regulations.

The first step was to restore the budgetary process as an instrument of presidential policy. As noted by Allen Schick, budget preparation had been "mostly bottom-up, with agencies preparing their requests with little policy guidance from the White House."[18] Reagan reversed the process and instituted a system whereby budgetary decisions are made at the top, with the agency role reduced to complying with White House orders. Budgets are now developed by the White House and the Office of Management and Budget, not by the spending agencies.[19]

Next, tight control was established over the appointments process. Presidents Nixon and Carter had permitted department heads some discretion in appointing their principal subordinates. Reagan's cabinet secretaries were allowed no such leeway and were told bluntly that the White House was going to handle the appointments process.[20] The primary selection criteria were loyalty to the president and support of his goals; a majority of appointees had no prior government experience whatsoever.[21]

18. Allen Schick, "The Budget as an Instrument of Presidential Policy," in *The Reagan Presidency and Governing America,* Lester M. Salamon and Michael S. Lund, eds., Urban Institute, 1985, p. 95.

19. Ibid., p. 113.

20. Lou Cannon, "Appointments by the White House Take Right Turn," *Washington Post,* June 18, 1981.

21. Calvin MacKenzie, "Cabinet and Subcabinet Personnel Selection in Reagan's First Year," paper presented to the American Political Science Association Convention, 1981.

Decision making was centralized in the White House through establishment of seven Cabinet Councils: Economic Affairs, Natural Resources and Environment, Human Resources, Food and Agriculture, Legal Policy, Commerce and Trade, and Management and Administration. The councils "served more as communicators and enforcers of centrally determined policy positions than as mechanisms for active deliberation over priorities."[22] As described by Edwin Meese III, Reagan used the Cabinet Council system "so that cabinet members feel closer to him than they do to their departments—and he gives them a lot of opportunity to remember that."[23]

In April 1985 the Cabinet Councils were abolished and replaced with an Economic Policy Council and a Domestic Policy Council, chaired by former White House aides Secretary of the Treasury Baker and Attorney General Meese. This action was proclaimed by President Reagan as embracing his "commitment to Cabinet government," but it was interpreted generally as further centralizing of power in the White House.

Government by regulation is the inevitable concomitant of government by proxy. If the government wishes to control or influence the nonfederal agencies that administer federal programs, it must do so either by grant and contract provisions or by regulations. Interpretation and application of rules and regulations are also the only available means for controlling the so-called entitlement programs, which account for $382.7 billion in the 1985 budget, or 39.9 percent of federal outlays. These programs permit minimal administrative discretion. In her study of public assistance grants in Massachusetts, Martha Derthick concluded that, to the extent federal administrators attempt to realize sub-

22. Lester M. Salamon and Michael S. Lund, "Governance in the Reagan Era: an Overview," in *The Reagan Presidency and the Governing of America,* Salamon and Lund, eds., p. 9. For analysis and evaluation of the Cabinet Councils, see Chester A. Newland, "Executive Office Policy Apparatus: Enforcing the Reagan Agenda" in the same volume.

23. Dick Kirschten, "Decision Making in the White House: How Well Does It Serve the President?" *National Journal,* April 3, 1982.

stantive ends, they are "likely to do so indirectly, through the use of administrative conditions" or regulations.[24] If one cannot control the players, then the next best thing is to dictate the rules of the game.

In the past the contest between the president and the Congress for power to direct executive policies and actions focused mainly on issues related to executive branch structure. The contest has shifted to a new arena with jurisdiction over the review and control of regulations providing the major source of conflict. The 1970s witnessed a concerted campaign by the Congress to obtain the dominant position. Executive and independent agency rules and regulations were increasingly subjected to veto by one or both houses of the Congress. Twenty-three bills calling for legislative veto of rules and regulations were introduced in the 96th Congress (1979–80). In 1982 the Senate voted to make almost all agency regulations subject to a veto procedure. The Congress temporarily lost the battle when the Supreme Court held the legislative veto to be unconstitutional.[25] The Congress is actively exploring alternative methods for reasserting its control.

Commencing with the so-called Quality of Life Reviews initiated in 1971 under Richard Nixon, presidents began to take an interest in reviewing agency regulations. The Quality of Life Reviews were aimed at all agencies having regulatory jurisdiction over environmental, occupational safety, and consumer protection matters. In practice, review was limited almost exclusively to regulations of the Environmental Protection Administration. President Gerald Ford tried another approach by directing his Council on Wage and Price Stability to analyze the inflationary impact of proposed regulations. The Inflation Impact Statement and its successor, the Economic Impact Statement, were credited

---

24. Martha Derthick, *The Influence of Federal Grants,* Harvard University Press, 1970, p. 198.

25. *Immigration and Naturalization Service* v. *Chadha,* 103 S. Ct. 2764 (1983). For an analysis of congressional control of regulation, see Barbara H. Craig, *The Legislative Veto: Congressional Control of Regulation,* Westview Press, 1983.

with little more than stimulating agency economic and policy analysis of their regulatory outputs.[26]

A highly complex system for "improving" and reviewing regulations was established by Executive Order No. 12044, March 23, 1978, promulgated by President Carter. The Carter order required agencies to review and revise procedures for developing significant regulations with a view to minimizing paperwork. Agency procedures were, at a minimum, to provide for a semiannual agenda of significant regulations, agency head oversight, opportunity for public participation, and compliance with criteria specified in the order, including an evaluation of alternative approaches, direct and indirect effects, and potential costs. Agencies were also required to submit a paperwork budget to the Office of Management and Budget. Administration of the Carter directives was vested in a regulatory council, the Council on Wage and Price Stability, and a regulatory analysis review group.

One result of the Nixon, Ford, and Carter measures was to broaden somewhat the president's authority over the regulations, but it is evident that the central objective was to stem the mounting flood of regulations and to reduce the burden on the private sector. No one yet perceived that review of regulations would take its place with budgetary review as one of the principal management tools available to the president.

Reagan had the insight to sense the significance of regulations in a government that depended increasingly on outsiders to do its job. He stressed that "Hamilton's admonition that the executive 'produce a good administration' requires careful, continuous atention to regulatory and managerial reform."[27] It was no coincidence that President Reagan referred first to regulatory reform. In establishing review and control of regulations by Execu-

26. Robert S. Gilmour, "Presidential Clearance of Regulation," paper presented to the National Conference of the American Society for Public Administration, April 17, 1983.

27. Ronald W. Reagan, "The Presidency: Roles and Responsibilities," *National Forum*, Fall 1984.

tive Order No. 12291, February 17, 1981, and Executive Order No. 12498, January 4, 1985, Reagan underscored that it was his intent to "increase the accountability of agency heads for the regulatory actions of their agencies" and to "provide for presidential oversight of the regulatory process." He argued that his authority to review and control regulations derived directly from his constitutional power to "take care that the laws be faithfully executed."[28]

Although some in the Congress complained that Executive Order No. 12291 raised serious constitutional issues,[29] the Congress itself unwittingly created the foundation on which President Reagan built when it enacted the Paperwork Reduction Act of 1980 establishing a statutory Office of Information and Regulatory Affairs in the Office of Management and Budget. President Reagan abolished Carter's Council on Wage and Price Stability and Regulatory Council and transferred responsibility for reviewing regulations to his principal management arm, the Office of Management and Budget.

The guidelines contained in Executive Order No. 12291 made it unequivocally clear that a cost-benefit test would be applied to all rules and regulations. The thrust of the order was directed at "major rules," those having an economic impact of $100 million or more annually, but the OMB was given authority to prescribe criteria for determining what was "major." The OMB's hand was further strengthened by Executive Order No. 12498, which requires each agency to submit "an overview of the agency's regulatory policies, goals and objectives for the program year and such information concerning all significant regulatory actions of the agency, planned or underway . . . as the director [OMB] deems necessary to develop the administration's regulatory program." The order's announced purpose is to "assure consistency with administration policy" and to "enable the president to guide and supervise the implementation of administration pol-

28. *Presidential Control of Agency Rulemaking*, Committee Print 97–0, 97th Congress, 1st Session, June 15, 1981, p. 80.

29. Ibid., pp. 46–73.

icy."[30] There can be little doubt that the Reagan administration is in charge of the regulatory process.[31]

Reagan's organization strategy is custom tailored to his distinct operating style and conservative agenda. It has worked because of his ability to remain above the battle and his willingness to delegate authority to a chief executive officer or officers in the White House—Donald Regan in his second term and the triumvirate of James Baker, Edwin Meese, and Michael Deaver in the first. It is doubtful that it would work as well for a president with a different role concept who was desirous of promoting new programs—the approach is not well adapted to building coalitions in support of innovative program initiatives.

If President Reagan were to examine the long-range implications of current trends, he might not be as sanguine about the state of the Union. Contrary to his expressed intentions, the policies and procedures now in force are calculated to produce a federal government that is more centralized, more intrusive, and more bureaucratic. Growth of the regulatory state has converted the one unelected branch of government, the Judiciary, from a relatively neutral umpire or referee to an active player in the administrative game.

The tightly controlled decision-making process installed by President Reagan bears a striking resemblance to Richard Nixon's abortive plan for fundamentally altering the chain of command within the White House and executive branch. It again raises the question of whether or not undue centralization of power in the White House would upset the delicate constitutional system of checks and balances deemed by the founding fathers to be essential for protection of our liberties.

Privatization is certain to multiply the number of federal corporate dependents who look to Washington for sustenance and whose economic welfare depends more on political skills than on

30. Memorandum to Agency Heads from Douglas H. Ginsburg, administrator for Information and Regulatory Affairs, January 14, 1985.

31. For assessment of the OMB's clearance of regulations, see Gilmour, "Presidential Clearance of Regulation," and *The Reagan Regulatory Strategy*, George C. Eads and Michael Fix, eds., Urban Institute, 1984.

entrepreneurship and managerial ability. The U.S. government has become the "major philanthropist," outstripping foundations, private individuals, and corporations as provider of revenues to nonprofit corporations. Through grants and service contracts, nonprofit service corporations now receive the largest share of their income from the federal government.[32] The stepped-up defense program has meant an increase both in the number of companies competing for government contracts and in the percentage of their income derived from government sales.[33]

When it is acting through third parties, the federal government is not subject to some of the constitutional limits on its powers. Provisions included in grants and contracts may be utilized vastly to expand the federal outreach and intrusiveness. The Advisory Commission on Intergovernmental Relations correctly observed that "he who pays the piper calls the tune."[34] The Supreme Court held that conditions attached to grants are a legitimate exercise of Congress' power to fix the terms by which federal funds are expended, although Justice Benjamin Cardozo foresaw that the point "at which pressure turns into compulsion and ceases to be inducement" is "a question of degree—at times, perhaps, of fact."[35] Consolidation of categorical grants into massive block grants has made it even more difficult for state and local governments to resist federal pressure. A proliferation of mandates and requirements have been attached to federal grants running the gamut from nondiscrimination, environmental protection, and labor standards to cost principles and audit. Comparable provisions may be included in contracts with private companies supplying goods and services to the government.

Indirect administration vastly complicates the problems of es-

---

32. Lester Salamon, "The Invisible Partnership: Government and the Nonprofit Sector," *Bell Atlantic Quarterly,* Vol. 1, No. 1, Autumn 1984.

33. Defense obligations for research and development have increased from $26,408 million in 1984 to an estimated $39,426 million in 1986.

34. Advisory Commission on Intergovernmental Relations, *The Federal Role in the Federal System: Dynamics of Growth* (A–86), June 1981.

35. David B. Walker, *Toward a Functioning Federalism,* Winthrop Publishers, 1981, p. 146.

tablishing accountability for program results, not to mention maintaining simple honesty and integrity. More than twenty years ago the Bureau of Budget stressed the following in a report to the Congress on contracting for research and development:

> No matter how heavily the government relies on private contractors, it should never lose a strong internal competence in research and development. By maintaining such competence it can be sure of being able to make the difficult but extraordinarily important program decisions which rest on scientific and technical judgments. Moreover, the government's research facilities are a significant source of management personnel.[36]

Federal agencies have not been able to maintain adequate in-house competence to supervise and evaluate contractor performance. Most disturbing are the implications of current trends for the quality and character of the federal career service.

Something is drastically wrong when more than 70 percent of the senior career executives advise bright young people to seek employment outside the federal government.[37] This disillusionment with the career service is generally attributed to politicization, working environment, and lack of material incentives. Important as these factors may be, the basic causes of lowered morale run much deeper, to the changing role of the federal government itself.

In the past, the senior career service has been distinguished from classic bureaucracies by its identification with program and professional objectives. With some exceptions, it has attracted "doers" rather than careerists seeking status and prestige. Opportunities for doers are becoming increasingly restricted in the regulatory state.

Administration through third parties has converted the role of many senior career executives to that of grant and contract administrators, paymasters, and regulation writers and enforcers.

36. Senate Document No. 94, 87th Congress, 2nd Session, May 17, 1962, pp. 21–22.

37. Federal Executive Institute Alumni Association, newsletter, January 1983.

Emphasis inevitably has shifted from delivering services and evaluating results to complying with rules and regulations. David Lilienthal, almost twenty years ago, posed the crucial issue:

> I can think of few things that . . . can be more demoralizing to the dignity and strength of the federal career service: the creation and proliferation of a body of super civil servants, men who perform government functions, yet who are independent of government and its obligations as carried by federal employees, men recruited and paid and supervised as if they were in private employment but who are in fact doing the public's work.[38]

Conservative rhetoric portrays federal civil servants as masters of red tape who do not care what you do, as long as you comply with the rules and complete the necessary paperwork. Unless present trends are reversed, this image may become fact in the United States. In the regulatory state there will be fewer career civil servants but more bureaucrats. In the Reagan administration, under the supervision of a centralized and deeply politicized managerial structure in the OMB and elsewhere,[39] these trends have thus far been accentuated by design.

38. David E. Lilienthal, "Skeptical Look at 'Scientific Experts,' " *New York Times Magazine,* September 29, 1963.

39. See Chester A. Newland, "A Mid-Term Appraisal—The Reagan Presidency: Limited Government and Political Administration," *Public Administration Review,* January–February 1983, pp. 1–21.

7

Administration by Judiciary

Perhaps the most important consequence of the growth of the regulatory state is the increasing involvement of the courts in administrative decision making and execution. Up to now public administration literature and theories have almost totally ignored the role of the judicial branch. This is no longer possible when substantially less than 10 percent of the federal budget is spent on domestic programs performed directly by federal employees and the lions share of federal programs are administered by independent third parties through grants, contracts, and transfer payments.[1] Such arrangements not only invite litigation, but since disputes among parties in these relationships cannot be resolved authoritatively within the executive branch, they virtually command a litigation strategy by third parties and their supporting interest associations as vital means of dealing effectively with federal monitors, rulemakers, and enforcers. In addition, Congress has added commands of its own in the form of direct requirements for public participation in and judicial review of administrative decision making and appropriations for attorneys' fee awards. Once judges accepted the appropriateness of their

1. See Frederick C. Mosher, "The Changing Responsibilities and Tactics of the Federal Government," *Public Administration Review*, November–December 1980, pp. 541–48.

courts as sites for the resolution of such disputes, they became significant, sometimes the most significant actors in the administrative process.

Traditionally, American courts have maintained a deferential posture toward the discretionary powers of public administrators. At common law, administrative actions were generally held by judges to be "unreviewable." In one such case in 1840, the Supreme Court turned down an invitation to review a disputed naval pension with the comment that "the interference of the Courts with the performance of ordinary duties of the executive departments of the government would be productive of nothing but mischief; and we are quite satisfied that such a power was never intended to be given to them."[2] During the first half of this century, however, this presumption gradually evolved to its polar opposite—to a doctrine favoring review of agency action. Restrictive judicial theories nevertheless remained in the path that would take agencies and their officials to court.

During the decade and a half since publication of the first edition of this volume, even these remaining barriers have been seriously eroded, even abandoned to the point that courts are now content to entertain suits that would have been thought laughable by the standards of an earlier time. In still other departures from traditional restraints, courts now routinely maintain jurisdictional control over even the most minute details of agency activity for periods that have extended many years.

For the better part of a century after the Civil War, the Supreme Court led an aggressive judicial campaign in the so-called *substantive due process* cases to shield citizens and their corporate employers from loss of their "right of contract" as a protected "liberty" interest of the Fifth and Fourteenth Amendments. The Court was similarly active in prohibiting undue expansion of Congress' constitutional role in the regulation of interstate commerce. In particular, federal and state wages and hours legislation, laws regulating labor relations, disability compensation,

2. *Decatur* v. *Pauling*, 39 U.S. (14 Pet) 497 (1840).

and public utility rates were relatively consistently put aside as constitutional aberrations. At the high water mark of this period of judicial activism, the Court struck down the centerpiece of the New Deal's economic program, holding in 1935 that the National Industrial Recovery Act was not only an impermissible incursion of the Congress into a state's regulation of commerce within its own borders; it was also an unconstitutional delegation of legislative power to the executive branch.[3]

Two years later, although questions fundamental to the nature and scope of the regulatory state had in no way been resolved, the high Court abruptly left the field, announcing in a series of decisions that it would no longer stand in the way of the government's regulation of economic relations. Expansion of the national power to regulate commerce, combined with already established doctrines permitting the imposition of conditional requirements to federal grants-in-aid worked a "revolution" in the relationship between the federal government and the states.

As early as 1923, the Supreme Court determined that congressionally imposed grant conditions did not invade state powers as long as "statute imposes no obligation but simply extends an option which a state is free to accept or reject." According to this logic, even if the purpose of the grant-in-aid program is to tempt the states to yield to federal demands, "that purpose may be effectively frustrated by the simple expedient of not yielding."[4] The Court later held more explicitly that Congress possessed the "power to fix the terms upon which its money allotments to the states shall be disbursed."[5] With the exception of one limited and short-lived holding in deference to state power,[6] the Court's "open eyes" attitude toward state acceptance of federal grants persists unabated. As long as grant-in-aid conditions attached to

3. *Schechter Poultry Corp.* v. *United States,* 295 U.S. 495 (1935).

4. *Massachusetts* v. *Mellon,* 262 U.S. 447 (1923).

5. *Oklahoma* v. *Civil Service Commission,* 330 U.S. 127 (1947).

6. *National League of Cities* v. *Usery,* 426 U.S. 833 (1976), overturned by *Garcia* v. *San Antonio Transit Authority,* 469 U.S. ___, 83 L. Ed. 2d 1016 (1985).

the "contract" are reasonably related to a national purpose, they are understood merely to "induce," not to "coerce," and are immune to legal attack.[7]

As for the principle that would prohibit congressional delegation of legislative power to the executive without adequate standards, it was not overturned but simply left slumbering in the receding pages of the *U.S. Reports* without further judicial mention for nearly forty years. The pendulum had swung.

The Judiciary may be said to have retreated from its position as a pivotal arbiter of public policy at just the point when New Deal administrators, with their positive programs and restrictive regulations, were flourishing. At the same time, though not conceding their ultimate right to review administrative actions, in most fields of regulatory policy judges largely became content to leave discretionary judgments firmly in the hands of "experts," characteristically asserting "neither the technical competence nor legal authority to pronounce upon the wisdom of the course of action taken by [agency administrators]."[8] During the several decades beginning in the late 1930s, as Bernard Schwartz puts it, "The history of the development of administrative law was one of constant expansion of administrative authority accompanied by a correlative restriction of judicial power. . . . The scope of judicial review of administrative decisions was consistently narrowed."[9]

Despite the newfound judicial deference to Congress and its designated "experts" in the agencies, the national debate over positive government was far from over. Conservatives had, almost inevitably, to attack the administrative process as a symbol of substantive policies they opposed. The idea of reinvolving the Judiciary in administrative decision making held great appeal. Liberals, on the other hand, had only to recall the recently dis-

7. See Advisory Commission on Intergovernmental Relations, *Regulatory Federalism: Policy, Process, Impact and Reform* (A–95), February 1984.

8. *Board of Trade* v. *United States*, 314 U.S. 534, 548 (1942).

9. Bernard Schwartz, *Administrative Law*, 2nd ed., Little, Brown and Co., 1984, p. 24.

continued substantive due process decisions to find danger in such proposals. Nonetheless, the wide diversity of agency policy and practice in dealings with their respective clienteles eventually fostered near unanimous consensus in support of a uniform set of minimum standards for agency procedure. These standards were adopted as the Administrative Procedure Act (APA) of 1946. "The major effects of the Act," as Kenneth Davis has it, "were to satisfy the political will for reform, to improve and strengthen the administrative process, and to preserve the basic limits upon judicial review of administrative action."[10]

Although the APA did not initiate a new period of judicial activism and administrative review, it did identify standards for agency compliance and explicitly provided for court intervention when those standards were not met. Ironically, it was the liberals who would later use appeals to the Judiciary most vigorously, both to cripple agency actions they opposed and to propel others that they favored. In another generation, the Judiciary would respond to the call for a renewed substantive due process doctrine, in the cause not of protecting economic interests but rather of advancing civil rights and social justice. At the same time, the Judiciary would begin to take a far less deferential look at administrative expertise.

"We stand on the threshold of a new era in the history of the long and fruitful collaboration of administrative agencies and reviewing courts,"[11] Chief Judge Bazelon announced from the federal appellate bench in 1971. During the same year his colleague, Judge Leventhal, spoke judicially of a "new partnership" between courts and agencies.[12] Whatever the course of this new collaboration, it took no great acuity to discern who was intended to be the junior "partner." A "new era" of judicial participation in administrative decision making had indeed arrived.

10. Kenneth Davis, *Administrative Law Treatise,* 2nd ed., vol. 24, K. C. Davis Publishing Co., 1978.

11. *Environmental Defense Fund* v. *Ruckelshaus,* 439 F.2d 584 (D.C. Cir. 1971).

12. *Greater Boston Television Corp.* v. *FCC,* 444 F.2d 841 (D.C. Cir. 1971).

Most of the long-standing barriers to judicial participation in administrative affairs were essentially self-imposed limits to court jurisdiction over or involvement in policy decisions. By and large such limits were developed as a matter of practical jurisprudence, protecting courts from the most severe buffetings of political storms stirred up by troubling public choices. As to the courts' jurisdictional reach, Article III of the Constitution was tightly interpreted as extending only to *actual* "cases in law and equity" arising under the Constitution and federal law or occasioned by diversity of citizenship and to *genuine* "controversies" involving more than one eligible "party."

Accordingly, judicial "advisory opinions" were ruled out as early as the administration of President Washington; in-house disputes of the agency-versus-agency variety were beyond the courts' reach; and heated "political questions" were "nonjusticiable," inappropriate for judicial action. In addition, to protect the courts from unnecessary exposure and delimit the case load, elaborate jurisdictional doctrines such as those involving the "standing" of parties to sue or "intervene" in cases already at bar and the maturation or "ripeness" of controversies to a point that would be suitable for adjudication were built up.

While federal courts have retained their aversion to advisory opinions, in recent years most other doctrinal restraints on judicial involvement in administrative decisions have been finessed or ignored. Interagency lawsuits, once completely barred as lacking diversity of parties in interest (i.e., the government would be suing the government), are still uncommon as a matter of executive policy but hardly unknown. Congress has made increasingly explicit provisions for government corporations and other government-sponsored enterprises to sue and be sued independently as a matter of law.

Otherwise, statutory provisions extending special duties and responsibilities to executive and independent agencies have been interpreted to imply federal court jurisdiction to hear their disagreements. In a controversy between the secretary of the interior and the Federal Power Commission over the location of a hydroelectric project on Washington's Snake River, for example, the Supreme Court easily found in the Anadromous Fish Act of 1965 "a special mandate from Congress . . . that gives [the secretary] special standing to appear, to intervene, to introduce evidence on the proposed river development program, and to participate fully in the administrative proceedings [of the FPC]."[13] That the secretary also had standing to sue fellow administrators in federal court passed without comment.

The most extreme extension of this departure from the historic understanding of the "case" and "controversy" requirement came, of course, when the U.S. special prosecutor was permitted by the Supreme Court to sue his ultimate boss, President Nixon. Sufficient basis for this suit was found by the Court in a regulation issued earlier by the attorney general.[14]

When it is inappropriate or impolitic for administrators to haul their colleagues from other departments into court, it may be entirely feasible for them to leak vital particulars to a supportive interest group or to one of the burgeoning public interest law firms, thus arming a surrogate to carry their legal challenges forward. This is precisely what Labor Department administrators did to attack Office of Management and Budget regulatory clearance (and alleged actual change) of proposed departmental rules governing the exposure of hospital workers to ethylene oxide used in sterilizing medical equipment. Labor Department scientists publicly attacked OMB interference as dictates "to the agency by OMB without input from the Occupational Safety and Health Administration professionals."[15] Privately, an OSHA administrator placed a call to Ralph Nader's "law firm," the Public Citizen Litigation Group, with a tip that, to meet a court-imposed deadline, OSHA's original ethylene oxide rules had been rushed to the *Federal Register* without retyping, complete with OMB scratchouts and editorial revisions. Public Citizen

13. *Udall* v. *FPC*, 387 U.S. 428 (1967).
14. *United States* v. *Nixon*, 418 U.S. 683 (1974).
15. *The New York Times*, April 10, 1985, p. A20.

lawyers had only to visit the National Archive Building for a copy of the damaging evidence. Some months later Public Citizen, joined by a host of employees unions, entered a federal suit charging "plainly unlawful" pressure from OMB in the writing of rules that were legally the responsibility of the Department of Labor.[16]

Until recently the characteristic judicial approach toward the standing of organizations and individual citizens to sue the government was expressed in a case appealed to the Supreme Court in 1937 by 18 private power companies. With their revenues threatened by direct competition from the Tennessee Valley Authority, the companies charged that heavily subsidized TVA operations violated the Constitution. The Court stopped well short of the constitutional claim, however, holding that "the damage consequent on competition, otherwise lawful" was in these circumstances loss without injury in any legal sense and would "not support a cause of action or right to sue."[17] The power companies were caught in a "Catch 22" situation. Without standing to sue, they had no way to make the case that TVA's operations were "otherwise unlawful" in constitutional terms. During the same era, taxpayers who hoped to press charges that certain other government activities were illegal were similarly told that their interest—taxpaying—was "comparatively minute and indeterminable; and the effect upon future taxation, of any payment out of funds, so remote, fluctuating and uncertain, that no basis is afforded . . ." such a challenge to federal expenditures.[18]

"Old era" legal doctrines requiring "ripeness" of controversies for judicial settlement and "exhaustion of administrative remedies" were almost equally forbidding to those who would bring suit against the execution of federal policy. Typical of the highly restrictive holdings that predominated in the earlier period was the case of twelve federal workers who sued to enjoin the en-

16. Brief for Petitioners at 60, *Public Citizen Health Research Group* v. *Rowland,* No. 84–1252 & No. 85–1014 (D.C. Cir. filed March 4, 1985).

17. *Tennessee Electric Power Co.* v. *TVA,* 306 U.S. 118 (1937).

18. *Frothingham* v. *Mellon,* 262 U.S. 447 (1923).

forcement of regulations promulgated under the Hatch Act forbidding their participation in organized political campaigns. According to the Supreme Court's rendering in 1947, the "personal interest" of such employees in their "civil rights" and "the general threat of possible interference with those rights by the Civil Service Commission under its rules . . . does not make a justiciable case or controversy."[19]

The classic judicial statement on exhaustion held that "no one is entitled to judicial relief for a supposed or threatened injury until the prescribed administrative remedy has been exhausted."[20] Such principles would clearly keep litigants out of the courts for at least as long as an agency made creative use of inaction and delay. If an agency could avoid obviously improper actions and those that would cause "irreparable injury," it controlled the schedule of events.

Modern doctrines of jurisdiction not only have unlocked the courtroom doors to the government's challengers, but some would suggest that the doors have been flung off their hinges. In the early 1970s, an unincorporated group of law students advanced the seemingly improbable claim that because they enjoyed camping, hiking, fishing, and other recreational activities in Washington, D.C., and environs, they should be able to take the Interstate Commerce Commission to task in federal court for permitting a 2.5 percent increase in railroad freight rates without producing a proper environmental impact statement. As Solicitor General Griswold stated the matter on appeal to the Supreme Court,

> We have a rather remarkable situation here—five law students, though I'm told they are a changing group . . . proceeding not as lawyers but as plaintiffs . . . have tied up all the railroads in the country, and with the aid of the district court, have prevented the railroads from collecting from 500,000 to a million dollars a month for the past eight months on ship-

19. *United Public Workers* v. *Mitchell,* 330 U.S. 75, 89 (1947).
20. *Meyers* v. *Bethlehem Shipbuilding Corp.,* 303 U.S. 41, 50–51 (1938).

> ments of recyclable materials. . . . It is not said which forest,
> river, stream or mountain . . . is used by any member of
> SCRAP [Students Challenging Regulatory Agency Procedures].
> It's obvious that these allegations could be made by any mem-
> ber of the public who wishes to make them. . . . There is no
> evidence to support their standing. . . .[21]

Notwithstanding such arguments, a majority of the Court
found a sufficient logical connection between SCRAP's recreational and aesthetic interests, as well as its economic claims—
higher costs for finished goods—and the adverse consequences for
those concerns as the result of a modified rate structure for railroad freight, to grant the standing requested by the students.[22]
In the *SCRAP* case and elsewhere, the high Court has made it
plain that the required "injury in fact" that must be shown to
achieve legal standing is not confined to "economic harm" but
may include a variety of aesthetic interests as well.

In addition, the Supreme Court has also opened judicial doors
to taxpayers and to disadvantaged competitors, once explicitly
denied access, holding that, "the question of standing is related
only to whether the dispute sought to be adjudicated will be presented in an adversary context and in a form historically viewed
as capable of judicial resolution."[23]

In the mid-1960s, executives at Abbott Laboratories found
themselves in a situation analogous to that of the politically
active federal workers confronted by threatening Hatch Act regulations some twenty years earlier. Faced with a Food and Drug
Administration regulation requiring costly changes in prescrip-
tion drug labeling and advertising, which Abbott Labs and
thirty-seven other drug manufacturers thought to exceed statutory authority, the companies sued to enjoin enforcement. As far
as the government was concerned, without enforcement of the

21. Quoted in Richard C. Cortner, *The Bureaucracy in Court,* Kennikat
Press, 1982, p. 31.

22. *United States* v. *SCRAP,* 412 U.S. 669 (1973).

23. *Flast* v. *Cohen,* 392 U.S. 83,101 (1968), quoted in *Assn. of Data Processing
Service Organizations* v. *Camp,* 397 U.S. 150 (1970).

rule there was no "actual case or controversy." The appellate court agreed. At this point, however, the Supreme Court recognized the difficulty of such a view that it had earlier ignored: "If petitioners [the drug companies] wish to comply they must change all their labels, advertisements, and promotional materials; they must destroy stocks of printed matter; and they must invest heavily in new printing type and new supplies. The alternative to compliance—continued use of material which they believe in good faith meets the statutory requirements, but which clearly does not meet the regulation of the Commissioner—may be even more costly. That course would risk serious criminal and civil penalties for the unlawful distribution of 'misbranded' drugs."[24] This landmark statement made it evident that the courts would henceforth be granted jurisdiction in such situations.

As to "the long settled rule" requiring exhaustion of administrative remedies prior to judicial involvement in a dispute, the rule on "exhaustion" actually applied by courts in recent years seems to be that *"sometimes* it is required and *sometimes not."*[25] Though the courtroom doors may not be off the hinges, they are surely ajar.

The most ancient of all of the judicial walls erected to protect Anglo-American governments from private litigants, the doctrine of "sovereign immunity," is the one that has fallen the farthest in recent times. Initially derived from the thirteenth-century maximum that a vassal could sue his lord only in the court of a higher lord, it followed that the English King, the "sovereign" at the apex of the feudal hierarchy, could not be sued at all— there existed no higher court than the King's Bench. Just why such a doctrine was embraced by the newly seceded American Republic remains one of the mysteries of *stare decisis.* Indeed, it was not only preserved but extended to protect the government and its officials at all levels of the federal system.

24. *Abbott Laboratories* v. *Gardner,* 387 U.S. 136 (1967).

25. Kenneth Culp Davis, *Administrative Law Text,* 3rd ed., West Publishing Co., 1972.

The doctrine of sovereign immunity wore thin as scholars and jurists could discover no logical reason why a tort suffered as the result of government action had no judicial remedy whereas the same wrong, committed by a private party, offered an actionable, clear-cut case for judicial relief. Governmental immunity was nonetheless invoked with constancy and success until checked to some extent by the Federal Tort Claims Act of 1946. Even then the statute's thirteen categoric exceptions, including an exemption for a range of damage claims from assault, battery, false imprisonment, false arrest, malicious prosecution, defamation, misrepresentation, and other intentional torts, left injured individuals at the mercy of Congress for recovery. Also exempt was the performance of any "discretionary function or duty." As long as officials acted "within the outer perimeter of [their] line of duty," both they and the government held "absolute immunity" from suit in the exempted areas.[26] With that protection, the jurisdiction of federal courts was foreclosed to injured parties.

In 1971, after a string of warrantless, early-hour raids, involving particularly egregious behavior by federal law enforcement officers in the wrong private residences, the Supreme Court declared that when government torts violated constitutional rights, they were judicially actionable.[27] During the same period, the courts were also rapidly expanding the protections of the century-old Civil Rights of 1871 to those charging violations by state and local officials.

This process of case law development culminated in 1974 in the aftermath of the shooting of thirteen students at Kent State University by the Ohio National Guard. In this case, the Supreme Court allowed suit against the governor of Ohio and the adjutant general of the Guard, subject to a "qualified immunity," which was said to depend on the varied scope of discretion and responsibility of such officials and on "the existence of reasonable grounds for belief formed at the time and in light of all

26. *Barr* v. *Matteo,* 360 U.S. 564 (1959).

27. *Bivens* v. *Six Unknown Named Agents of the Federal Bureau of Narcotics,* 403 U.S. 388 (1971).

circumstances, coupled with good-faith belief" that the acts committed were "performed in the course of official conduct."[28]
Plaintiffs in the Kent State suit ultimately failed this test on the
merits, but the principle of "qualified" rather than "absolute"
immunity remained. Parties injured by the state could now have
their day in court.

Also in 1974, Congress passed the Intentional Tort Amendment, exposing the federal government to liability for many of
the intentionally inflicted wrongs exempted by the original Tort
Claims Act. Two years later, Congress amended the Civil Rights
Act to permit court assessment of "a reasonable attorney's fee"
in connection with successful civil rights actions. Subsequently,
the Supreme Court continued on this logical path by dropping
the barrier of "absolute immunity" to suits against high-ranking
officials of the federal government and applying the "qualified
immunity" standard to them as well.[29]

In sum, changing doctrines of jurisdiction, along with parallel
statutory changes, have made federal agencies and state jurisdictions far more accessible in court to aggrieved clients and
constituents. Public agencies and their managers have become
appealing targets of opportunity for claimants, proponents of
policy change, and their attorneys. Lowered barriers to judicial
review have also allowed the courts to become crucial centers of
administrative decision making and oversight as federal judges
began to probe the substantive merits of administrative action as
well as procedural adequacy.

Taken collectively, the most important, if undramatic, judicial
incursions into administrative realms are surely those involving
managerial activities that were once informal, highly discretionary, and most often assumed to depend on the wisdom and good
judgment of public managers. Undoubtedly, most such cases
would have been kept out of court for want of jurisdiction or, if
entertained, would have been pronounced "unreviewable" or
"committed to administrative discretion" in years past. However,
the "new era" of judicial assertiveness has been one that formal-

28. *Scheuer* v. *Rhodes,* 416 U.S. 232 (1974).
29. *Butz* v. *Economou,* 438 U.S. 478 (1978).

ized what were once informal processes, forcing administrators closer to the role of judges and to the anticipation of increasingly penetrating reviews by their newfound colleagues on the bench.

Agency lawmaking procedure—"rulemaking"—as set out in the Administrative Procedure Act epitomizes informal process. The essential model is that of the legislative committee. Notice of the particulars of a proposed new regulation (rule) must be posted in the *Federal Register* and a time announced to give "interested persons an opportunity to participate in the rulemaking."[30]

Like its legislative committee counterpart, the rulemaking agency may or may not actually "hear" the testimony of those "interested persons"; the receipt of written testimony will suffice. And, also like the committee, if the agency finds it "impracticable, unnecessary, or contrary to the public interest," in the language of the APA, even the informal notice-and-comment proceedings may be dispensed with. In any case, as this model presents it, both legislative committees and agencies make their own judgments and decisions with regard to the "record" thus generated, take their own "notice" of relevant factors that may or may not be on that record, and, based on their own specialized knowledge, experience, and expertise, make binding legislative decisions.

The "record" of notice-and-comment rulemaking minimally described in the APA is hardly a record at all in any judicial sense. It is merely a collection, perhaps a woefully incomplete and haphazard collection, of unexamined statements, reports, observations, and letters. In the words of the statute, the "relevant matter presented" in such a collection has at least to be given "consideration" by the agency lawmaker.[31] Presumably, congressional lawmakers are at liberty to ignore their "records" altogether.

Since passage of the APA forty years ago, the most significant changes in the regulatory process—a "reformation" as Richard

---

30. 5 U.S.C.A. 553.

31. See Martin Shapiro, "On Predicting the Future of Administrative Law," *Regulation*, May–June 1982, pp. 19–20.

Stewart calls them—have been made by reviewing courts rather than by Congress.[32] In gradual case-by-case increments, courts have required rulemaking to be thoroughly documented and supported by an exclusive administrative record, which will be fully available for judicial review. The change was fundamentally a switch in decision-making models—from the give and take and discretionary openness of the legislative model to the protections, rigidities, and rituals of the judicial model.

According to the legislative model, the products of both congressmen and administrators are constrained by limiting commands of the Constitution. Administrators, in addition, are confined by "statutory jurisdiction, authority, or limitations" and prohibited from "actions, findings, and conclusions found to be . . . arbitrary, capricious, [or] an abuse of discretion. . . ."[33]

Practical limits of administrative discretion typically revolve around the current judicial understanding of just what is meant by "arbitrary and capricious" behavior. The traditional standard, as we have seen, was a relatively limited and narrow one. More recently, judges have commonly recited the "arbitrary and capricious" standard as a preface to demanding more thoroughgoing regulatory procedures. When Judge Leventhal announced the "new partnership" between agencies and reviewing courts, he also commanded administrative rulemakers to take a "hard look" at the materials presented and the issues raised.[34] Subsequent cases have found that reviewing courts also must undertake a "substantial inquiry," and one that is "searching and careful," into the facts of a rulemaking procedure. In keeping with this approach, courts have begun to require that rulemaking agencies base their decisions on "substantial evidence" on the record.[35]

---

32. Richard B. Stewart, "The Reformation of American Administrative Law," *Harvard Law Review*, Vol. 88, 1975, p. 1667.

33. 5 U.S.C. 706.

34. *Greater Boston Television Corp.* v. *FCC*, 444 F.2d 841, 851 (D.C. Cir. 1971).

35. *Pacific Legal Foundation* v. *Department of Transportation*, 593 F.2d 1338, 1343, n. 35 (D.C. Cir.), cert. denied, 444 U.S. 830 (1979).

In the logical train of these requirements comes a long list of judge-made additions to rulemaking that have long been associated with the courtroom and formal adjudication rather than informal process. It has been held that a rulemaking has a duty "to identify vital material questions raised during the proceedings and indicate the agency's response to those concerns"; that the evidence relied on must be exposed to "full public scrutiny"; that interested parties must have an opportunity to study, analyze, and respond to such data; and that the agency has a responsibility to reconsider its decision if new information is presented after the comment period is closed. Although none of these procedures is mentioned in the APA itself with regard to rulemaking, more often than not appellate courts have treated them as implicit commands of the act. As one appellate opinion put it, "fairness may require more than the APA minimum" if, as others have said, critical policy issues are to be properly "ventilated."[36]

The judicial interest in administrative "fairness" has prompted some judges to go even further in judicializing the basic model for rulemaking. At least one decision suggested that "cross-examination [of witnesses] may be necessary if critical issues cannot be resolved" in the notice-and-comment process. Others have devoted considerable attention to the troublesome role of *ex parte* contacts, which had long been barred in quasi-judicial though not in lawmaking procedures. At the extreme, the District of Columbia appellate bench found that such contacts led to "the possibility [of] one administrative record for the public and this court and another for the [Federal Communications] Commission and those in the know." This the court held to be "intolerable."[37] In other situations judges have held that agency rulemakers, after "reasoned consideration of all material facts . . . must articulate with reasonable clarity their reasons for deci-

36. *Kennecott Copper Corp.* v. *Environmental Protection Agency,* 462 F.2d 846, 850 (D.C. Cir. 1972); *Natural Resources Defense Council* v. *United States Nuclear Regulatory Commission,* 547 F.2d 633, 655 (D.C. Cir. 1976).

37. *Home Box Office, Inc.* v. *Federal Communications Commission,* 567 F.2d 9 (D.C. Cir. 1971).

sion" and that the administrator must "supply an implementing statement that will enlighten the court as to the basis on which he reached . . . the standard from the material presented."[38]

Curiously, one of the strongest voices raised in opposition to these judicial additions to the APA has been that of the Supreme Court itself. Read literally, Justice Rehnquist's monumental opinion in the *Vermont Yankee* case of 1978 would have called a halt to the judge-made regulatory reforms of a decade. Upon review of a Nuclear Regulatory Commission regulation overturned by the court below, the Supreme Court concluded that "the majority of the Court of Appeals struck down the rule because of perceived inadequacies of the procedures employed in rulemaking proceedings." The underlying premise of such a decision, the high Court determined, could not be supported: "Agencies are free to grant additional procedural rights in the exercise of this discretion, but reviewing courts are generally not free to impose them if agencies have not chosen to grant them." Otherwise, court-imposed regulatory procedures would constitute a "sort of Monday morning quarterbacking [that] not only encourages but almost compels the agency to conduct all rulemaking proceedings with the full panoply of procedural devices normally associated with adjudicatory hearings." Not only was this unnecessary, but the Court could find no statutory basis that "permitted the court to review and overturn the rulemaking proceeding on the basis of the procedural devices employed (or not employed) by the Commission so long as the Commission employed the statutory minima. . . ."[39]

Despite the sweep of the *Vermont Yankee* decision, it was not entirely surprising that the Supreme Court's dicta were accorded less than full deference by the judicial hierarchy below. In the first place, the high court has itself added requirements to informal rulemaking, demanding, for example, that OSHA develop

38. See William E. Pederson, Jr., "Formal Records and Informal Rulemaking," *Yale Law Journal*, Vol. 65, 1975, p. 38.

39. *Vermont Yankee Nuclear Power Corp.* v. *Natural Resources Defense Council, Inc.*, 435 U.S. 519 (1978).

"findings" that a revised standard for worker exposure to benzine is "reasonably necessary or appropriate," and that the new regulation would significantly reduce the health hazard to workers."[40]

Second, federal agencies take their primary judicial cues not from the Supreme Court but rather from the U.S. Court of Appeals of the District of Columbia. The D.C. Appellate Court has long been regarded as the preeminent administrative court in America. It handles the most critical cases and, in terms of sheer volume, the bulk of the administrative case load. Such a position of primacy is not easily and probably not willingly surrendered. The point could hardly be made clearer by the Appellate Court's treatment of the *Vermont Yankee* case on second appeal. Here the appellate court's "giant step sideways from an analysis rejected unanimously by the Supreme Court in Vermont Yankee II" caused Judge Wilkey to remark in dissent: "The majority has deviated from a clearly presented path—charted by the Supreme Court itself—to lead this court again on a confusing and unauthorized incursion into a policymaking area reserved by the Congress to the NRC."[41] Ultimately, the "arbitrary and capricious" standard entails substantive supervision of the agency's record, however well the reviewing court may couch its findings in the language of procedural adequacy. This is precisely the point that Judge Wilkey and others have uncovered and underscored.

Finally, in at least two cases the Supreme Court has already acquiesced in judicial additions to minimum statutory requirements of rulemaking that were supplied by courts below—disallowing an agency's use of extrarecord data[42] and enforcing demands that an agency "pinpoint" the evidence on which it relied.[43] And in numerous other cases that have not reached the

---

40. *Industrial Union Dept., AFL–CIO* v. *American Petroleum Institute*, 448 U.S. 607 (1980).

41. *Natural Resources Defense Council, Inc.* v. *United States Nuclear Regulatory Commission*, 685 F.2d 459, 524 (D.C. Cir. 1982).

42. *National Crushed Stone Ass'n.* v. *Environmental Protection Agency*, 449 U.S. 64 (1980).

43. *AFL–CIO* v. *Marshall*, 101 S.Ct. 2478, 2506 (1981).

Supreme Court, appellate courts have continued their embellishment of APA rulemaking requirements almost as if the Supreme Court's *Vermont Yankee* dictum did not exist.

Judicialization of the administrative decision making does not end with the rulemaking process. And apart from its restrained position on rulemaking, the Supreme Court has shown remarkably little reluctance to add procedural requirements and to intrude boldly into what used to be important but unstructured and rarely challenged choices of responsible officials.

Perhaps the most telling and also highly precedential example was provided by the high Court's handling of a complaint brought by a group of concerned Tennessee citizens and national conservation organizations against Secretary of Transportation John Volpe. The conservationists argued that Secretary Volpe had violated terms of the Department of Transportation Act and the Federal-Aid Highway Act by approving expressway construction across twenty-six acres of Overton Park in the City of Memphis. They pointed out that these statutes prohibited the secretary's approval of any such "program or project . . . unless (1) there is no feasible and prudent alternative to the use of such land, and (2) such program includes all possible planning to minimize harm to such park. . . ."[44] This meant, they argued, that the secretary was obliged to make his own "formal findings" to support the highway's approval and that he could not simply rely on the public hearing and subsequent judgment of the Memphis City Council. Although the Court did not agree to require formal findings of the secretary, neither would it accept the secretary's affidavits later made to support his actions. The Court held that the secretary's decision should be subject to "a thorough, probing, in-depth review" to determine whether or not he "could have reasonably believed that in this case there are no feasible alternatives or that alternatives do not involve unique problems," but that the administrative record was not yet before the courts:[45]

44. 23 U.S.C. 138; 49 U.S.C. 1653(f).

45. *Citizens to Preserve Overton Park* v. *Volpe*, 401 U.S. 402 (1971).

The lower courts based their review on the litigation affidavits that were presented. These affidavits were merely "post hoc" rationalizations, which have traditionally been found to be an inadequate basis for review. . . . Thus it is necessary to remand this case to the District Court for plenary review of the Secretary's decision. That review is to be based on the full administrative record that was before the Secretary at the time he made his decision. . . .

The court may require the administrative officials who participated in the decision to give testimony explaining their action. Of course, such inquiry into the mental processes of administrative decisionmakers is usually to be avoided. . . . And where there are administrative findings that were made at the same time as the decision . . . there must be a strong showing of bad faith or improper behavior before such inquiry may be made. But here there are no such formal findings and it may be that the only way there can be effective judicial review is by examining the decisionmakers themselves.

In other words, the secretary does not have to prepare formal findings each time an important decision is made (as a judge must at the conclusion of a case), but if he does not, he and his subordinates risk being hauled onto the witness stand where cross-examining attorneys will be all too delighted to create a record in court and formally recommend findings of their own.

In some situations in which an administrator is disinclined to pursue a course of action or to prosecute a violation, courts have begun to hold that such officials must produce an "explanation" or "statement of reasons" for their delay or inaction. In this, courts have gone a step beyond the requirements currently made of judicial prosecutors. The leading Supreme Court holding of this sort was prompted by complaints from an unsuccessful candidate for union office who alleged election frauds and sought action from the secretary of labor. Under terms of the Labor–Management Reporting and Disclosure Act of 1959, after investigating such complaints, the secretary then must decide whether or not to initiate a court action to set aside the election. In this case the secretary uncovered election irregularities but nonetheless informed the defeated candidate that, "based upon the investigative findings, it has been determined . . . that civil action to set aside the election is not warranted." The Supreme Court disagreed: "it is necessary for [the Secretary] to delineate and make explicit the basis upon which discretionary action is taken, particularly in a case such as this where the decision taken consists of a failure to act after the finding of union election irregularities." The Court noted further that such "a statement of reasons serves purposes other than judicial review." These purposes, the Court said, involved promoting "thought by the Secretary" and compelling "him to cover the relevant points and eschew irrelevancies" in order "to assure careful administrative consideration. . . ."[46]

Administrative practices have become more formalized in other ways as well. In 1972, the hearing examiners used by a handful of regulatory agencies for formal proceedings were rechristened "administrative law judges." As their pay and civil service status were elevated, so were their numbers increased. Six years later the General Accounting Office reported that "More than 1,000 Administrative Law Judges, with virtually guaranteed tenure until retirement, serve in 28 agencies as quasi-judicial officers presiding at formal administrative hearings to resolve disputes." According to the GAO study, these agencies "collectively process a larger case load than U.S. courts, affect the rights of more citizens, and employ more than twice as many Administrative Law Judges as there are active judges in Federal trial courts."[47]

The increasing prestige and numbers of administrative "judges" correspond squarely with judicial demands for greater formality in the handling of individual cases. As government benefits—welfare, public housing, education, and the like—came to be firmly defined as propertylike "entitlements," it followed that beneficiaries could not be denied these benefits without "due process of law."

Even though the overwhelming majority of case-type decisions

46. *Dunlop* v. *Bachowski*, 421 U.S. 560 (1975).

47. Comptroller General of the United States, "Administrative Law Process: Better Management Is Needed," May 15, 1978, pp. 3–4.

continued to be handled in an informal manner as a matter of administrative discretion, this increasingly meant that those affected could successfully demand and get the full panoply of judicial protections. In the leading decision on the termination of welfare benefits, for example, the Supreme Court went beyond even the requirements of the APA, requiring proceedings "tailored to the capacities and circumstances of those who are to be heard," in addition to sufficient advance notice and the right to appear in person with an attorney, to testify orally, and "to confront and cross-examine the witnesses." What is more, the final decision must be based solely on the evidence adduced at the hearing, and such a process must be completed *before* benefits may be discontinued.[48] Although this decision was directed toward state and local welfare administrators, its impact has been felt throughout the federal system. The effect on the lower courts, as Judge Friendly observed, "has been profound. The trend in one area after another has been to say, 'If there, why not here?' "[49] Examples may be found in cases ranging from termination of Social Security and medical benefits to eviction from public housing and school suspension. The principle has also been applied to applicants *for* welfare benefits.

In fashioning the legal principles so far discussed, the judicial focus has been on the reform of *procedures* as a means of gaining greater "fairness." That is not to say that judges are unconcerned with results. On the contrary, judicial opinions couched in the language of procedure are often enough thinly clad efforts to reach a particular conclusion in substance. In one area, however—in the so-called institutional reform cases that affect prisons, mental hospitals, school districts, and a host of other public service institutions—even the veil of proper procedure has been stripped away. There, the policy preferences of judges have become diamond-hard "decrees" mandating the most detailed reforms and public expenditures to match.

Over the past fifteen years, in well over a hundred federal dis-

48. *Goldberg* v. *Kelly,* 397 U.S. 254 (1970).

49. Henry J. Friendly, "Some Kind of Hearing," *Pennsylvania Law Review,* Vol. 123, 1973, pp. 1267, 1299–1300.

trict court cases that have largely been supported by the appellate bench, judges have begun to articulate novel and mostly undifferentiated doctrines of equity in administrative settings. In the past, equitable relief coupled with continued jurisdiction for extended periods, was extraordinary, limited to a relatively few situations, such as bankruptcy and estate administration. Otherwise, judges were at pains to avoid involvement in equitable judgments requiring complex remedies and prolonged judicial supervision. By and large, parties seeking relief from government action had to be content with money damages if their cases could be heard at all. As the Supreme Court stated this restrained approach in 1949, "in the absence of a claim of constitutional limitation, the necessity of permitting the Government to carry out its functions unhampered by direct judicial intervention outweighs the possible disadvantage to the citizen in being relegated to the recovery of money damages after the event."[50]

Contemporary administrative equity cases have been brought to the courts on a variety of constitutional and statutory grounds, most notably on the basis of the Eighth Amendment's prohibition of "cruel and unusual punishment" and the Fourteenth Amendment's "privileges or immunities," "due Process," and "equal protection" clauses. It should be added that most of the constitutional claims would not have been recognized as such in an earlier time. Many have been brought as class actions, reflecting, as Abram Chayes says, "our growing awareness that a host of important public and private interactions—perhaps the most important in defining the conditions and opportunities of life for most people—are conducted on a routine or bureaucratized basis and can no longer be visualized as bilateral transactions between private individuals."[51]

Of equal interest in many of these cases, adversary process has yielded to mutual advocacy proceedings. Wardens and institution directors ostensibly sued by inmates and clients have joined

50. *Larson v. Domestic & Foreign Commerce Corp.*, 337 U.S. 682 (1949).

51. Abram Chayes, "The Role of the Judge in Public Law Litigation," *Harvard Law Review*, Vol. 89, 1976, p. 129.

forces with their erstwhile adversaries in the cause of better conditions and larger budgets. Representation for the public fisc is often nowhere in view and seemingly irrelevant to the judicial principles at issue.

In 1970, when a federal district court in Arkansas decided eight consolidated class action suits brought by inmates in different units of the state's penitentiary system, Chief Judge Henley noted that this was the "first time that convicts [through their court-appointed attorneys] have attacked an entire penitentiary system in any court." Citing a catalog of abuses, ranging from widespread torture of and brutality toward inmates to chronically dangerous, unhealthy, and segregated facilities and practices without any pretense of an attempt to rehabilitate, the court found the very fact of "confinement in the Arkansas Penitentiary System under existing conditions amounts to a cruel and unusual punishment constitutionally prohibited." Short of issuing an injunction in this pathbreaking case, Judge Henley gave the respondents "an opportunity to come forward with a plan to eliminate existing unconstitutionalities" under guidelines drawn by the court as "minimum requirements if persons are going to continue to be confined in the Penitentiary."[52]

Two years later, Alabama District Judge Frank M. Johnson took this development one step further on review of conditions at that state's largest mental health facility and at the state school and hospital for the retarded. Although plainly revulsed at the "intolerable and deplorable" levels of treatment and "extremely dangerous conditions" he found there, he at first directed the Alabama Department of Mental Health to devise its own plan to improve the system. Then, after two court-imposed deadlines had passed without signs of progress, the court declared firmly that, as a matter of Fourteenth Amendment "due process," inmates "unquestionably have a constitutional right to receive such individual treatment as will give each of them a realistic opportunity to be cured or to improve his or her mental condi-

52. *Holt* v. *Sarver*, 309 F. Supp. 362 (E.D. Ark. 1970).

tion. . . ." To support this declaration, the court defined detailed constitutional standards of care, treatment, and habilitation and ordered compliance.[53] Evidently, the "substance" of the "due process" clause had been relocated.[54]

These cases provided models for a host of others that would follow. Judges have experimented with any number of remedies in order to gain compliance. In most, however, the "centerpiece" of the institutional reform cases, including the school desegregation and equalization cases, has been the judicial "decree," often entered into as a "consent decree" by the parties. Typical of such decrees are elaborate and minutely detailed directives for the accomplishment of specific reforms. In Louisiana, District Judge Christenberry ordered "immediate" implementation of reforms in the New Orleans Parish Prison, which specified additional medical services; construction of a new hospital-infirmary; establishment of arrangements to provide "adequate security for medical personnel to facilitate the needs of the medical program"; provision of psychiatric and dental care services; maintenance of a year-round recreational program; construction of an indoor recreation area; and limitation of the number of prisoners in the main prison facility. In addition, the judge directed that "the management and operation of the prison be improved immediately," specifying the employment of qualified professionals to fill personnel vacancies, and demanding the upgrading of recruitment standards and training programs, increases in wages and other incentives, and implementation of an affirmative action plan.[55]

Often such decrees are not only elaborate but numerous. Former Boston Superintendent of Schools Robert Wood reports that, during the control of Boston's public schools by Judge Garrity's court, "well over 200 court orders to the school department [were] outstanding, ranging from major efforts at plan-

53. *Wyatt* v. *Stickney*, 344 F.Supp. 373; 344 F.Supp. 387 (M.D. Ala. 1972).

54. See Judge Frank M. Johnson's own explanation in, "The Constitution and the Federal District Judge," *Texas Law Review*, Vol. 54, 1976, pp. 903–16.

55. *Hamilton* v. *Schiro*, 338 F.Supp. 1016 (E.D. La. 1970).

ning to the repair and maintenance of individual classrooms. When I once asked an able department counsel whether we were inadvertently in contempt of court in any way, he shrugged his reply, 'Who knows—it's hard enough to count the orders, let alone read them.' "[56]

Because the administrative equity cases inevitably have substantial financial implications, the question of appropriations authority can hardly be avoided. Whatever the constitutional standard applied to public institutions and services, ultimately the power of the purse was understood to reside with legislatures, not with courts. In the main, courts have treated the issue obliquely, leveraging their decrees with implied threats against noncompliance or nonappropriation—typically the prospect of closing institutions and releasing inmates. Federal judges have also appointed masters, monitors, and receivers to take over entirely the management of public facilities. In extreme situations, courts have even gone so far as to levy fines, assess compensating damages for inmates, and threaten the dismissal and incarceration of recalcitrant officials. In order to pay for the mandated reforms in Alabama, Judge Johnson wrote that it might "be necessary for the court to take affirmative steps . . . to ensure the proper funding is realized."[57] Taking note of the fact that "special sessions of the Legislature are frequent occurrences in Alabama," the court suggested that "there has never been a time when such a session was more urgently required."[58] Failing prompt legislative action, the court made plain its intention "to utilize other avenues of fund raising," hinting darkly at the judicial sale of Alabama state lands.[59]

The administrative agencies taken into receivership by federal courts have been predominantly those of states and municipalities. But federal agencies may also become, in effect, "captive of

56. Robert Wood, "Professionals at Bay: Managing Boston's Public Schools," *Journal of Policy Analysis and Management*, Vol. 1, Summer 1982, 461–62.

57. *Wyatt* v. *Stickney*, 344 F.Supp. 373, 382 (M.D. Ala. 1972).

58. Ibid., 394, n. 14.

59. Ibid.; *Wyatt* v. *Aderholt*, 503 F.2d at 1318 (5th Cir. 1974).

the court."[60] A decade and a half ago, a suit brought on behalf of a black public school student in Mississippi charged that the federal Office of Civil Rights (OCR) had failed to enforce Title VI of the Civil Rights Act of 1964 with sufficient vigor. That title prohibits "discrimination on the basis of race, color or national origin" in "any program or activity receiving federal financial assistance" and authorizes the termination of federal funding to any recipient that persists in discriminatory practices.

For fully fifteen years Federal District Judge John Pratt maintained jurisdiction in the case, issued numerous orders with demanding deadlines, and allowed additional party interveners to introduce new issues long after pleas of the initial complainant ceased to have any meaning. According to Jeremy Rabkin, one indisputable outcome of these orders and other pressures brought to bear by the action was to "shift OCR very heavily, at times almost exclusively, toward complaint-based enforcement," despite strong evidence "that compliance reviews initiated by the agency itself . . . are a more productive use of resources than processing individual complaints." In some ways, Rabkin finds, the protracted lawsuit made the introduction of administrative improvements more difficult rather than easier: "Managers knew that any controversial initiative could be quickly challenged by leaks from recalcitrant subordinates or second-guessing from resentful predecessors. At the same time, the intervening authority of the court inhibited successive secretaries from imposing on OCR the discipline and direction which their own broader perspective and higher status could provide."[61]

It may be, as Judge Richard Neely contends, that judicial encroachment on the functions of the coordinate branches is more the fault of legislative and executive inadequacy than of overzealous judges.[62] It is certainly true that Congress has specifically invited judicial review in numerous statutes in addition to the APA. In some, notably the Clean Air Act Amendments of 1977,

60. Jeremy Rabkin, "Captive of the Court: A Federal Agency in Receivership," *Regulation*, May–June 1984, pp. 16–26.

61. Ibid., p. 26.

62. Richard Neely, *How Courts Govern America*, Yale University Press, 1981.

accompanying committee reports urged "that the courts continue their thorough, comprehensive review which has characterized judicial proceedings under the Clean Air Act thus far."[63] There is an implication here that such reviews might be advisable under other statutes as well. There is also no doubt that the Congress, institutionally, and through individual members, has made greatly increased use of the judiciary both to challenge executive action and to attempt to gain advantage in intramural struggles.[64] As to the penal and mental institutions managed by state executives, and a number of school districts as well, their failures and excesses have been legion and the stuff of public (and judicial) revulsion.

Judges were initially reluctant to become involved in active administrative oversight, particularly to the point of superintending whole institutions. But once pathbreaking precedents appeared, others followed in rapid order. Since the early 1970s, courts seemingly have been eager to take on the most complex and politically sensitive cases, often at odds with a coordinate (and elected) branch of the government. In recent cases involving the presidential effort to reduce the costs of federal regulation, for example, David Beam likens the courts to interest groups as a "countervailing force." The Reagan administration "has sought to lighten the [regulatory] burden on grantees, but," as he points out, "the judiciary, with few exceptions, has interpreted laws in a manner that extends and intensifies grantee's obligations. . . . Overall, the executive and judicial branches appear to be marching to different drummers."[65]

As to the institutional reform cases, Cornell Law School Dean Roger Cramton warns that the judge in administrative equity cases "may gradually lose his neutrality, becoming a partisan

63. Davis, *Administrative Law Treatise*, Vol. 5, 364–65.

64. See "Notes—Executive Discretion and the Congressional Defense of Statutes," *Yale Law Journal*, Vol. 92, 1983, pp. 970–1000.

65. David R. Beam, "New Federalism, Old Realities: The Reagan Administration and Intergovernmental Reform," in *The Reagan Presidency and the Governing of America*, Lester M. Salamon and Michael S. Lund, eds., Urban Institute Press, 1985, p. 439.

who is pursuing his own cause." Dean Cramton cites the example of one federal judge in a class action who took over substantial management of the case, appointed expert witnesses, suggested areas of inquiry, then ordered defendants to pay $250,000 toward social science research on the effectiveness of his final decree.[66]

Part of the difficulty with the expanded judicial role in administration is inherent in the structure of the judicial process as a site for administrative oversight and as a model for executive decision making. Because the judiciary depends on private initiatives to invoke its powers and continues to operate within the relatively narrow framework of case-by-case adjudication, it can only rarely be informed by a comprehensive view of the agency activities under examination. In the first instance, at least, the issues are framed by litigants acting in an adversarial relationship with the agency. The court's method of decision is fundamentally tied to the analytic method, reason, and theoretic standards rather than other modes of decision, particularly those of bargaining and compromise. Finally, the court's focus is inherently retrospective in character, lacking the essential resources for prediction, planning, and ready adaptation to unexpected consequences and altered circumstances.[67] At the same time, that focus is necessarily diffused by heavy dockets of other cases, many of them demanding and complex, clamoring for attention.

In some circumstances the Judiciary's "nonbureaucratic" structure no doubt offers greater flexibility in dealing with administrative issues. The judicial setting may also ensure more effective participation by inmates, constituents, even repressed administrative insiders, and the groups that represent them. But such advantages do not overcome the fundamental difficulty of administration by Judiciary in a representative democracy: the problem of accountability.

66. Roger C. Cramton, "Judicial Law Making and Administration," *Public Administration Review*, Vol. 36, 1976, p. 553.

67. See Donald L. Horowitz, *The Courts and Public Policy*, The Brookings Institution, 1977, pp. 33–56.

Even if there is a legislative default, Archibald Cox asks, "does a federal court—usually a single judge—have legitimate power to levy taxes on a people without their consent, and to decide how public money shall be spent?"[68] To this one may add the question, does such an unelected, life-tenured official have legitimate authority to take over the powers and managerial responsibilities of an elected chief executive? Where, after all, is the check on assumed judicial power?

It is not enough to answer that the Judiciary is held generally accountable through the financial and jurisdictional restraints of the legislature, through socialization in adherence to the law, or through the appointment process. Not only are congressional reins on the Judiciary of debatable scope, but they are cumbersome and unlikely to be exercised with any precision whatever. Legal training and the tradition of *stare decisis* may indeed encourage judicial reluctance to depart well-trodden paths of precedent. But once major legal landmarks are established, a new line of precedent is available for citation and elaboration in response to the eager claims of newly encouraged litigants and increasingly less reticent judges. Once appointed, federal judges are well insulated from both executive and legislative restraints, wholly unchecked by popular electorate, and more likely to respond to the pressing claims of the parties before them.

Rampant delegation of legislative power and the expansion of third-party government compounds enormously the accountability problem. As national governmental power has increased, so has it moved to the margins of the system where democratic control and responsiveness are already attenuated. In this shift, the Judiciary have been cast as the arbiters between official government and their constituencies or their unofficial proxies and surrogates. Inevitably, power attaches to such a role. As a result, the Judiciary are now more involved in governance and less accountable to the governed then ever before.

68. Archibald Cox, *The Role of the Supreme Court in American Government*, Oxford University Press, 1976, p. 96.

8

The Executive Establishment:
Culture and Personality

Until the Congress declared by law in 1978 that all presidential records were federal property, a president's office files were deemed to be his private property and were taken with him when he left the White House.[1] In theory at least, an incoming president started with a clean slate. Obviously a president's freedom is circumscribed by the need for continuity, political commitments, tradition, and accepted norms of presidential behavior, but within these limits he retains considerable discretion to organize and staff his household as he sees fit, determine his work priorities, and develop his own style and interpretation of the presidential role. In Woodrow Wilson's words, each president has the freedom "to be as big a man as he can."[2]

Department heads seldom start with a clean slate. Generally they must adapt to the institution rather than the institution to them. There are likely to be daily reminders that they are merely temporary custodians and spokespersons for organizations with distinct and multidimensional personalities and deeply ingrained cultures and subcultures reflecting institutional history, ideology, values, symbols, folklore, professional biases, behavior pat-

1. H. G. Jones, *The Records of a Nation*, Atheneum, 1969, p. 160.

2. Quoted in Richard E. Neustadt, *Presidential Power*, John Wiley & Sons, Inc., 1960, p. 5.

terns, heroes, and enemies. The individual style of department heads must not do violence to the institutional mystique, and the words they speak and the positions they advocate cannot ignore the precedents recorded in the departmental archives. Most department heads are free only to be as big as the president, the bureaucracy, the Congress, and their constituencies will allow them to be.

A Cabinet member is confronted with all the problems of an actor type-cast to take over the lead role in a long-running classical drama. The audience expects the part to be played in a certain way and will react hostilely to departures from the main lines of characterization set by generations of previous actors. Responses different from those in the prepared script are highly disturbing to the bureaucracy and the principal constituencies in the Congress and the outside community on whom a department head must rely for support. It would be as unthinkable for a secretary of agriculture to question the innate goodness of the rural way of life and the inherent virtues of the family farm as it would be for an OMB director to be against economy and efficiency.

Whatever his background and individual bent, a secretary of the treasury, for example, is obliged to play the part of a "sound" money man. Given the setting in which he performs, it would be very difficult for him to do otherwise. One has only to walk into the ancient Treasury Department building adjoining the White House to sense the atmosphere of a conservative financial institution. The money cage at the main entry way, the gilt pilasters, the gold-framed portraits on the walls all reinforce the Treasury "image." As the leader of a rugged "outdoors-type" department, a secretary of the interior is not out of character when he climbs mountains, shoots the Colorado River rapids, and organizes well-publicized hiking and jogging expeditions. Identical conduct by the secretary of the treasury would shake the financial community to its core.

Program transplants that are alien to the institutional culture and environment seldom take root and are threatened with rejection. Franklin Roosevelt recognized this risk when he vetoed the Brownlow Committee's suggestion that federal loan programs be placed under the Treasury. Roosevelt advised Brownlow: "That won't work. If they put them in the Treasury, not one of them will ever make a loan to anybody for any purpose. There are too many glass-eyed bankers in the Treasury."[3]

A department head who cannot adapt to the institutional environment also runs the risk of rejection. Appointment by the president and confirmation by the Senate are no guarantee of institutional loyalty. Former Attorney General and later Chief Justice Harlan F. Stone is reported to have said of FBI Director J. Edgar Hoover, "If Hoover trusted you, he would be absolutely loyal; if he did not, you had better look out; and he had to get used to his new chief each time."[4] Among bureau chiefs, Hoover was unique in power and influence, but not in his attitude toward his nominal political superiors.

Cabinet members have much in common with the university president who observed ruefully, "Universities may have presidents, but presidents don't have universities." The plain truth is that such powerful subordinate organizations as the Federal Highway Administration, Army Corps of Engineers, National Park Service, and Forest Service constitute the departmental power centers and are quite capable of making it on their own without secretarial help, except when challenged by strong hostile external forces. Often they can do more for the secretary than he or she can do for them.

Institutional loyalty is not as crucial when the secretarial role is discrete and separable from that of department head. The secretaries of state, treasury, and at times, defense tend to function more as staff advisers to the president than as administrators of complex institutions. Their effectiveness and influence are only coincidentally related to their access to institutional resources. On occasion, presidents have utilized Cabinet officers essentially

3. A. J. Wann, *The President as Chief Administrator—A Study of Franklin D. Roosevelt,* Public Affairs Press, 1968, pp. 103–4.

4. Francis Biddle, *In Brief Authority,* Doubleday & Co., Inc., 1962, p. 257.

as ministers without portfolio, notably the postmaster general and attorney general, offices that have been occupied by political party chairmen, campaign managers, legislative strategists, or others who were appointed to serve in a noninstitutional capacity as presidential advisers.

For the secretaries of agriculture, commerce, energy, health and human services, education, housing and urban development, interior, labor, and transportation, as well as the heads of the major independent agencies, the secretarial or agency head and institutional roles cannot be divorced. Without the loyalty, or at least neutrality, of their principal bureau chiefs, these officials can be little more than highly ornamental figureheads. As such, they are powerless to advance the president's objectives either within their agencies or with their constituencies. The paradox is that a president ultimately may be best served by an agency head who is willing to risk occasional presidential displeasure to defend his agency's territory and vital interests. Once he has established his credibility within his agency, he can be much more effective in achieving his own goals and mobilizng support for the president's program.

The political executive is the proverbial man in the middle—what James E. Webb identifies as "the main point of impact in the relationships between the endeavor and its environment."[5] Based on his experience as NASA administrator, Webb recognizes that a department head has twofold and sometimes conflicting responsibilities:

> . . . he has to represent within the endeavor the outside environmental factors—the Federal Government, the President and the administration in all its facets, the Congress, and the national public; he has to make sure that the endeavor's goals and activities are responsive to the requirements and desires of the environment under conditions of rapid change and uncertainty.
>
> At the same time, the executive represents the entire en-

5. James E. Webb, *Space-Age Management*, McGraw-Hill Book Co., 1969, p. 128.

deavor as against the environment. He has the ultimate responsibility for securing from the environment the support necessary for gaining and sustaining momentum, for safeguarding against dysfunctional forces seeking control and influence, for—in short—keeping the endeavor viable and on course toward its goals.

The executive can do none of these inside or outside tasks alone. He must bind his associates to his objectives and to his team, even though they may hardly understand all the forces that are at work.[6]

The restraints applicable to cabinet appointments are of two kinds. Custom still requires that the secretary of the interior be from the west and that the secretary of agriculture, if not a "dirt farmer," be from an agricultural state and have a farm background. The secretaries of commerce, labor, and treasury must be individuals who have the confidence of their respective constituencies—organized business, organized labor, and the financial community. President Reagan strictly conformed to custom when he named James G. Watt, a Colorado lawyer, secretary of the interior; John R. Block, an Illinois farmer, secretary of agriculture; Malcolm Baldridge, a Connecticut industrialist, secretary of commerce; Raymond Donovan, a New Jersey contractor who claimed membership in the Brewery Workers Union and International Brotherhood of Electrical Workers, secretary of labor; Donald T. Regan, board chairman and chief executive of a major stock brokerage company, secretary of the treasury; and Samuel R. Pierce Jr., a black New York lawyer, secretary of housing and urban development.

Generally speaking, in making appointments, presidents attempt to find individuals who are *simpatico* and subscribe to the basic institutional outlook, goals, and values. There may be bitter disagreements about methods and policies, but these tend to resemble family differences and do not threaten institutional survival. To appoint a known critic of an agency's program, as President Reagan did in naming Anne Gorsuch Burford as ad-

6. Ibid.

ministrator of environmental protection, is the equivalent of a presidential vote of "no confidence."

As one descends the hierarchical scale, the distinctive departmental colorations come into focus even more sharply. Undersecretaries and assistant secretaries are less likely than secretaries to be generalists or people with broad political background. Sub-Cabinet appointments tend to mirror the diverse clientele groups, dependencies such as defense contractors, construction companies, educational institutions, and professional organizations that constitute an agency's constituency.

Hubert Humphrey may have complained with some justice that "Every once in awhile one gets the view down here in Washington that the respective departments are members of the United Nations, and that each has a separate sovereignty."[7] But if all department heads were cast from the same mold and always spoke in unison with the president, could our pluralistic political system as we now know it survive? It may be doubted that either the national interests or, in the final analysis, those of the president himself would be best served if departments were headed by agnostics who did not believe in the goals and values of the institutions they administered.

Admittedly there are dangers in the present system. Institutional myths and symbols may be worshiped for their own sake long after they have lost their original meaning. Institutional loyalties may be internalized with the result that programatic goals are displaced and institutional, professional, or bureaucratic survival and aggrandizement become the overriding objectives. These dysfunctional influences are latent in almost all organizations. Most susceptible are agencies with obsolete, static, or contracting programs or those that are highly inbred, such as the military and Foreign Service.

Former Chairman of the Joint Chiefs of Staff, General David C. Jones, acknowledges that the military services "find it difficult to adapt to changing conditions because of understandable attachments to the past. The very foundation of each service rests

7. Speech before National Housing Policy Forum, February 14, 1967.

on imbuing its members with pride in its mission, its doctrine and its customs and discipline—all of which are steeped in tra-ditions."[8]

Organizational behavior can be modified and redirected by substituting new program goals, redesigning administrative sys-tems, altering standards for recruitment and promotion, reor-ganization, training, and indoctrination. To be effective as a "change-agent" takes what few secretaries possess—leadership, a profound knowledge of institutional mores and programs, and, above all, time. Turnover among secretaries is high, and few serve for a full presidential term. President Nixon exceeded Pres-ident Grant's record of twenty-six Cabinet appointees in eight years with thirty in five years. One fact is clear, however—presi-dents seldom evaluate Cabinet appointees in terms of their poten-tial as change-agents. As we have seen, appointments generally go to conformists.

In selecting their Cabinets, presidents tacitly acknowledge what the orthodox organization theorists ignore—each major agency and its component elements symbolize certain widely held social values and bring a unique perspective to the councils of government. What has been described as the "machinery of Government" is not a machine with interchangeable parts. The Hoover Commission remedies for the manifest ills besetting the executive branch—removal of legal impediments to presidential and secretarial control over their subordinates and a neater ar-rangement of the boxes on the organization chart—are simple and logical but treat the symptoms rather than the disease.

Attempts to solve structural defects without knowledge or un-derstanding of the institutional psyche or the environmental fac-tors that condition organizational behavior are bound to fail and may produce severe traumas. Reorganizations are major surgery and should not be prescribed as a cure for personality problems. If reorganizations are indicated, under no circumstances should a physician trained only in anatomy be allowed to operate.

8. David C. Jones, "What's Wrong with Our Defense Establishment," *New York Times Magazine,* November 7, 1982.

Government agencies are social institutions. Social psychologists would concur in the opening sentences of the official Labor Department history, which reads as follows: "In fifty years an institution, just as a person, takes on a character and develops attitudes which distinguish it from all others. The Department of Labor is no exception."[9] Such common expressions as "the military mind" and the "Navy way" recognize that institutions do have individual personalities and outlooks, but we rarely associate this phenomenon with civilian agencies. Although each of the major departments has its own special character, these personality traits may or may not be shared fully by its principal subordinate bureaus. Attorney General Robert Kennedy's failure to understand the unique culture and language of the FBI, what Victor Navasky calls "Bureau-speak," constituted a major obstacle to achieving Kennedy administration goals of promoting civil rights and combating organized crime.[10] Deviations occur most frequently among the professional officer corps and in bureaus with limited missions and narrow constituencies. The Bureau of the Budget once was advised bluntly that the "Secretary of State does not necessarily speak for the State Department" when it cited conflicts between the secretary's views and those advocated by a foreign service representative. There is a Department of Agriculture culture, but there are also Extension Service, REA, Soil Conservation Service, and Forest Service cultures. These are not always compatible and sometimes produce conflicts.

According to social psychologists, "social systems are anchored in the attitudes, perceptions, beliefs, motivations, habits, and expectations of human beings."[11] A major unifying force in any organization is what Chester Barnard terms "associational attrac-

9. U.S. Department of Labor, *The Anvil and the Plow*, Washington, D.C., 1963.

10. Victor S. Navasky, *Kennedy Justice*, Atheneum, 1971. For a discussion of bureaucratic culture, see Morton H. Halperin, *Bureaucratic Politics and Foreign Policy*, The Brookings Institution, 1974.

11. Daniel Katz and Robert L. Kahn, *The Social Psychology of Organization*, John Wiley & Sons, Inc., 1966, p. 33.

tiveness."[12] People seek favorable associational conditions from their viewpoint and tend to gravitate toward organizations that share their personal values and norms and where they can work comfortably with colleagues of the same professional, educational, and social backgrounds. For this reason, career executives do not transfer freely from one department to another. In 1975 approximately two thirds of the career executives had worked in the same agency since reaching the middle grade. Only 12 percent of supergrade executives had worked in three or more agencies after attaining the middle grade.[13] Whatever movement there is normally takes place within the foreign affairs, science, intelligence, and budgeting communities, where interagency relationships are particularly close, or within the established professions such as law, engineering, and accounting.

The American Civil Service emphasizes loyalty to one's profession, program, bureau, and department, probably in that order, and not to the Civil Service career system. The exceptions, again, are the Foreign Service, Public Health Service, and Environmental Science Service, which adhere more closely to the classic bureaucratic pattern. In those cases, loyalty is given to the service rather than to the program or to the department. The corps systems are characterized by rank-in-man (Civil Service grades depend on job classification), entry at junior levels with a commitment to a career within the service, periodic rotation in job assignments, and, perhaps most important, selection and promotion based on the judgment of one's senior officers. Like the military officers corps, these are "closed systems." Interference by politicians or other outsiders in the selection and promotion processes is viewed as the "gravest impropriety."[14]

12. Chester I. Barnard, *The Functions of the Executive,* Harvard University Press, 1942, p. 146.

13. Hugh Heclo, *A Government of Strangers: Executive Politics in Washington,* The Brookings Institution, 1977, p. 117.

14. A typical example is Admiral King's reaction to Secretary Forrestal's tampering with the established promotion processes in the U.S. Navy. See Ernest J. King and Walter M. Whitehill, *Fleet Admiral King—A Naval Record,* W. W. Norton & Co., Inc., 1952, p. 635.

To speak of the federal bureaucracy as if it were a homogeneous entity is obviously most misleading. About the only thing that some federal employees have in common is that they are paid by the U.S. Treasury. Each group or subgroup has identifiable characteristics that motivate its behavior. A congenial or tolerable organizational environment for one group may be highly repellent to another. Limited movement among the groups exists, but this is partly because of people seeking their right niche, as well as promotion opportunities. A small number have transferred by lateral entry from the Department of Agriculture and Defense establishment to the Foreign Service, but we doubt that any diplomat has ever seriously considered transfer to such agencies as the Post Office or Soil Conservation Service.

Most agencies conduct "orientation" programs for new employees, and several, notably the Forest Service and Marine Corps, have devised sophisticated techniques for making true believers out of their recruits.[15] Formal indoctrination is seldom necessary, however. Professional employees who remain with an agency for any length of time partly "co-opt" themselves. It is true that people shape an institution; but an institution also shapes its personnel.

The kinds of people an agency attracts, its organization, policy positions, and responses to environmental influences are conditioned by a complex of tangible and intangible forces. To understand an agency's organization and behavior, one must first know its history, program patterns, administrative processes, professional hierarchies, constituencies, and budget structure.

Many agency traits are acquired; others are inherited. For example, the Atomic Energy Commission's internal organization structure was modeled on that of the Tennessee Valley Authority, which furnished the commission's first chairman, David Lilienthal. The policy of hiring private concerns to manage and operate atomic energy facilities was initiated by the U.S. Army

15. For a description of the Forest Service technique, see Herbert Kaufman, *The Forest Ranger—A Study in Administrative Behavior*, The Johns Hopkins Press, 1960.

Corps of Engineers when it ran the Manhattan Project and could have been reversed by the Commission only at the risk of major disruptions to the program. While the AEC subsequently developed an elaborate rationale to justify the policy of contracting out its work, the Corps of Engineers was doing nothing more than conducting its business as usual when it commenced the practice.[16] The Corps traditionally has performed its civil functions through contractors, who provide much of its political muscle, and was not organized and staffed to construct and operate atomic energy facilities with its own personnel, even if it had believed that direct operations would be preferable.

Government officials have an instinctive drive to reproduce the organizations, systems, and procedures with which they are most familiar. When asked to develop a self-financing plan for the rural electrification program, Agriculture inevitably proposed an exact duplicate of the farm credit banks. The regulatory commissions invariably insist that new regulatory programs be administered by multiheaded bodies. Sometimes the motivation is self-protection. David Lilienthal believed that TVA would be vulnerable as long as it remained the only institution of its kind and, therefore, he wanted the TVA model to be duplicated in other parts of the country. Organizational eccentricities are often directly traceable to the institutional biases of the legislative drafters and first administrators.

It does not take much digging for an organization archeologist to uncover evidence of prior civilizations and cultures within the executive branch. The Department of the Interior was once the catchall department of internal affairs before it was transformed into a natural resources and conservation agency, and its Bureau of Indian Affairs and Office of Territories represent vestiges of this earlier period. Designation of the secretary of the Army to supervise the Panama Canal continues a precedent established when President Roosevelt asked the secretary of war to act as his representative in overseeing the construction of the in-

16. See Ninth Semiannual Report of the Atomic Energy Commission, January 31, 1951.

teroceanic seaway. At the time, the War Department was the government's public works agency and, in addition, was responsible for U.S. territories and possessions. The latter functions were transferred to the Department of the Interior in 1939.

Organization structure may provide clues to dimly remembered public controversies and catastrophes. The Forest Service might well be in the Interior Department today if the historic dispute between Secretary Ballinger and Gifford Pinchot had not left conservationists with a nearly pathological distrust of the department. A collision of two commercial airliners over the Grand Canyon brought about the removal of the Federal Aviation Agency from the Department of Commerce. Organization location may stem from such ephemeral factors as the personality or background of a former secretary. President Kennedy wanted a southerner to administer the Community Relations Service and enforce the public accommodations laws and mainly for this reason gave the job to Secretary of Commerce Luther Hodges, who was from North Carolina. It was only with some difficulty that President Johnson was able to transfer the Community Relations Service to the Department of Justice after Secretary Hodges was succeeded in office by Secretary Connor, a northerner.

There are discernible differences between departments created in response to outside pressures (Agriculture, Commerce, Education, and Labor) and those established primarily at executive initiative (Health and Human Services, Housing and Urban Development, and Transportation). Clientele groups have a somewhat less proprietary interest in the latter departments. They are more concerned with protecting their pet bureaus from departmental domination, as evidenced by statutory provisions according special status to the Federal Housing Administration, Federal Highway Administration, and Federal Aviation Administration.

Labor unions also have a proprietary interest in certain agencies and bureaus and will oppose reorganizations that threaten union jurisdictions. Lars H. Hydle, president, American Foreign Service Association, objected to Reorganization Plan No. 2 of

1977, creating the Agency for International Communications, because it would transfer State Department employees represented by his organization to a bargaining unit represented by another union.[17] Proposed transfer of immigration and naturalization service inspectors to the customs service raised comparable jurisdictional issues. The implications of public service unions and collective bargaining for government organization and reorganization are only beginning to be recognized.

The influence on organization structure of historical memory, clientele, and union pressures cannot be wholly eliminated. Greater discretion exists with respect to the choice of tools for accomplishing program objectives. There is yet insufficient awareness that "different tools of government have their own distinctive dynamics, their own 'political economics,' that affect the content of government action" and institutional behavior.[18]

Regardless of where they are located on the organization chart or their program objectives, agencies engaged in common types of activities, such as lending and insurance, regulation, or public works, require people with comparable professional skills and backgrounds and share much the same professional and institutional values.

Government loans and insurance probably would be employed less frequently than they are to accomplish basic social and economic objectives if it were known that these programs have a built-in conservative bias. The professional elites in a lending agency are bankers or those with banking or financial experience. Bankers judge their success by the number of loans made and the repayment record, not by what they have contributed to the achievement of vague goals. Congress and the president are disposed to apply the same standard because it is very difficult to measure whether and to what extent government loans have, in

17. Subcommittee of the House Committee on Government Operations, hearings on Reorganization Plan No. 2 of 1977, October 18 and 21, 1977, p. 99.

18. Lester M. Salamon, "Rethinking Public Management: Third Party Government and the Changing Forms of Government Action," *Public Policy*, Vol. 29, No. 3, Summer 1981.

fact, improved the relative position of small business in our economy, fostered regional development, or assisted developing nations.

The Federal Housing Administration has mirrored the professional values and prejudices of the real estate men and mortgage bankers who originally staffed the agency. The Douglas Commission found that "the main weakness of FHA from a social point of view has not been what it has done but in what it has failed to do—in its relative neglect of the inner cities and of the poor, and especially black poor."[19] Insurance was denied to the poor and blacks because they were considered to be bad credit risks. There was evidence of an agreement among the FHA, lending institutions, and fire insurance companies, to block off certain central city areas within "red lines" and not to loan or insure within these lines. FHA's policies would have been entirely justified if a remarkably low default rate were the sole criterion of program effectiveness.

Exactly the same tendencies have been exhibited by the farm credit banks, as illustrated by the following exchange between R. B. Tootell, governor, Farm Credit Administration, and Congressman Dante Fascell:

> *Mr. Fascell.* Is a nonbankable finding a prerequisite to an FCA loan?
>
> *Mr. Tootell.* It is not, sir.
>
> *Mr. Fascell.* By regulation or law, it is not?
>
> *Mr. Tootell.* By none of those things. If it were, we would be placed in the position, I am sure, where our banks would be solvent enterprises for only a limited period of time.
>
> *Mr. Fascell.* You mean by that you have to get in the fight for the cream of the money market in order to make your operation go?
>
> *Mr. Tootell.* Well, we have to get our share of sound business.
>
> *Mr. Fascell.* You have to get your share of straight, good banking business?

19. National Commission on Urban Problems, "Building the American City," report to the Congress and the President, December 12, 1968, p. 100.

Mr. Tootell. Yes, we call it banking business.
Mr. Fascell. That is what it is.[20]

A quite different set of professional norms is introduced by the regulatory process. The financing institution is the banker's domain, but the lawyer reigns supreme over the regulatory agencies. Lawyers approach problems as "cases" and rely primarily on precedent and highly formalized adversary proceedings to produce fair and just solutions. The lawyer's criterion for success is the number of cases won or the decisions sustained on appeal and, more recently, the correctness and completeness of the rulemaking process. The regulatory approach has obvious limitations, if what is called for is positive government leadership and initiative in protecting the public interest and maintaining the economic health and vigor of the regulated industries.

Public works also have drawbacks as a means for accomplishing social and economic objectives because of the dominance given to the engineering profession. Project approval may depend more on sound engineering design than on extraneous social values. Under the accelerated public works program, projects tended to be awarded to communities with well-drafted plans on the drawing boards rather than to those that needed them the most. By nature, engineers like to build things and are not social and economic planners.

Each profession seeks to mold and shape the decision-making process so that issues will be presented and resolved in accordance with its professional standards. Harold Orlans has found that "once a particular profession becomes entrenched in an agency or institute, it is not easily dislodged. Thus, research programs and institutes often concentrate on the methods and theories of one profession (even of one school within a profession) rather than employing whatever methods and theories are most pertinent to the problems at hand."[21]

20. House Committee on Government Operations, hearings on H.R. 8332 to amend the Government Corporation Control Act, February 24, 1958, p. 178.

21. Harold Orlans, "The Political Uses of Social Research," *Annals of the American Academy of Political and Social Sciences*, Vol. 384, March 1971.

Robert A. Katzmann graphically portrays how disagreements among professionals—lawyers and economists—within the Federal Trade Commission led to conflicts about antitrust policy. Each group is motivated by different professional norms and personal goals. Katzmann notes that "by training the economist is wary of interference with the market mechanism; he perceives his task as the prevention of unwarranted government action. . . . In contrast to the economist, the lawyer is trained to be prosecution-minded; his career prospects depend upon his securing trial experience."[22]

Professions are characterized by their "relative insularity" and "imperial proclivities."[23] Jockeying for position among various professions or for position among sects within professions is a prime cause of structural disequilibrium. Each profession wants to be represented at the apex of the departmental structure, preferably with its spokesperson reporting directly to the secretary. Scientists propagandize for assistant secretaries for science or science advisers; accountants for comptrollers; lawyers for general counsels at the assistant secretary level; archivists for autonomous archival services. None wants to be subject to officials trained in alien disciplines.

The accounting, medical, and legal professions dominated the second Hoover Commission task forces on budget and accounting, medical services, and legal services and procedures. Their influence is evidenced by recommendations that comptrollers be established in all agencies and an assistant director for accounting in the Bureau of the Budget; an assistant secretary for health be created in HEW; and legal staffs of each department and agency be integrated under an assistant secretary for legal affairs or a general counsel. Congressman Holifield, a commission member, expressed concern about the report on "Budget and Accounting" because it "tends to exalt the role of the accountant

22. Robert A. Katzmann, *Regulatory Bureaucracy*, The MIT Press, 1980, p. 51.

23. Orlans, "The Political Uses of Social Research."

in Government just as the Commission Report on Legal Services tends to exalt the role of the lawyer in Government."[24]

Arguments for status and autonomy are rationalized by an appeal to a "higher loyalty." Government lawyers are by no means the only professionals to claim that members of their profession are answerable to the people of the United States and their professions as well as to their immediate administrative superiors. Lawyers contend that "they must have a degree of independence from administrative control which will enable them to serve as lawyers in Government and not merely as employees of Government."[25]

Scientists argue that national policy for science is a matter to be determined primarily by scientists themselves. Alan T. Waterman, former director of the National Science Foundation, testified as follows: "In any recommendations . . . concerning a research effort of the country, any agency, public or private, should defer to the judgment of the active and capable research scientists in the field."[26]

A Brookings Institution study opposed a Department of Health, Education, and Welfare because it doubted "whether power over professional matters should be vested in a lay department head."[27] The fact that health, education, and welfare were separate professions, each with its distinctive body of knowledge and techniques, and that the bureau chiefs were leaders in their respective professions, meant for Brookings that anything other than a housekeeping and coordinative role for the secretary would be inappropriate. If a secretary attempted to do something to which the organizations of state, federal, and local professionals were

24. Commission on Organization of the Executive Branch of Government, report on "Budget and Accounting," June 1955, p. 70.

25. Commission on Organization of the Executive Branch of Government, report on "Legal Service and Procedures," March 1955, p. 17.

26. W. Henry Lambright, *Governing Science and Technology,* Oxford University Press, 1976, p. 146.

27. Commission on Organization of the Executive Branch of the Government, task force report on "Public Welfare," January 1949, p. 11.

opposed, he would have a difficult fight on his hands.[28] The Brookings Institution was correct in anticipating that establishment of a Department of Health, Education, and Welfare would not diminish significantly the power of the professional guilds.

Most HEW secretaries preferred not to get involved in disagreements among professional groups. Such modest legislative proposals as one giving a secretary discretion to waive the single-state agency provision on a governor's request were approached with extreme caution. Under these provisions, state agencies other than those designated by federal law were ineligible to administer grant-in-aid funds. The designated agency was generally a "professional" agency such as the Health or Education Department.

Wilbur J. Cohen, at the time assistant secretary of HEW, testified in 1965 that the proposal was undesirable because "it did not protect a Secretary or a Governor from being pressured by professional or other groups" and would expose the secretary to "these kinds of sharp differences of opinion, which provoke strong feelings of professional personnel in the health, education and welfare field." Cohen concluded that "If you want good administration you have ultimately to get the support of the professional people, the State people, and the local people, or it makes little sense to change the administrative structure and lose the support of the people whom you actually have to count on to administer something."[29] Contrary to the advice from many of his principal subordinates, Secretary Gardner withdrew HEW's objection to this legislation and it was enacted in 1968.

Professional guilds are by no means confined to the Department of Health and Human Services. No less powerful guilds include the National Conference on State Parks, Society of American Foresters, American Association of State Highway Officials, National Association of Housing and Redevelopment Officers, Interstate Conference of Employment Security Agencies, and the

28. Ibid., p. 6.

29. Senate Committee on Government Operations, hearings on S. 561, Intergovernmental Cooperation Act, March 31, 1965, pp. 196, 197, 199.

Society of American Archivists. Federal officials are very active in these organizations. The guilds constitute a form of private government and are regularly consulted about proposed federal policies and regulations, often before the policies and regulations are discussed with the secretary. Secretaries have almost no option but to approve when presented with pacts reached after several months of negotiations with a guild.

Organization issues may be sensitive because they spring from jurisdictional disputes among professional guilds or splinter groups within professions. Engineers and biomedical specialists vied for control of the environmental health program. The debate over organization was, at its root, a debate over whether environmental health was primarily a disease problem or an engineering problem. It was the surgeon general's view that "it is an engineering job to get pollutants out of the environment, but it is a biomedical job to know how much lead in the environment will not cause harm to human beings."[30] Business economists demanded that the Council of Economic Advisers be reconstituted so as to break the virtual monopoly that was held by academic economists over council appointments.[31]

Few developments have had more significance for public administration than the rapid growth in the proportion of professional and technical employees since World War II. This trend is not limited to the federal government. Frederick Mosher estimates that about one third of all government employees are engaged in professional and technical pursuits, more than three times the comparable proportion in the private sector.[32] Mosher defines profession to include both the general professions (i.e., law, medicine) and the predominantly public service professions (i.e., foresters, social workers, educators.)

30. *Congressional Quarterly,* January 24, 1969, p. 170.

31. Statement by William H. Chartener, assistant secretary of commerce for economic affairs, *Washington Post,* September 27, 1968.

32. Frederick C. Mosher, *Democracy and the Public Service,* 2nd ed., Oxford University Press, 1982, p. 113. For a discussion of the role of lawyers, economists, engineers, accountants, and scientists, see "Symposium on Professions in Government," *Public Administration Review,* Vol. 38, No. 2, March–April 1978.

The consequences of increasing professionalization for federal organization structure are only beginning to be perceived. Professional concepts of status and autonomy are difficult to reconcile with orthodox doctrines of economy and efficiency, hierarchy, span of control, and straight lines of authority and accountability. The most sacred tenets of the orthodox theology are being openly challenged. Educators insist that "education is a unique activity—so different in its essential nature that it withers in an atmosphere of control to which most state activities can accustom themselves."[33] Archivists argued that "no mere concept of administrative efficiency could be permitted to deflect the object for which historians had labored so long," an independent National Archives.[34] From time to time scientists, lawyers, doctors, and other professionals have voiced similar heresies.

Mosher warns of the danger that "the developments in the public service of the mid-century decades may be subtly, gradually, but profoundly moving the weight toward the partial, the corporate, the professional perspective and away from that of the general interest."[35] In and of itself, professionalization is a major force for dividing the executive branch into separate narrow compartmentalized units. When professionalization is mixed with the centrifugal forces generated by clienteles, dependents, congressional committees, the politics of fund raising, and collective bargaining, the pressures for further balkanization of the executive branch become nearly irresistible.

Clientele groups and dependencies fear agencies with divided loyalties. They want agencies to represent their interests and their alone. Some years ago, rumors of a pending reorganization of bank supervisory agencies inspired this banner front-page headline in the *United States Investor:* NATIONAL BANKS NEED SPOKESMAN: OFFICE OF THE COMPTROLLER OF CURRENCY SHOULD BE PRESERVED.[36] It is clear from positions taken on banking legisla-

33. Malcolm Moos and Francis E. Rourke, *The Campus and the State,* The Johns Hopkins Press, 1959, p. 6.

34. H. G. Jones, *The Records of a Nation,* p. 21.

35. Mosher, *Democracy and the Public Service,* p. 230.

36. *United States Investor,* February 23, 1946.

tion that the comptroller of currency still speaks for the national banks, although few present-day comptrollers would express it as baldly as the comptroller's annual report in 1923: "The Comptroller of the Currency should, in the governmental organization, be the representative and partisan of the national banks."[37] President Truman's plan to strengthen the secretary of the treasury's control of the comptroller of the currency was defeated.

Certain agencies are admittedly partisans and representatives of particular interests within our society, and some were deliberately established for that purpose. President Truman thought it entirely proper that the Department of Commerce should be "a channel to the White House for business and industry" and regretted that organized labor did not use the Department of Labor in the same way.[38] President Nixon cited the need for preserving the Department of Agriculture as a "vigorous advocate" of farm interests when he abandoned his plan to abolish the department in order to divide its functions among the proposed departments of Community Development, Economic Affairs, Human Resources, and Natural Resources.[39]

Clientele interests rarely focus, however, at the departmental level. The department is valued mainly as a symbol. Departmental constituencies, even for acknowledged partisans such as Agriculture, Commerce, and Labor, represent a diversity of interests and may speak with conflicting voices. That there is a contest for access and power among the diverse elements in each constituency is demonstrated by the struggles between the Farm Bureau, the Grange, and the Farmer's Union, and, before the merger, the American Federation of Labor and the Congress of Industrial Organizations.

Pressures are most intense when constituencies are narrowly based and united by a common interest in preserving tangible economic privileges granted to them by federal law. It is the in-

37. Comptroller of the Currency, *Annual Report*, 1923, p. 18.

38. Harry S Truman, *Memoirs of Harry S Truman*, Vol. 1, Doubleday Co., Inc., 1955, p. 110.

39. *The New York Times*, November 12, 1971.

dependent agency or the bureau that is most likely to be seized upon as the vehicle for safeguarding and advancing these interests.

Congress does not encourage departmental scrutiny of bureaus with close constituency ties. Secretary of Agriculture Benson, for example, had his knuckles rapped for invoking his statutory powers to approve REA loans of over $500,000. Senator Humphrey denounced the secretary for "downgrading" the Rural Electrification Administrator "to the detriment of the REA program." He called on the secretary to cease and desist his "interference with the REA administrator's authority," or the Congress would take appropriate action.[40]

The REA's power derives in part from the strength of the organization representing the beneficiaries of REA loans—the National Rural Electric Cooperative Association. Each of the agencies dispensing federal largesse has its personal lobby: the Corps of Engineers has the Rivers and Harbors Congress; the Bureau of Reclamation has the National Reclamation Association; the Soil Conservation Service has the National Association of Soil and Water Conservation Districts. The Department of Agriculture's precedent in organizing its own support organization, the Farm Bureau, has been followed by many other agencies.

These groups are very jealous of the special relationship with their government sponsor. Interlopers are not treated kindly. Programs that may dilute the sponsor's single-minded concern with their interests are vigorously opposed. The Farm Bureau attempted to throttle at their birth the agricultural adjustment, farm security, and soil conservation programs that threatened the Extension Service–land grant college monopoly consummated by a 1914 agreement with the secretary of agriculture. Unless courted continually with suitable favors, an interest group may turn on its patron. The Department of Agriculture learned, to its sorrow, that the price of Farm Bureau allegiance was complete subservience.

Administrative systems are no more neutral than organization

40. *Congressional Record*, July 31, 1958, p. 14385.

arrangements. Professional, dependency, and bureaucratic interests may be as much affected by *how* a program is administered
as by *where* it is administered. The far-reaching policy implications of TVA's decision to channel its agricultural programs
through the land grant colleges are brilliantly documented in
Philip Selznick's *TVA and the Grass Roots*. TVA became firmly
locked into the Farm Bureau–Extension axis.

Federal agencies may be more responsive to the middle man
or their administrative agents than they are to the ultimate consumers of goods and services. The Department of Health and
Human Services, which channels most of its funds through state
agencies, is subject to quite a different set of influences from the
Small Business Administration and Veterans Administration,
which provide services directly to the people. The Department
of Housing and Urban Development, which deals with urban
agencies, responds differently than the Department of Agriculture, which administers its programs through land grant colleges, chosen instruments such as Soil Conservation districts, and
elected farmer committees. The Corps of Engineers is wholly dependent on its contractors—in contrast to the Tennessee Valley
Authority, which, as a matter of long-standing policy, does almost all its own work.

Difficulties occur when agencies and their clienteles develop a
vested interest in the way things are done. New approaches are
resisted for no other reason than that they require major modifications in existing administrative patterns or complicate constituency relationships. John Gardner has observed that, if agencies become prisoners of their systems and procedures, "the rule
book grows fatter as the ideas grow fewer. Almost every well-
established organization is a coral reef of procedures that were
laid down to achieve some long-forgotten objective."[41] The
Atomic Energy Commission was practically incapable of operating anything except by contract, and went so far as to contract
out administration of the city of Oak Ridge. This has become a

41. John Gardner, *No Easy Victories*, Harper & Row, 1968, p. 44.

major problem for the Department of Energy, which has had to assimilate the AEC functions.

Original purposes may be submerged in an overlay of myths, sentiment, and slogans. The farmer committee system is venerated as the most perfect expression of the principles of "grassroots" democracy. Forgotten are the system's humble beginnings as the offspring of a marriage of convenience between New Deal idealism and old-fashioned agricultural politics. The system was inaugurated at a time when the Farm Bureau and its state and local government allies were making a determined effort to capture the new action programs providing cash benefits to farmers. Whatever his public explanations, it is clear that Secretary Wallace was motivated as much by a desire to establish an effective counterweight to the Farm Bureau's political power as he was by ideological considerations. Soil conservation districts under elected boards were organized with much the same objective in mind.[42]

Clientele-oriented policies also may be engraved in stone. Devotion to these "historic" policies endures in the face of changing circumstances and challenges by presidents and prestigious study commissions. The U.S. Army Corps of Engineers adheres rigidly to the policy first enunciated in 1787 that inland waterways should be regarded "as public highways open to use of the public generally without restriction," although every president since Franklin Roosevelt has recommended the imposition of user charges. It was the Corps' unswerving dedication to this policy, rather than admiration for its engineering skills, that caused user organizations to lobby for Corps of Engineers' control of the St. Lawrence Seaway. The campaign did not succeed, but the House Commitee report directed that the St. Lawrence Seaway Corporation utilize the services of the Corps of Engineers for de-

42. For origins of the farmer committtee system and soil conservation districts, see John M. Gaus, "The Citizen as Administrator," in *Public Administration and Democracy*, Roscoe Martin, ed., Syracuse University Press, 1965, pp. 175–76; Robert J. Morgan, *Governing Soil Conservation*, The Johns Hopkins Press, 1965, pp. 317, 318, 353, 354; Morton Grodzins, *The American System*, Rand McNally & Co., 1966, pp. 351, 352, 356.

sign, construction, maintenance, and operation of the seaway and emphasized that in approving tolls it was "not digressing from the firm and long-standing toll-free policy established with respect to inland waterways."[43]

Interest groups have fascinated a generation of American scholars.[44] Political pluralists consider competition among interest groups as an integral and indispensable element in the democratic process. Those who deem all interest groups by definition to be evil and picture government agencies as marionettes dangling from strings manipulated by "special interests" are indulging in gross oversimplifications. The relationship between an agency and its constituency is based on a mutuality of interests—a mutuality generally established by the provisions of laws enacted by the Congress. The government agency often does the manipulating, not the reverse. The Forest Service, for example, maintains a roster of "key men" who can be called on in time of need for succor.[45] Other agencies maintain similar networks of individuals and organizations.

Interest groups are not monoliths. Their power is essentially negative. They are most effective in blocking actions—modification of the 2 percent interest rate on REA loans, transfer of the Maritime Administration to the Department of Transportation, imposition of user charges. These issues do not generate internal disputes. It is far more difficult to obtain unanimity when new proposals are being advanced, for then the sharp differences that exist in any organization quickly come to the surface.

Once systems are developed and patterns of organization behavior are established, in most instances they cannot be altered

43. House Report No. 1215, 83rd Congress, 2nd Session.

44. See E. Pendleton Herring, *Public Administration and the Public Interest*, McGraw-Hill Book Co., 1936; David Truman, *The Governmental Process*, Alfred A. Knopf, 1964; Harmon Zeigler, *Interest Groups in American Society*, Prentice-Hall, Inc., 1964; Grant McConnell, *Private Power and American Democracy*, Alfred A. Knopf, 1967. Theodore J. Lowi, *The End of Liberalism*, W. W. Norton Co., 1969.

45. Donal V. Allison, "The Development and Use of Political Power by Federal Agencies: A Case Study of the U.S. Forest Service," May 1965 (unpublished thesis, University of Virginia).

significantly by interdepartmental reorganizations. This is particularly true when bureaus, such as the U.S. Employment Service, are moved intact from one department to another. Reorganizations may result in scarcely more than a new name on the letterhead. Where changes are produced, they are seldom those anticipated or intended by the proponents of reorganization.[46] *Vin ordinaire* cannot be transformed into champagne merely by shifting the location of the bottle in the wine cellar.

The behavior of adult institutions can be altered. But this generally requires a combination of organization and nonorganizational measures, which enlarge the agency's constituency, compel redesign of the administrative system, and call for a different mix of professional skills. Important as it was, the transfer of the U.S. Coast Guard from the Treasury Department to a more compatible environment in the Department of Transportation would not by itself have been sufficient to bring about the dramatic change in the service's self-image and concept of role and mission. For the first time in the Department of Transportation, the Coast Guard was asked to participate in the formulation of departmental policies. By legislation and executive action the Coast Guard's mission was enlarged to include new regulatory activities, such as boating safety and environmental protection, which transferred "Coast Guard men and women from deck to desk."[47] The end result was, according to Lieutenant Commander Lawrence I. Kiern, to compel the Coast Guard "to abandon its traditionally apolitical character in regard to departmental affairs."[48]

The *first* organization decision is crucial. The course of institutional development may be set irrevocably by the initial choice of administrative agency and by how the program is designed.

46. Harold Seidman, Dominic Del Guidice, and Charles Warren, *Reorganization by Presidential Plan: Three Case Studies*, National Academy of Public Administration, 1971.

47. William Macleish, "The United States Coast Guard: Poor, But Proud and Looking Ahead," *Smithsonian*, Vol. 13, No. 4, 1982.

48. Lieutenant Commander Lawrence I. Kiern, "Changing the Guard," *Naval Institute Proceedings*, February 1985.

Unless these choices are made with full awareness of environmental and cultural influences, the program may fail or its goals may be seriously distorted.

Herbert Hoover believed that the simple physical grouping of functions "cheek-by-jowl" in departments organized by major purposes would automatically make it possible to eliminate overlaps and produce coordinated policies. This hypothesis assumes that department heads are or should be chief executives, as the term is used in business or military organizations, with authority reaching down through every step of the organization.

Luther Gulick defined the work of a chief executive by the acronym POSDCORB: planning, organizing, staffing, directing, coordinating, reporting, and budgeting.[49] In major or minor degree, department heads do perform all of these functions, but POSDCORB by itself provides an inadequate and unrealistic description of a secretary's job. Statutes that contemplate that a department head will "control" his agency are equally unrealistic.

A department head's job is akin to that of a major university president and is subject to the same frustrations. His principal duties involve matters that are unrelated to the internal administration and management of the institution. As far as his subordinates are concerned, he is the institution's ceremonial head, chief fund raiser, and protector of institutional values and territory. An informal check reveals that a department head may spend 25 percent or more of his time in meetings with members of the Congress and appearances before congressional committees, and probably an equivalent amount of time in public relations work such as speech-making and cultivating agency constituencies. One administrator reported that he was required to keep thirty-five full committees and seventy-five subcommittees informed of his agency's activities.[50] Another block of time is de-

49. Luther Gulick, "Notes on the Theory of Organization" in *Papers on the Science of Administration*, Luther Gulick and L. Urwick, eds., Institute of Public Administration, 1937.

50. Michael J. Malbin, "You Can Please Some of the Senators Some of the Time," *National Journal*, January 15, 1977.

voted to White House conferences and meetings of interagency and advisory committees. Minimal time is left for managing the department, even if a secretary is one of the rare political executives with a taste for administration.

A department head's managerial role is primarily that of a "mediator-initiator." In the words of Clark Kerr, former president of the University of California, who was referring to university presidents, "he must be content to hold the constituent elements loosely together and to move the whole enterprise another foot ahead in what often seems an unequal race with history."[51] He has opportunities to set directions and exercise significant influence only when new programs are being developed or when major increases in expenditures are being requested for old programs. Normally a department head has neither the time nor the inclination to concern himself with ongoing operations that appear to raise no problems.

The prime quality required of a department head, and most often lacking, is political leadership. Hugh Heclo correctly diagnosed the problem when he wrote the following:

> A political executive who does not know what he wants to accomplish is in no position to assess the bureaucracy's performance in helping him to do it. Likewise, an executive whose aims bear little relation to the chances for accomplishment is in an equally weak position to stimulate help from officials below. By trying to select goals in relation to available opportunities, political appointees create a strategic resource for leadership in the bureaucracy.[52]

Too often department heads equate management with control. Instead of providing positive policy leadership and coordination, departments may have a negative influence and impose restraints that hamper operating agencies in carrying out their missions. The congressional panel on social security was critical of the role

51. Quoted in the *Washington Post,* June 8, 1969, p. B1.

52. Hugh Heclo, "Political Executives and the Washington Bureaucracy," *Political Science Quarterly,* Vol. 92, Fall 1977.

played by the Department of Health and Human Services and its failure to adequately consider the Social Security Administration's special needs when imposing regulations to achieve departmental uniformity.[53]

Almost forty years ago the Bureau of the Budget found that "the outstanding weakness in federal administration today lies in deficiencies in administrative leadership, coordination and control at the top of federal departments and agencies."[54] Since then the number of assistant secretaries and special assistants have multiplied, staff resources available to a secretary have been augmented, and sophisticated systems have been installed to enhance a secretary's decision-making powers. However, department heads remain the weakest link in the chain of federal administration. Unless departmental management can be improved, reorganization cannot be counted on to yield more than marginal benefits.

If we are to do something meaningful about the organization and management of the executive branch, we must start first with department and agency heads. New approaches are needed— approaches based on what the political executives' functions really are—not on obsolete concepts of what they should be.

53. S. Prt. 98–204, Congressional Panel on Social Security Organization, "A Plan to Establish an Independent Agency for Social Security," June 12, 1984, p. 32.

54. Memorandum to staff of Division of Administrative Management from Donald C. Stone, assistant director for administrative management, April 5, 1948.

9

Cooperative Feudalism

Federal "professional" agencies and their state and local counterparts may have their differences, but they are as one when it comes to combating attempts by outsiders to encroach on their fiefdoms. Outsiders include lay administrators and competing professions, but the most feared are elected executives charged with representing the broader public interests—the president of the United States, governors, and mayors—and those such as budget officers who assist political executives in a general staff capacity. This bias is clearly evident in replies by federal grant-in-aid administrators to a questionnaire prepared by the Senate Subcommittee on Intergovernmental Relations. The subcommittee found that, "In the administration of these programs, counterparts tend and prefer to deal with counterparts. Chief executives and top management generalists are viewed by these program administrators as potential or actual enemies, subject to the fluctuating whims of the electorate."[1]

These alliances among professional counterparts and their constituencies in and outside of the Congress are variously referred to as subgovernments or "iron triangles." Presidents Nixon, Carter, and Reagan have attempted systematically to curb the

1. Senate Committee on Government Operations, Subcommittee on Intergovernmental Relations, "The Federal System as Seen by Federal Aid Officials," December 15, 1965, p. 55.

power of the subgovernments through grant consolidation, decentralization, and budgetary restraints. Although the alliances
are presently on the defensive, there is no evidence that they are
prepared to surrender.

The federal system as seen by federal and local program specialists and as it now in fact operates bears little resemblance to
classic concepts of federalism, which emphasize the independence of each of the levels of government and separation of powers. Traditional, or "layer-cake," theory assumes that the functions appropriate to each level can be defined with reasonable
precision and should be kept distinct from and independent of
each other. The problems of federalism are believed to relate
mainly to the proper allocation of responsibilities. President Eisenhower's Commission on Intergovernmental Relations and the
Joint Federal-State Action Committee organized by President Eisenhower and the Governors' Conference in 1957 took this approach. As stated by the commission, its task was "to determine,
within the constitutional limits of National and State powers,
and in the light of 165 years of practical experience, what division of responsibilities is best calculated to sustain a workable
basis for intergovernmental relations in the future."[2]

President Reagan's "New Federalism" is in many respects
merely a restatement of traditional concepts. He was proposing
to reestablish a separation between the functions of the federal
and state governments when he stated in his 1981 inaugural
address:

> It is my intention to curb the size and influence of the federal
> establishment and to demand recognition of the distinction
> between the powers granted to the federal government and
> those reserved to the states or to the people.

In contrast there are those who argue that "the functions of
the three levels of government are no longer distinguishable.
Their revenue sources are both interdependent and overlapping

2. The Commission on Intergovernmental Relations, a report to the President, June 1955, p. 33.

and there often is a wide gulf between the point of decision and the visibility of governmental action."[3] Layer-cake theory is rejected by some students of the federal system, notably Morton Grodzins and Daniel J. Elazar, whose culinary tastes run to "marble cake."[4] The marble cake school rejects separateness as the keystone of federalism. Separation of functions by levels of government is considered to be both impractical and undesirable when governments operate in the same clienteles and seek comparable goals. Although the system involves both competition and cooperation, the latter is the most important. As far as it goes, this description of "cooperative federalism" comes much closer to reality than traditional theories. Yet it is seriously deficient in failing to recognize that separatism can and has developed within the system without clear-cut separation of functions by levels of government.

What we have in several important functional areas are largely self-governing professional guilds, or what the Advisory Commission on Intergovernmental Relations calls "vertical functional autocracies."[5] In other areas federal agencies have established their own independent local government systems. Former governor of North Carolina, Terry Sanford, was speaking of the "vertical functional autocracies" when he wrote:

> The lines of authority, the concerns and interests, the flow of money, and the direction of programs run straight down like a number of pickets stuck into the ground. There is, as in a picket fence, a connecting cross slat, but that does little to support anything. In this metaphor it stands for the government. It holds the pickets in line; it does not bring them together. The picket-like programs are not connected at the bottom.[6]

3. George E. Hale and Marian Lief Palley, *The Politics of Federal Grants,* Congressional Quarterly Press, 1981, p. 2.

4. Senate Committee on Government Operations, p. 95.

5. Advisory Commission on Intergovernmental Relations, Tenth Annual Report, January 31, 1969, p. 8.

6. Terry Sanford, *Storm Over the States,* McGraw-Hill Book Co., 1967, p. 80.

The Advisory Commission on Intergovernmental Relations (ACIR) has observed that federal grant programs become "institutionalized" in networks of program specialists in the executive and legislative branches, as well as organized beneficiary groups. According to the ACIR, the existence of these professional guilds "creates serious obstacles to the exercise of political leadership by the occupants of the White House, the Congress, or the political parties."[7]

A survey by the ACIR reveals that the picket fence is still in place, although it has ceased to be of the sturdy, solid wood variety. David B. Walker suggests that "bamboo fence" federalism now more accurately "captures the vertical functionalism, continuing professionalism, greater flexibility and realism" of contemporary administrators.[8] Although the emphasis continues to be on functionalism and program protectionism, the standpatism and indifference to broader intergovernmental issues evident in the earlier responses to the Senate Subcommittee on Intergovernmental Relations have become somewhat muted.

The federal system is not a single system, but a loose grouping of relatively autonomous confederations of federal, state, and local professional agencies. Senator Edmund Muskie was one of the first to discern and describe accurately the true character of twentieth-century federalism. He classified intergovernmental relations "as almost a fourth branch of government," but one that "has no direct electorate, operates from no set perspective, is under no special control, and moves in no particular direction. . . ."[9]

No one deliberately planned to create this fourth branch of government. In fostering the establishment of autonomous local

7. Advisory Commission on Intergovernmental Relations, "The Federal Role in the Federal System: The Dynamics of Growth" (A-86), June 1981, p. 93.

8. David B. Walker, *Toward a Functioning Federalism,* Winthrop Publishers, Inc., 1981, p. 128.

9. Senate Committee on Government Operations, Subcommittee on Intergovernmental Relations, "The Federal System as Seen by State and Local Officials," 1963, p. 2.

units or in organizing special districts and independent para-governments, the federal government was responding to existing patterns of state and local organization and, in some instances, endeavoring to compensate for some of its more obvious weaknesses. Fragmentation of authority, both horizontal and vertical, is the distinguishing feature of our local government systems. As in the Congress, "power is nowhere concentrated; it is rather deliberately and of set policy scattered amongst many small chiefs."

Power is diffused among 50 states and over 82,000 local governments including, in round numbers 3000 counties, 19,000 municipalities, 18,000 townships, 14,000 school districts, and 28,000 special districts.[10] Within one city there may be five or more "governments" (county, city, school district, sanitary district, fire district, water district, library district, etc.) levying taxes and exercising authority over the same citizens.

Although significant progress has been made since the 1960s, particularly in strengthening the authority of state governors, executive power in many jurisdictions remains weak and fragmented. In some states a governor's powers with respect to the budget, planning, organization structure, executive appointments, and administration continue to be hedged with restrictions.

Executive power may be shared with five or more independently elected officials who owe no allegiance to the governor and who may be his political enemies. The number of states with a short executive ballot (four offices or less) has increased from three in the 1960s to nine, but eleven states have added officials making their ballot even longer.[11]

The planning and supervisory role of the governor and his central management units are undercut by federal regulations, which foster the autonomy of program specialists. It is no coin-

10. U.S. Department of Commerce, Bureau of Census, *Statistical Abstract of the United States*, 1985, p. 283.

11. David B. Walker, "The States and the System: Changes and Choices," *Intergovernmental Perspective*, Vol. 6, No. 4, Fall 1980.

cidence that executive power is likely to be weakest with respect to state agencies that are heavily dependent on federal funds. A study by George E. Hale and Marian Lief Palley found that "federal grants change the behavior of state administrators and that executive and legislative control suffers."[12] Approximately 38 percent of the unaided agencies lobbied for supplements to the executive budget compared with 60 percent from agencies with federal sponsors.

At the outset, there was no intention to create privileged sanctuaries or to thwart governors in the exercise of whatever legitimate powers they might possess. Safeguards were believed necessary to simplify administrative relationships between the federal government and the recipients of federal grants, to maintain accountability, and, above all, to ensure that the national purposes of programs authorized by the Congress were not obscured or lost by dividing up administrative responsibility among the host of state agencies that could advance jurisdictional claims.

National objectives were a matter of little moment during the early years of the republic when federal assistance consisted mainly of land grants to the states. Congress specified the general purposes for which the proceeds from land sales could be used (generally education or internal improvements), but it imposed few other restrictions and made no provision for federal supervision. The Morrill Act of 1862 marked the beginning of a trend toward increased emphasis on national objectives with federal supervision and regulations to see that grants were used for the intended purposes. With the proliferation of grant-in-aid programs and the growing dependence on grants to promote national purposes, either through stimulation of state action or through cooperative education, health, welfare, and employment security programs, the organizational and administrative disarray within most state governments could no longer be safely ignored.

The single-state-agency requirement was devised as one means

12. Hale and Palley, *The Politics of Federal Grants*, pp. 105–6.

for bringing some order out of administrative chaos. Provisions designating the state agency to administer or supervise federal grants and establishing direct relationships between the designated agency and its federal counterpart first appear in the 1916 Federal Highway Act. To be eligible for federal highway assistance, a state must have "a State highway department which shall have adequate powers and be suitably equipped and organized to discharge to the satisfaction of the Secretary the duties required by this title. Among other things, the organization shall include a secondary road unit." The secretary (now the secretary of transportation) is directed to enter into "formal project agreements" with state highway departments and to "certify to each of the departments the sums which he has apportioned." There is no requirement that the secretary seek a governor's advice and approval before concluding project agreements or even that he keep the governor informed.

The 1917 Smith-Hughes Act stipulates that to receive the benefits of federal appropriations for vocational education a state must designate or create as the administering agency a state board consisting of no fewer than three members, and having "all necessary powers" to cooperate with the federal program agency, or designate the state board of education for this purpose. Again, no role is specified for the governor. Vocational education grants are treated as the exclusive concern of the federal government and its chosen state instrument.

Congress went beyond the requirement for a "sole local agency" in authorizing grants for vocational rehabilitation services and provided, in addition, that the vocational rehabilitation bureau, division, or other unit of a state vocational education agency designated under the Act "shall be subject only to the supervision and direction of such agency or its executive officer."

Perhaps the most extreme example of federal organizational dictates is to be found in the National Health Planning and Resources Development Act of 1974, which requires states to designate a Health Planning and Development Agency to perform the planning under the act as well as to administer the program.

States are also directed to create state Health Coordinating Councils, which are to approve state plans and review all applications for federal health care grants.

At one time or another, federal laws have called for designation of a "single state agency" or "sole agency" for such programs as school lunch, highways, maternal and child health care, maternity and infant care, child welfare, community health, mental retardation, library services, urban planning, manpower development and training, water pollution control, national defense education, vocational education, vocational rehabilitation, civil defense, public assistance, hospital and medical facilities construction, and law enforcement assistance.

Without question these requirements have served to rationalize state administration within prescribed functional areas and have helped to improve the quality of state personnel by introducing professional standards and merit-system principles. As tangible evidences of "success," one can cite the state highway and welfare departments and vocational education boards, which were established as the direct result of federal "stimulation." Integration within functional areas has been obtained, however, at the cost of professional inbreeding, organizational and administrative rigidity, further impairment of central executive authority, and loss of political responsibility.

Until very recently, few worried about the adverse effects, although a survey group reported to the Commission on Intergovernmental Relations in 1955, based on its study of Michigan State government, that

> Federal grant programs have done nothing to strengthen the State government as a political entity. Rather, the divisive elements in the political situation have been emphasized by the close professional and functional relationships that have grown up in the grant fields between Federal and State program officials. In the Federal-State grant relationship the political leadership of the State often has been ignored to the detriment of sound statewide development.
>
> Professional association of administrators and private citi-

zens has promoted further compartmentalization of interest
and loyalty along program lines to the detriment of overall
government unity.[13]

Strict construction of the single-state-agency provision has enabled state program administrators to evade central fiscal controls and to block attempts at administrative reform. Channeling
of requests for vocational education and child welfare services
grants through state budget bureaus was opposed because it
"would undermine the 'single agency' requirement."[14] The Department of Health, Education, and Welfare vetoed a proposal
by Oregon to establish a state agency in its own image. Objections were raised because (1) the head of the proposed Department of Social Services would be interposed between the governor and the administrators of federally assisted programs; (2)
program administrators would be appointed outside the merit
system; and (3) administrative authority would be subject to review beyond that of the respective divisions.[15] The Department
of Health, Education, and Welfare also disapproved the Florida
Department of Health and Rehabilitative Service's 1976 vocational rehabilitation plan because it violated the single-state-
agency provision. HEW Secretary Joseph A. Califano denied the
Florida governor's request for a waiver. Secretary Califano gave
the following explanation: "The decision is reached because of
restrictions in the law and does not reflect my personal view
that states should have more latitude than at present to organize
and manage programs funded by the Federal government."[16]

Wilbur Cohen's sensitivity about allowing any modifications
of the single-state-agency provision is understandable. For the
professional guilds, these statutory provisions are the equivalent

13. Commission on Intergovernmental Relations, "The Fiscal and Administrative Impact of Federal Grants-in-Aid," June 1955, p. 38.

14. Senate Committee on Government Operations, "The Federal System as
Seen by Federal Aid Officials," p. 53.

15. Ibid., p. 45.

16. National Academy of Public Administration, *Reorganization in Florida*,
Washington, D.C., September 1977, p. 65.

of corporate charters, the indispensable source of both power and legitimacy. Any questioning of the single-state-agency concept represents a challenge to their existence.

The consequences of organizational compartmentalization and functionalism within both the executive and the legislative branches of the federal and state governments are to be seen in the multiplication of narrow categorical programs. By restricting the purposes for which federal grants may be utilized, each legislative committee and subcommittee, and professional discipline and subdiscipline, seeks to reinforce its jurisdictional claims and to make certain that funds cannot be diverted to competing programs. Support of general health has become submerged in a multiplicity of separate grants for heart disease, cancer, venereal disease, mental retardation, maternal and child health, mental health, communicable disease, and so forth. The Partnership for Health Act in 1966 made some progress by consolidating and combining several categorical health grants, but progress was to be short-lived. The Congress soon backslid by enacting new categorical health programs for migrant workers, alcoholics, and drug addicts.

A major objective of Reagan's "New Federalism" has been to reduce the number of categorical grants and to provide assistance through broad-based block grants. At last count there were 392 categorical grants, 142 fewer than in 1980.[17] Nonetheless, categorical grants remain the principal form of federal assistance and in 1984 represented 87 percent of federal aid.[18]

Single state agencies are established within the framework of the state government and are subject, at least nominally, to control by the governor and the legislature. This is not true of federally sponsored organizations at the local level, which are outside and independent of the established city and county governments. These include special districts, authorities, and, more recently, private nonprofit organizations, which have become

17. Advisory Commission on Intergovernmental Relations, *A Catalog of Federal Grant-in-Aid Programs to State and Local Governments,* fiscal year 1984.

18. Office of Management and Budget, *Special Analysis, Budget of the United States Government,* fiscal year 1986, p. H–21.

strong competitors with state and local governments for federal grants.

In the mid-1960s about a quarter of federal programs affecting urban development induced or even required special districts for their administration.[19] Federally encouraged special districts have included law enforcement districts, community action agencies, comprehensive area manpower programs, comprehensive health and area planning agencies, air quality regions, local development districts within the Appalachian area, and resource conservation development districts. Another approach was illustrated by the public housing program and, to a lesser extent, by urban renewal, for which federal officials demonstrated a preference for independent or semi-independent local authorities.

There was some grumbling about federal encroachment on local domains, but local officials were hardly in a position to argue in principle against a few more special districts and independent authorities. Development of federal "little governments" attracted no public attention or outright opposition until the poverty program. Mayors and county executives were accustomed to being bypassed; but federally financed assaults against "the establishment" hit them in their political vitals, where it hurt the most.

Ironically, the community action agency was initially considered by the Bureau of the Budget as a unifying force to meld together the resources of the federal, state, and local governments and the private community in the war against poverty. There was no desire to fight city hall. The original Economic Opportunity Act gave the local community the option to designate either a "public or private nonprofit agency" to administer a community action program, provided that the program "was developed, conducted, and administered with the maximum feasible participation of the areas and members of the groups served." The public agency could be an extension of the mayor's office or under his control.

The Bureau of the Budget's vehicle for "institutional coopera-

19. Advisory Commission on Intergovernmental Relations, "Fiscal Balance in the American Federal System," Vol. 1, October 1967, p. 72.

tion" was transformed by the Office of Economic Opportunity into an instrument to promote "institutional change." Some went so far as to interpret community action "as a mandate for Federal assistance in the effort to create political organizations for the poor."[20] Emphasis was shifted from coordination and collaboration with established federal, state, and local agencies to competition.

Some community action agencies developed their own constituencies and sufficient political power to earn the respect, if not the enthusiastic support, of most elected local officials. A measure of accommodation was achieved, as demonstrated by the fact that fewer than 2 percent of the communities exercised the option accorded local officials under 1968 amendments to the Economic Opportunity Act to convert private community action agencies to public agencies.[21]

The Model Cities Act also called for "citizen participation." City development agencies bore a striking resemblance to community action agencies, but the Department of Housing and Urban Development profited from OEO's experience. HUD stressed that problems would never be resolved if city hall and the city development agency got "tangled up in the rhetoric of total control." Citizen access to and influence on the decision-making processes was provided, but subject to the rights of responsible elected city officials to make final decisions and to supervise and control the use of public funds.[22] Though they had somewhat different objectives, the extent of overlap between city development agencies and community action agencies further complicated the problems of coordinating federal urban assistance programs.

20. Daniel P. Moynihan, *Maximum Feasible Misunderstanding*, The Free Press, 1969, p. 131.

21. Comptroller General of the United States, Review of Economic Opportunity Programs, March 10, 1969, p. 21.

22. Remarks of H. Ralph Taylor, assistant secretary for Model Cities and Governmental Relations, Department of Housing and Urban Development, before the Model Cities Midwest Regional Conference, September 6, 1968.

As of December 1978, citizen participation requirements were extended to include 155 separate federal grant programs, accounting for more than 80 percent of grant funds. The Advisory Commission on Intergovernmental Relations observed that, taken as a whole, these requirements were "diverse, complex, confusing, sometimes arbitrary, less effective than they might be, and difficult for some federal aid recipients to comply with."[23]

"Citizen participation" is a very slippery term and means very different things to different people. If participation is measured by the number of citizens who participate in public hearing or vote for members of citizen boards, it rests on a very narrow base. The "citizen participant" is generally the representative of an interest group.[24] Citizen participation can be and has been used as a means for transferring power from officials who have at least some political responsibility to the community at large to self-perpetuating local cliques or the bureaucracy. It can operate in ways that provide symbolic citizen participation, but minimal individual citizen influence and maximum citizen frustration.

Former White House counselor and present U.S. senator Daniel P. Moynihan has observed that citizen participation is a "bureaucratic ideology." "The bureaucracy increasingly gets its way, and acquires a weapon against the elected officers of 'representative' government, but it is not clear that it gets its results. A process of cooptation, of diminished rather than enhanced energies, somehow seems to occur." Moynihan concludes that

> The Federal Government should constantly encourage and provide incentives for the reorganization of local government in response to the reality of metropolitan conditions. The objective of the Federal Government should be that local government be stronger and more effective, more visible, accessible, and meaningful to local inhabitants. To this end the Federal

23. Advisory Commission on Intergovernmental Relations, "The Federal Influence on State and Local Roles in the Federal System" (A–89), November 1981, p. 44.

24. Ibid. p. 45.

> Government should discourage the creation of paragovern-
> ments designed to deal with special problems by evading or
> avoiding the jurisdiction of established local authorities, and
> should encourage effective decentralization.[25]

Some of the chosen federal instruments are not unlike para-
sitic growths living on the body of their federal hosts. Their
appetite for power and appropriations can be satisfied only by
what is fed into the host agency. Any reduction in appropriations, elimination or transfer of programs, or tightening of
political controls is strongly resisted. To be separated from the
host is to risk survival.

The antipolitical biases, conflicts, and pressures present within
the intergovernmental system have been transmitted to the federal body politic. As the price for congressional approval of the
reorganization plan creating the Department of Health, Education, and Welfare, President Eisenhower was compelled to provide assurances that "the Office of Education and the Public
Health Service retain the professional and substantive responsibilities vested by law in those agencies or in their heads."[26]
Seeming irrationalities in the federal structure have their roots
in jurisdictional disputes among vertical functional autocracies.

President Kennedy underestimated the influence of the vocational education guild when he proposed to break its monopoly
over vocational training established by the Smith-Hughes Act.
The administration manpower development and training bill
sent to the Congress in 1961 provided for a direct federal operation administered by the secretary of labor and financed wholly
from federal funds. State vocational education facilities were to
be employed at the discretion of the secretary of labor by individual agreements negotiated through the Department of
Health, Education, and Welfare, but principal emphasis was to
be given to on-the-job training.

25. Daniel P. Moynihan, "Toward a National Urban Policy," speech delivered
at Syracuse University, May 8, 1969.

26. Message transmitting Reorganization Plan No. 1 of 1953, March 12, 1953.

The American Vocational Association centered its attack on the sections of the administration bill that permitted manpower development and training programs to be conducted without reference to the states or to HEW. It wanted HEW to control the program, with money to be distributed to the states by formula grants. The compromise bill enacted by the Congress in 1962 split jurisdictional responsibility between Labor and HEW. Except for on-the-job training, the law provided for state administration and financing by funds apportioned to the states in accordance with "uniform standards" agreed on by the secretaries of Labor and HEW.[27]

Within the Department of Labor, the U.S. Employment Service, which has an independent power base in the Interstate Conference of Employment Security agencies, the Bureau of Apprenticeship and Training supported by its allies in the AFL–CIO, and the Office of Manpower, Automation, and Training, all competed for control. Secretary Wirtz's announced plans to consolidate departmental manpower programs in a new Manpower Administration had to be withdrawn because of widespread state complaints that the proposed reorganization was both "surprising and detrimental."[28] The opposition was spearheaded by one of the most powerful guilds, the Interstate Conference of Employment Security Agencies. The daily work of the conference was carried out by an executive secretary on the Department of Labor payroll. Former Manpower Administrator and Assistant Secretary of Labor Stanley H. Ruttenberg complained, "Taking a stubborn stance of unremitting opposition to almost any suggestion for change, the Interstate Conference offers protective cover for those who would use the employment service to prevent change instead of making it a positive instrument of social reform."[29]

27. For the legislative history of the Manpower Development and Training Act, see James L. Sundquist, *Politics and Policy,* The Brookings Institution, 1968, pp. 85–91.

28. *The New York Times,* November 28, 1968.

29. Stanley H. Ruttenberg and Jocelyn Gutches, *The Federal-State Employ-*

The Council of Chief State School Officers, the National Association of State School Boards, and the National Education Association had the necessary political muscle to secure passage of a Senate amendment transferring the popular Head Start program from the Office of Economic Opportunity to the Office of Education over protests by OEO and the secretary of HEW. Senator Clark condemned the amendment as a power play by the education lobby. He stated the following:

> Of course, the education lobby is for this transfer. Why would it not be? They would like to run the program just as they would like to run all the rest of the programs which are not under their jurisdiction now, whether they are education programs, or not. . . .[30]

The Senate amendment did not stand up in the House of Representatives, and language was substituted directing the president to make a special study of whether responsibility for administering the Head Start program should be left with OEO or transferred to another agency. President Nixon determined that Head Start should be delegated to HEW, but with the important proviso that the program be lodged directly under the secretary, not in the Office of Education.[31] The education guild had won something of a Pyrrhic victory.

As long as a guild can maintain its support within the Congress, it has little to fear from executive reorganization proposals. When it loses congressional confidence, it is in serious trouble. Successive measures to reorganize federal water pollution programs were designed deliberately to wrest power from the Public Health Service and the state health departments. Members of Congress were fed up with what they considered to be "footdragging" by the health agencies. Congressman John Blatnik

---

ment Service: A Critique, The Johns Hopkins Press, 1970. Emmette S. Redford and Marlin Blisset, *Organizing the Executive Branch: The Johnson Presidency,* University of Chicago Press, 1981, pp. 180–83.

30. *Congressional Record,* July 17, 1968, p. S8811.

31. *Weekly Compilation of Presidential Documents,* February 24, 1969.

complained that all he could get from the Public Health Service were bland assurances that "Everything is fine. The States are doing a good job. The municipalities are doing a good job. We are getting along well with them." Meanwhile "year by year pollution was getting worse and worse."[32] Blatnik sympathized with the problems faced by HEW Secretary Gardner and told him:

> We are dealing with the Public Health Service. They did not care who was the Secretary of HEW. In fact, their attitude was an open, brazen one: "These Secretaries upstairs come and go. We are going to tell you."[33]

Congress enacted legislation to transfer water pollution control functions from the Public Health Service to a new Water Pollution Control Administration in the Department of Health, Education, and Welfare, but this reorganization did not wholly sever the ties with the Public Health Service. Complete separation was achieved by Reorganization Plan No. 2 of 1966, which transferred the program to the Department of the Interior, except for certain limited health functions retained by the secretary of HEW. Four years later the program was transferred to a new independent Environmental Protection Agency.

Governors and mayors are only now beginning to appreciate the political implications of federal organization structure, administrative arrangements and procedures. Some of the reports for the 1955 Commission on Intergovernmental Relations showed that federal aid programs could have a significant impact on the balance of power within a state, but the commission did not think the problem was worth mentioning in its final report. As late as 1962, the Council of State Governments reported that federal grants had a minor influence on state governmental structure and organization, a view not shared by the Governor's

32. House Committee on Government Operations, hearings on Reorganization Plan No. 2 of 1966 (Water Pollution Control), March 30 and May 4, 1966, p. 42.

33. Ibid., p. 10.

Conference, which in 1961 deplored "the tendency of Federal agencies to dictate the organizational form and structure through which States carry out Federally supported programs."[34] Almost 47 percent of the state and local officials who responded to a 1962 questionnaire circulated by the Senate Committee on Intergovernmental Relations answered "no" to the question: "Has the kind of State and local government required by Federal grant-in-aid statute or administrative ruling hampered the flexibility of State and local organization structure?"[35] Few governors and mayors would answer "no" today.

Governors have endeavored to strengthen their power position by establishing an office in Washington wholly dedicated to their interests. Until this office was organized, many governors had to rely for intelligence about federal policies and operations on information filtered through communications channels controlled by the guilds. Many states, cities, and counties have established liaison offices in Washington, but most of these offices do not act as the "eyes and ears" of the governors and mayors. Their activities are concentrated principally on obtaining federal grants and contracts and "casework."[36]

In contrast with governors and mayors, the guilds are supported by strong power bases within the federal establishment and have developed a close rapport with functionally oriented congressional committees. They have the capacity to block or delay reform measures they suspect contain hidden traps. As a result, progress in obtaining needed reforms has been painfully slow.

Decentralization is viewed as a subterfuge to strengthen the power of local politicians. The National Education Association

34. Senate Committee on Government Operations, "The Federal System as Seen by Federal Aid Officials," pp. 40, 41.

35. Senate Committee on Government Operations, Subcommittee on Intergovernmental Relations, "The Federal System as Seen by State and Local Officials," 1963, pp. 42, 43.

36. Advisory Commission on Intergovernmental Relations, "The Federal Role in the Federal System: Dynamics of Growth" (A–86), June 1981, pp. 144–48.

was able to bring sufficient pressure to bear through the Appropriations Committees to compel the Office of Education to rescind its plans for decentralized administration of Titles I, II, and III of the Elementary and Secondary Education Act and Titles III and V of the National Defense Education Act. The Office of Education had been urged by the White House and the secretary of HEW to decentralize its operations. The NEA and other school organizations argued that establishment of Office of Education regional offices would conflict with the policy that all elementary and secondary educational programs should be channeled through the state departments of education.

Highway interests were early successful in their attempt to cut off funds for the administration of Section 204 of Model Cities Act requiring coordinated review and comment at the metropolitan level on federal grant-in-aid applications submitted by individual local agencies and political subdivisions. The intention was merely to "subject highway planners," among others, "to other points of view and to some more persuasion,"[37] but for the highway guild this raised the possibility that metropolitan agencies could mobilize public support against freeways and overturn plans promoted by the state highway departments and Bureau of Public Roads. Section 204 also drew fire from critics who believed that any strengthening of metropolitan agencies was part of a plot to impose white suburban control on the black inner cities.[38]

Guilds are politically powerful, but not invincible. Recent measures to strengthen the relative power of the generalists within the system at least provide the opportunity over the long run to produce significant change.

Passage of the Intergovernmental Cooperation Act was held up for three years, but it was finally enacted in 1968. In addition to authorizing waiver of the single-state-agency provision, the

37. Senate Committee on Government Operations, hearings on S.561, Intergovernmental Cooperation Act of 1965, March–April 1965, p. 218.

38. Frances Fox Piven and Richard A. Cloward, "Black Control of Cities," *The New Republic*, September 30, 1967, and October 7, 1967.

act provides that (1) governors and state legislatures shall be informed of federal grants to state agencies; (2) federal aid, to the extent possible, shall be consistent with and further the objectives of state, regional, and local comprehensive planning; and (3) loans and grants should be made to units of general local government rather than to special purpose units.

Following enactment of the Intergovernmental Cooperation Act, the number of special districts, authorities, and other independent units encouraged by federal programs declined.[39] At the same time that the federal government has increased its support of general purpose local governments, it has promoted the establishment of a variety of substate regional organizations for such diverse activities as planning, economic development, health systems, services to the aging, and community action.[40]

Reorganization by region or area is perhaps the most commonly prescribed antidote to functional parochialism. When a geographic area is used as the basis of organization, the influence of the functional specialist is reduced. The proliferation of federally sponsored substate planning organizations, however, is not calculated to enhance the relative power position of mayors and governors. Regional organizations often constitute another layer of government and exacerbate the power struggle among the states, cities, counties, and special districts. It is contended that "under the guise of supporting decentralized governments close to the people, regional planning and grants delivery become even more complex, confusing and obscure."[41]

President Nixon's aim was to transfer significant decision-making power with respect to federal grants from functional specialists to ten federal councils chaired by presidential appointees and subject to direction by the Office of Management and Budget. Department and Agency representatives were generalist political appointees who had "the responsibility for intersect-

39. Advisory Commission on Intergovernmental Relations, "The Federal Influence on State and Local Roles in the Federal System," pp. 16–17.

40. Ibid.

41. Hale and Palley, *The Politics of Federal Grants*, p. 118.

ing the strong functionalist-specialist lines."[42] The attempt to superimpose a system of regional administration on an executive branch structure organized by function and purpose proved to unworkable. Although useful as networking organizations for intergovernmental management, the councils were incapable of either administering or coordinating categorical grants.[43] President Reagan first reduced the size of and then abolished the regional councils in 1983. Regionalization may strengthen the president, but it has the opposite effect on state and local political executives. If a regional council were able, in fact, to control the flow of federal funds into a region, then the council chairman could well become the dominant political force within the region—superior to governors and mayors. Federal influence over local decisions would be increased, not decreased.

Block grants have the potential for containing the power of the guilds and shifting control to the generalists. Block grants occupy a middle position between categorical aids and general revenue sharing and permit greater local discretion within broad functional areas such as health, employment and training, and community development. The benefits of increased local discretion may well be offset, however, by the greater leverage given to the federal government through the concentration of funding in a single grant. Rejection of a block grant raises serious political and fiscal problems for a state or city. Consequently, it is more difficult to resist imposition of across-the-board mandates such as those that now apply to nondiscrimination, environmental protection, planning and project coordination, relocation and real property acquisition, labor and procurement standards, public employee standards, and access to government information and decision processes.

Block grants, together with devolution and budgetary reduc-

42. Leigh E. Grosenick, ed., *The Administration of the New Federalism: Objectives and Issues,* American Society for Public Administration, 1973, p. 52.

43. Robert W. Gage, "Federal Regional Councils: Networking Organizations for Policy Management in the Intergovernmental System," *Public Administration Review,* Vol. 44, No. 2, March–April 1984.

tions, were seen by the Reagan administration as the most effective instruments for wresting control from the guilds. This intent was made clear by a White House official who made the following statement:

> We have consciously set out to force political decisions and the struggles that accompany them down to the state and local level. The so-called iron triangles in Washington for too long have had a virtual monopoly on political influence in Congress and the agencies.[44]

President Reagan in 1981 called for consolidation of twenty-five health programs into two block grants and thirteen social service programs into one grant and for consolidation of a few energy programs.[45] What he obtained from the Congress was considerably less. Pressure from the more powerful guilds compelled major compromises in his original proposals. Congress decreased the funds covered by the consolidations from $16.5 billion to $7.5 billion and increased the number of block grants to nine.[46] Restrictions and limitations attached to some of the grants made some question whether or not the term *block grant* was an accurate description.[47] Except for one new block grant to replace the Comprehensive Employment Training Act, President Reagan has been unsuccessful in his attempts to consolidate additional grant programs. One student of the intergovernmental system concluded that, "When the dust had settled, the categorical grant system had survived in reasonably good health the most resolute attack on it to date by the most powerful political antagonist it had yet encountered."[48]

A further step toward devolution was taken by Executive Or-

44. Quoted in Claude E. Barfield, *Rethinking Federalism*, American Enterprise Institute, 1981, p. 24.

45. Lawrence D. Brown, James W. Fossett, and Kenneth T. Palmer, *The Changing Politics of Federal Grants*, The Brookings Institution, 1984, pp. 104–5.

46. Ibid., p. 106.

47. Ibid.

48. Ibid.

der No. 12372, which went into effect on October 1, 1983. The order delegates to the states authority to establish their own procedures for reviewing and coordinating requests for federal assistance and federal programs and projects in their jurisdictions. Federal administrators are directed to be more responsive to state and local concerns. The order replaces Office of Management and Budget circular A–95, which had prescribed the review process.

The net impact of Reagan's "New Federalism" has been to reduce somewhat the number of categorical grants and to restrain grant-in-aid outlays. Grant-in-aid spending is projected to decline from $107.0 billion in 1985 to $100.7 billion in 1986 and $99.2 billion in 1987.[49] Enthusiasm for reforming the intergovernmental system appears to have waned in the second Reagan term. Except for relatively modest changes, the pre-Reagan structure basically remains intact.

The ACIR has viewed with deep concern "the almost unbridled tendency of the part of the national government and the political process that sustains it to thrust nearly all of the nation's most national domestic concerns, as well as an ever-multiplying number of parochial and even private concerns into the intergovernmental arena."[50] The result of creeping intergovernmentalization has been to permit "the national government to avoid some of its most basic governmental responsibilities, while cluttering up its agenda with issues that more properly belong on that of a municipal or county council, a school board, or a state legislature."[51]

David B. Walker attributes the present feeble functioning of the federal system to the "fractured concept of public responsibility spawned by . . . intrusive intergovernmentalization"[52] He

49. Office of Management and Budget, p. H–1.

50. Advisory Commission on Intergovernmental Relations, "The Federal Role in the Federal System: The Dynamics of Growth" (A–86), p. 108.

51. Ibid.

52. David B. Walker, "The State of American Federalism—1977," *Publius*, Vol. 8, No. 1, Winter 1978.

believes that something more than slogans and incremental adjustment is necessary to restore public confidence in the system. Walker argues for "a new public philosophy" and a shift in emphasis from special to national interests.[53] The obstacles to developing such a new philosophy in a government system now characterized by diffusion of power and responsibility at every level are enormous.

53. Walker, *Toward a Functioning Federalism*, p. 246.

IO

Coordination: The Search for the Philosopher's Stone

In ancient times alchemists believed implicitly in the existence of a philosopher's stone, which would provide the key to the universe and, in effect, solve all of the problems of humankind. The quest for coordination is in many respects the twentieth-century equivalent of the medieval search for the philosopher's stone. If only we can find the right formula for coordination, we can reconcile the irreconcilable, harmonize competing and wholly divergent interests, overcome irrationalities in our government structures, and make hard policy choices to which no one will dissent.

When interagency committees such as the Economic Opportunity Council fail as coordinators, the fault is sought in the formula, not in deeper underlying causes. The council's inability to perform its statutory duties as coordinator of the federal government's antipoverty efforts was attributed to the fact that the law (1) placed coordinating responsibility on a body of peers who could not be expected voluntarily to relinquish decision-making control over planning for or operation of programs, and (2) designated the director of the Office of Economic Opportunity, then a non-Cabinet-level official, as chairman with coordinative authority over officials of greater status. The formula was changed to provide that the council have an independent chairman and staff, but with no better results. The original council at least met a few times; the restructured council was never convened at all. Again, revision of the formula was prescribed as the remedy. The comptroller general proposed that the council's functions be transferred to an Office of Community Resources in the Executive Office of the President, which would provide staff support for President Nixon's interdepartmental Urban Affairs Council.[1]

Whether we are dealing with poverty, science, telecommunications, or international and national security programs, the search for a coordinating formula seems to follow almost a set pattern: (1) establishment of an interagency committee chaired by an agency head and with no staff or contributed staff; (2) designation of a "neutral" chairman and provision for independent staff; and (3) transfer of coordinating functions to the White House or Executive Office of the President, establishment of a special presidential assistant, and reconstitution of the interagency committee as a presidential advisory council.

Our efforts to discover effective means for coordinating international and national security programs have taken us the complete cycle.

PHASE ONE

1944   State-War-Navy Coordinating Committee created by agreement of respective secretaries (Air Force added in 1947).

1947   National Security Council established.

1949   State-War-Navy-Air Coordinating Committee abolished and functions assumed by National Security Council staff. NSC staff nominated by agencies represented on the council.

---

1. Comptroller General of the United States, "Review of Economic Opportunity Programs," March 18, 1969, pp. 163–65.

PHASE TWO

1950   NSC staff group reconstituted and designated as "senior staff."

1953   NSC "senior staff" formalized as Planning Board. Operations Coordinating Board, chaired by undersecretary of state, created with responsibility for coordinating implementation of national security policies.

1953   Special assistant to the president for National Security Affairs established and designated as chairman of the Planning Board.

1957   OCB incorporated in NSC structure. Provision made for presidential appointment of chairman and vice-chairman.

PHASE THREE

1961   Senate Subcommittee on National Policy Machinery criticizes "overinstitutionalization" of NSC system and overreliance on the Planning Board and OCB. Recommends OCB be abolished and "responsibility for implementation of policies cutting across departmental lines . . . be assigned to a particular department or a particular action officer."

1961   President Kennedy reduces NSC staff, downgrades NSC role, and abolishes OCB. Responsibility for coordinating policy and operations assigned to the secretary of state.

PHASE FOUR

1966   National Security Action Memorandum 341 ostensibly "provides the authority and machinery for the effective leadership of the country's foreign affairs by the Department of State." NSAM 341 established a two-tiered structure of interagency committees: (1) interdepartmental regional groups chaired by the assistant secretary of state for each regional bureau; (2) a senior interdepartmental group chaired by the undersecretary of state. Theoretically, the chairman of each group was empowered to decide all matters within the purview of the group, subject to appeal to next higher authority.

The Nixon administration changed the names of the committees to interdepartmental groups and the undersecretaries committee and restricted the latter to "operational matters." Both committees reported to an NSC review group chaired by Henry Kissinger. The NSC committee structure was again reorganized by President Carter with the stated purpose of placing "more responsibility in the departments and agencies while insuring that the NSC, with my assistant for National Security Affairs, continues to integrate and facilitate foreign and defense policy decisions."[2] The number of NSC staff committees was reduced from seven to two, the Policy Review Committee and Special Coordination Committee. The latter was chaired by the assistant for National Security Affairs and the former by the secretary of state.

President Reagan replaced the Policy Review Committee and Special Coordination Committee with three senior interagency groups for foreign policy, defense policy, and intelligence under each of the senior interagency groups; lower-level interagency groups are organized by either geographic area or function.[3]

Defective machinery may contribute to the difficulties of co-ordinating multifaceted federal programs, which cut across traditional agency jurisdictions, but it is seldom, if ever, at the root of the problem. The power to coordinate does not normally carry with it the authority to issue binding orders. Executive orders customarily confer broad powers "to facilitate and co-ordinate" federal programs and direct each department and agency to "cooperate" with the official designated as coordinator. However, buried in the boiler plate at the end of the order there is usually a section reading "Nothing in this order shall be construed as subjecting any function vested by law in, or assigned

2. Presidential Directive/NSC-2, January 20, 1977.

3. White House press release, National Security Council Structure, January 12, 1982.

pursuant to law to, any Federal department or agency or head thereof to the authority of any other agency or officer or as abrogating or restricting any such function in any manner."[4]

Neither the president nor a coordinator appointed by him can perform the functions vested by law in the heads of departments and agencies. When conflicts result from clashes in statutory missions or differences in legislative mandates, they cannot be reconciled through the magic of coordination. Too often organic disease is mistakenly diagnosed as a simple case of inadequate coordination.

If agencies are to work together harmoniously, they must share at least some community of interests about basic goals. Without such a community of interests and compatible objectives, problems cannot be resolved by coordination. Senator Frank Moss ascribed the conflict between the National Park Service and the Army Corps of Engineers over the Florida Everglades to "uncoordinated activities." Park Service officials complained that the Engineers drained the Everglades National Park almost dry in their efforts to halt wetlands flooding and reclaim glade country for agriculture. The Engineers argued that wetlands were "for the birds" and flood control for the people.[5] Coordinating devices may reveal or even exacerbate the conflict, but they cannot produce agreement among the agencies when a choice must be made as to whether a single piece of land should be drained for flood control and reclaimed for agriculture or maintained as wetlands to preserve unique and valuable forms of aquatic life.

Coordination is rarely neutral. To the extent that it results in mutual agreement or a decision on some policy, course of action, or inaction, it inevitably advances some interests at the expense of others or more than others. Coordination contains no more magic than the philosopher's stone. In does, however, contain

4. See, for example, Section 4 of Executive Order No. 11452, January 23, 1969, establishing the Council for Urban Affairs.

5. Senate Committee on Government Operations, hearings on S.886 to redesignate the Department of the Interior as a Department of Natural Resources, October 17, 1967, p. 16.

a good deal of the substance with which alchemists were concerned—the proper placement and relationship of the elements to achieve a given result.

Coordinators are seldom judged objectively or evaluated by realistic standards. Coordination may influence people, but it makes few friends. The tendency is to consider that coordination most effective which operates to one's own advantage. Few coordinating systems have worked as successfully as OMB's procedures for clearing proposed legislation and reports on legislation and advising agencies as to the relationship of legislative proposals to "the Administration's program," but the legislative clearance process is by no means universally admired. By doing its job well, OMB has gained few friends among members of Congress and interest groups whose pet bills have been held "not in accord with the Administration's program."

The term coordination is used in laws and executive orders as if it had a precise, commonly understood meaning. Yet probably no word in our administrative terminology raises more difficult problems of definition. For James D. Mooney, coordination is no less than "the determining principle of organization, the form which contains all other principles, the beginning and the end of all organized effort."[6] Coordination is also defined as concerted action, animated by a common purpose, responding to recognized signals and utilizing practiced skills. Coordination describes both a process—the act of coordinating—and a goal: the bringing together of diverse elements into a harmonious relationship in support of common objectives. The power to coordinate in and of itself confers no additional legal authority, but merely provides a license to seek harmonious action by whatever means may be available under existing authorities.

In current usage, coordination has come to be identified primarily with the formal processes by which we attempt to adjudicate disagreements among agencies. Mooney would regard the

6. James D. Mooney, "The Principles of Organization," in *Papers on the Science of Administration,* Luther Gulick and L. Urwick, eds., Institute of Public Administration, 1937, p. 93.

proliferation of coordinating mechanisms, such as interagency committees, as prima facie evidence of "lack of coordinated effort" resulting from inexact definitions of jobs and functions.[7] Coordinating machinery becomes necessary only when coordination cannot be achieved by sound organization, good management, and informal cooperation among agencies engaged in related and mutually supporting activities.

Formal coordinating processes are time-consuming and the results are generally inconclusive. True coordination sometimes may be obtained only by going outside the formal processes.

By overemphasizing coordinating machinery, we have created the false impression that most federal activities are uncoordinated. This is by no means the case. Without informal or so-called lateral coordination, which takes place at almost every stage in the development and execution of national programs and at every level within the federal structure, the government probably would grind to a halt. Skilled bureaucrats develop their own informational networks. Managers who are motivated by a desire to get something done find ways and means of bridging the jurisdictional gaps. Informal coordination is greatly facilitated when people share the same goals, operate from a common set of legal authorities and information assumptions, agree on standards, have compatible professional outlooks, and can help each other. Where these conditions exist, there is no need for the intervention of third parties to secure harmonious action.

Politicization of the senior career service inevitably disrupts the networks and impedes lateral coordination. It is argued by some that the networks are instruments of bureaucratic ideologies that must be controlled if an administration is to achieve its political objectives.[8]

Coordination does not necessarily require imposition of authority from the top. State and local governments have the crucial role in the process of administering and coordinating federal

7. Ibid.

8. Stuart M. Butler, Michael Sanera, and W. Bruce Weinrod, *Mandate for Leadership* II, The Heritage Foundation, 1984, p. 484.

assistance programs. The functions of establishing state, regional, and local goals, developing comprehensive plans, and determining priorities among grant proposals in terms of these goals and financial restraints is a local responsibility. Effective performance of these functions by state and local governments can reduce or eliminate need for coordinating arrangements at the federal level.

Complete reliance on voluntary cooperation is not feasible, however, except in Utopia. The goals of our pluralistic society, as reflected in federal programs, are frequently contradictory. No matter how the government is organized, it is impossible to define jobs and design programs in such a way as to eliminate all overlaps and potential conflicts among agencies. Even when the will to cooperate is present, good intentions may be thwarted by the size of the federal establishment, the growing complexity and compartmentalized character of federal programs, differences among professional groups, and the absence of a clear sense of direction and coherence of policy either in the White House or in the Congress. We cannot produce harmony by synthetic substitutes when the essential ingredients are lacking within the governmental system. The much maligned interagency committees are the result, not the cause, of our inability to agree on coherent national objectives and to find a workable solution to our organizational dilemma.

Interagency committees are the crabgrass in the garden of government institutions. Nobody wants them, but everyone has them. Committees seem to thrive on scorn and ridicule and multiply so rapidly that attempts to weed them out appear futile. For every committee uprooted by Presidents Kennedy, Johnson, and Carter's much publicized "committee-killing" exercises, another has been born to take it place.

Interagency committees as a general institutional class have no admirers and few defenders. Former Secretary of Defense Robert Lovett ascribed the proliferation of interagency committees to the "foul-up factor," or the tendency of every agency with even the most peripheral interest to insist on getting into the act. According to Lovett, committees have now so blanketed the whole executive branch as to give it "an embalmed atmosphere."[9] From his observation, committees are composed of "some rather lonely, melancholy men who have been assigned a responsibility but haven't the authority to make decisions at their levels, and so they tend to seek their own kind. They thereupon coagulate into a sort of glutinous mass, and suddenly come out as a committee."[10] Lovett concluded that "two heads are not always better than one, particularly when they are growing on the same body."[11]

Nelson Rockefeller, W. Averell Harriman, and Lyndon B. Johnson were no less critical. Rockefeller contended that interagency committees "reduce the level of Government action to the least bold or imaginative—to the lowest common denominator among many varying positions. In such circumstances, policy may be determined not for the sake of its rightness—but the sake of agreement."[12] Harriman condemned committees as organs of "bureaucratic espionage" employed by agencies to obtain information about the plans of other departments that could be used to "obstruct programs which did not meet with their own departmental bureaucratic objectives."[13] In a memorandum to the heads of departments and agencies, President Johnson cautioned that "improper use of committees can waste time, delay action, and result in undesirable compromise."[14]

Like most things in nature, interagency committees do fulfill a purpose, although this may at times be poorly defined or understood. The harshest critics have been unable as yet to devise satisfactory substitutes. Those who condemn interagency committees as a class are not in the least inhibited when it comes to

9. Senate Committee on Government Operations, Subcommittee on National Policy Machinery, "Organizing for National Security," hearing, Vol. 1, p. 15.

10. Ibid., p. 30.

11. Ibid., p. 17.

12. Ibid., p. 945.

13. Ibid., p. 635.

14. Lyndon B. Johnson, Memorandum for Heads of Departments and Agencies, February 25, 1965.

safeguarding "their committees" or in proposing new ones when it suits their purposes, even though they may feel obliged to resort to such high-sounding titles as "council" as a form of disguise. It depends on whose ox is being gored.

Presidents may be unenthusiastic about interagency committees in general, but they object most to those created by the Congress. As we have indicated in Chapter 2, interagency committees are effectively utilized by the Congress as a means for circumscribing and limiting the president's powers. Bureau of the Budget Circular No. A–63, March 2, 1964, admonished agencies that "Committees should be established, insofar as possible, by means which permit maximum flexibility in determining the membership, functions, and duration of the group. Therefore, agencies should not propose the establishment of committees by legislation unless there is a clear need to do so." This language was echoed in President Johnson's message transmitting Reorganization Plan No. 4 of 1965 in which he argued that statutory provisions "are rarely sufficiently flexible to permit the membership or role of the committees to be accommodated to changing circumstances or to permit their termination when they have outlived their usefulness." The plan abolished nine statutory committees, but the Board of Foreign Service and the National Advisory Council on International Monetary and Financial Problems were quickly reestablished by executive action.

The Congress also professes a distaste for interagency committees, but its fire is directed mainly against those created by the president or department heads. Senator Edmund Muskie was highly critical of the twenty odd interagency committees with responsibility for coordinating federal grant-in-aid programs, but his solution was a bill to establish another interagency committee to be called the National Intergovernmental Affairs Council with a strong executive secretary directly responsible to the president.[15]

15. Senate Committee on Government Operations, Subcommittee on Intergovernmental Relations, hearings on "Creative Federalism," Part I, "The Federal Level," p. 5.

Use of interagency committees as a legal subterfuge to get around the provisions of a 1909 law (31 U.S.C. 673) prohibiting the use of federal funds to finance commissions, councils, boards, and similar bodies not created or authorized by the Congress has contributed to congressional hostility. The one exception to the law is a statute (31 U.S.C. 691) permitting agencies to use their funds to pay the expenses of "interagency groups engaged in authorized activities of common interest." These restrictions are not applicable to the president's emergency and special projects funds, which are subject, however, to the Russell rider establishing one-year limitation for commissions financed from these funds.

Interagency committees have been created by the president solely for the purpose of making it possible legally to divert agency appropriations to pay the costs of controversial bodies such as the Consumer Advisory Council and various study commissions. Congress called a halt to this in 1968 by including language in appropriation acts prohibiting the use of funds appropriated to agencies to finance interagency groups "which do not have prior congressional approval of such method of financial support."[16]

Contributory financing is an irritant, but the Congress has more basic concerns about committees that are wholly creatures of the executive. Interagency committees may be employed to alter subtly the balance of power among executive agencies and, consequently, the balance of power among congressional committees with program jurisdiction. If the president were to establish a committee chaired by the OMB director or the chairman of the Council of Economic Advisers to coordinate water resources programs, it would bring an immediate and violent response from the Interior Committees.

Congressional mistrust of presidential committees was evidenced by the Federal Aviation Act of 1958, which provided that the FAA administrator "shall not submit his decisions for the approval of, nor be bound by the decisions or recommendations

16. Public Law 90–479, Section 510.

of, any committee, board or other organization created by Executive order."

Interagency committees cannot be discussed rationally without distinguishing among the distinct types of committees and the varied purposes they serve. These differences relate primarily to method of establishment, duration, chairman, membership, staff, financing, and functions.

Statutory committees financed by separate appropriations and employing their own staff are nothing more or less than an independent agency headed by an interagency board. The president may be authorized to designate the chairman, or the law may designate a Cabinet officer or agency head as chairman. The president may be given some discretion in selecting committee members, or membership may be determined by statute.

Difficulties occur when the law endows these agencies with something more than advisory functions. Budget Bureau Circular No. A-63 observed that "committees should be used for such functions as advising, investigating, making reports, exchanging views, etc." As a matter of executive branch policy, the circular instructed agencies that "responsibility for performance of operating or executive functions, such as making determinations or administering programs should not be assigned to committees." This admonition is repeated in the Federal Advisory Committee Act of 1972, which declares that "committees should be advisory only, and that all matters under their consideration should be determined, in accordance with law, by the official, agency, or officer involved."

The bureau's directive was intended to head off the establishment of interagency committees on the model of the National Advisory Council on International Monetary and Financial Problems and comparable bodies. NAC's statutory authorities included such broad and far-reaching powers as (1) "coordination by consultation or otherwise" of the U.S. representatives in international financial institutions and all federal agencies engaged in international monetary and financial transactions; (2) approval on behalf of the United States of the Articles of Agreement of various international institutions; (3) issuance of binding instructions to U.S. representatives to the World Bank and similar institutions. Consonant with its status as an independent agency, the NAC was directed to submit special reports to both the president and the Congress.

Most of the powers of the NAC were exercised, not by the Council as a whole, but by the Treasury and the NAC staff. During the regime of George Humphrey as secretary of the treasury, the council itself seldom met. The staff concentrated its attention on reviewing individual loan applications and day-to-day agency operations. The council's role as a "coordinator" and policy adviser to the president, except to the extent this function was performed in scrutinizing loan applications, ceased to be its major focus. The net effort of these statutory provisions and the NAC mode of operations were severely to restrict the president's discretion in his choice of advisers on international monetary and financial policy and in organizing, coordinating, and administering executive branch activities.

By far the largest number of interagency committees deal with highly technical problems and provide a convenient vehicle for exchanging information and bringing the technical people together on a regular basis to discuss problems of mutual concern. These include the Ship Structure Committee, Committee on Exports, Committee on Atmospheric Water Resources, and Range Weed Research Group. Other than providing a source of fun for columnists on dull days—the Interdepartmental Screw Thread Committee is always worth a chuckle—technical committees present few problems except in controversial areas such as pesticides, in which there are deep divergencies in agency objectives and policies that cannot be resolved by technicians. There are many professional "communities" in the federal government that cut across jurisdictional lines, and the committees in part serve as a forum and meeting place for the "law enforcement," "intelligence," "foreign affairs," "scientific," and "educational" communities, among others.

Controversy centers principally on a relatively limited number of interagency committees that have become, in the words of the Jackson Subcommittee, "the gray and bloodless ground of bureaucratic warfare—a warfare of position not of decisive battles."[17] The battle for position is never-ending and grows more intense as agencies seek to gain control or at least exercise influence over the growing number of new and important programs that cut across established jurisdictional lines. Sometimes a stalemate is evidenced by cochairmen or rotating chairmanships. Occasionally, the stalemate is resolved by making the vice president or some other "neutral" the chairman.

Members of these committees act as instructed delegates of their agencies. They judge their effectiveness by how many points they win for their side. With this emphasis on gamesmanship, agency staff assigned to the committee become highly expert in identifying and escalating interagency differences, even when the issues are insignificant or nonexistent. Staff of the NSC Planning Board, before the board was abolished by President Kennedy, were among the leading exponents of this art.

Whatever their other drawbacks, interagency committees can be useful in setting the metes and bounds of agency jurisdictions and areas of legitimate interest. Without them, or a reasonable substitute, we would have no criteria for discriminating claims in such areas as education, water resources, science, poverty, economic and trade policy, and manpower. Agencies vie for membership on committees established by the Congress or the president, not necessarily because they expect the committee to play a decisive role, but to establish their right to request information and to be consulted about matters that concern them. Otherwise their colleagues could charge them with "meddling." The fact that the committee may never meet, or, if it does, only third- and fourth-echelon officials might attend, becomes a matter of relatively little importance.

Chairmanship of a committee establishes primacy within a given program area but confers no authority, other than that

17. Senate Committee on Government Operations, Subcommittee on National Policy Machinery, Vol. 3, p. 50.

which the chairman already possesses by law. Membership in an exclusive club such as the National Security Council carries with it a certain amount of prestige but, in and of itself, little influence.

Membership can provide greater access to the president when the president meets frequently with a committee and looks upon it as a part of his council. The informal committee dubbed the "Troika," composed of the secretary of the treasury, the budget director, and the chairman of the Council of Economic Advisers, exercised a dominant influence over financial and economic policy during the Kennedy and Johnson administrations. The committee was called the "Quadriad" when it included the chairman of the Federal Reserve Board.

The seven cabinet councils or committees established by President Reagan did provide access to the president and limited participation in the policy process. According to Chester A. Newland, the councils served primarily as coordinators of "secondary-level domestic policy development, interpretation, and implementation" and were concerned mainly with the details to carry out policies determined elsewhere in the Executive Office of the President.[18] The seven councils were abolished in 1985 and replaced by an Economic Policy Council and a Domestic Policy Council.

Much of the criticism of interagency committees is directed at the wrong target. Committees can perform effectively when they are assigned appropriate tasks that are within their competence. The Alaska Reconstruction Commission was successful because each of the committee members had the statutory authority and motivation to do things that were necessary to assist Alaska's recovery from the disastrous Good Friday earthquake. The committee was not called on to revise basic government policies, except for a few modifications it recommended to meet the special

18. Chester A. Newland, "Executive Office Policy Apparatus: Enforcing the Reagan Agenda," in *The Reagan Presidency and the Governing of America,* Lester M. Salamon and Michael S. Lund, eds., The Urban Institute Press, 1985, pp. 153–61.

circumstances in Alaska, but to obtain agreement among the agencies on the work that needed to be done and to see that it was carried out on a phased time schedule.

On the other hand, the federal executive boards proved totally ineffective in dealing with critical urban problems because they were given a job that they were inherently incapable of accomplishing and that was wholly alien to the purpose for which they were organized. President Kennedy established federal executive boards in ten of the largest cities in 1961. The number was, by the end of 1969, increased to twenty-five. Board membership was limited to the principal federal civilian and military officials who happened to be located within the designated geographic area. Unless the agencies most concerned with critical urban problems—the Departments of Housing and Urban Development, Health, Education, and Welfare, and Labor, and the Office of Economic Opportunity—had offices in a city, they were not represented on the federal executive board. When they were represented, it might be by someone from a specialized bureau, such as the Food and Drug Administration, who was not competent to discuss departmental programs.

The objectives in creating the boards were reasonably modest and attainable: improvement of communications between Washington and the field and among federal officials in the field; encouragement of cooperation among federal agencies in areas where cooperation might be to their mutual advantage; support of community activities such as blood donor drives and community chest campaigns. In each of these areas, members of the boards had the authority to act. As long as the boards confined their activities to such programs as equipment sharing, joint training, and improved public services, they were able to make a valuable contribution.

The boards failed when they were directed in 1965 to identify unmet urban needs and to devise and carry out interagency and intergovernmental efforts to help solve critical urban problems. A 1969 Bureau of the Budget-Civil Service Commission evaluation identifies three principal reasons for this failure, all of which should have been anticipated before the assignment was made: (1) interagency committee have no decision-making authority and cannot resolve fundamental conflicts about agency priorities; (2) collaborative efforts among members of the boards could not be effective because of the weaknesses in the boards' composition and the disparity among the boards' members in the powers delegated to them by their respective agencies; and (3) members of the boards with full-time jobs elsewhere could not be expected to devote the necessary time to activities that were extraneous to their official duties.[19]

The federal executive boards' manifest failure as coordinators did not deter efforts to assign comparable functions to a somewhat differently constituted group of interagency committees, the ten federal regional councils. It should have come as no surprise that the councils also proved incapable of reconciling "conflicting policies and practices among their member agencies."[20]

The deficiencies associated with interagency committes can be avoided or minimized if (1) missions are tailored to their capabilities; (2) membership is kept as small as possible; (3) institutionalization of staff and procedures is held to a minimum; and (4) the end product is advice to someone who has authority to decide and who wants the advice. Committees perform poorly when compelled to act as collective decision makers, either as program administrators or as policy coordinators.

Standing interagency committees with responsibility to coordinate *in general* are to be distinguished from *ad hoc* interagency groups organized by the president or agency heads to study and report on *specific problems,* such as delays in the processing of federal grants, management of automatic data processing equipment, and contracting for research and development. These com-

19. Bureau of the Budget and U.S. Civil Service Commission, Memorandum for the President, "Evaluation of Federal Executive Boards," July 22, 1969.

20. Robert W. Gage, "Federal Regional Councils: Networking Organizations for Policy Management," *Public Administration Review,* Vol. 44, No. 2, March–April 1984.

mittees operate with a high degree of informality and are staffed by agency personnel with the requisite professional skills rather than by professional coordinators. The committees go out of business once their assigned task is accomplished. Problem-oriented working committees have been extremely useful.

President Johnson's executive orders directing the secretaries of housing and urban development and agriculture to act as "conveners" represented an attempt to institutionalize the problem-oriented approach to coordination.[21] The secretary of HUD had proposed an interdepartmental council as a means for carrying out his statutory responsibility "to exercise leadership at the direction of the President in coordinating Federal activities affecting housing and urban development." As an alternative to a standing committee, the Bureau of the Budget suggested that the secretary be given responsibility by executive order to convene, or authorize his representatives to convene, meetings at appropriate times and places of the heads, or representatives designated by them, of such federal departments and agencies with programs affecting urban areas as he deemed necessary to seek solutions to identified or anticipated urban development problems. Comparable responsibility with respect to rural development was to be given to the secretary of agriculture.

Budget Director Charles L. Schultze argued that "coordination is best done when it is done with respect to specific identifiable problems on a case-by-case basis."[22] The executive orders conferred no authority on the secretaries but it held them accountable for seeing to it that the right people were brought together at the right time to solve specific problems. Matters requiring a decision were to be referred promptly to the person with the authority to act, up to and including the president.

The very simplicity of the convener concept guaranteed that it would be almost universally misunderstood. Senator Muskie

21. Executive Order No. 11297, August 11, 1966; Executive Order No. 11307, September 30, 1966.

22. Senate Committee on Government Operations, Subcommittee on Intergovernmental Relations, hearings on "Creative Federalism," Part 1, "The Federal Level," November 1966, p. 399.

was convinced that the convener order did nothing more than establish another interagency committee.[23] Others contended that the orders merely confirmed powers that every secretary already possessed. Secretary Robert Weaver, on the other hand, thought the convener authority was so significant that he was unwilling to delegate it to any of his subordinates, although the Bureau of the Budget had contemplated that the key role would be assigned to HUD regional administrators so that problems could be tackled immediately at their points of origin. For all these reasons, the convener approach had only a minimal impact and, despite some minor success, proved only slightly more effective than the traditional coordinating formulas.

A variant of the convener approach is to be found in Bureau of the Budget circulars designating "lead" agencies for coordinating meteorological programs and federal activities in the acquisition of water data. For example, the Department of the Interior is made responsible "for exercising leadership in achieving effective coordination of national network and specialized water data acquisition activities" and is directed to "prepare and keep current a federal plan, and the status of its implementation, for the efficient utilization of network and related water data acquisition activities."[24] These arrangements have raised few of the questions associated with the convener orders, mainly because the issues tend to be more technical than political.

Problems are created when multiple lead agencies share responsibility for coordinating the implementation of similar and overlapping policies. Five lead agencies are concerned with enforcing fair employment practices in the administration of federal grants. Functions are assigned according to type of discrimination such as discrimination against the handicapped or under construction contracts.[25]

Interagency committees, conveners, and lead agencies are basi-

23. Ibid., p. 116.

24. Bureau of the Budget Circular No. A-67, "Coordination of Federal Activities in the Acquisition of Certain Water Data," August 28, 1964.

25. Advisory Commission on Intergovernmental Relations, *Categorical Grants: Their Role and Design,* 1977, pp. 262–63.

cally organized ways of promoting voluntary cooperation. Many believe that they are fatally flawed because there is no provision for a central directive authority. The Area Redevelopment Act of 1961 attempted to overcome this deficiency by centralizing authority and funding in a small coordinating agency—the Area Redevelopment Administration—and requiring decentralized operations through delegate agencies. The ARA was thought of as the "prime contractor" for federal depressed-area assistance, with the delegate agencies performing in the role of subcontractors.[26] The administration's primary focus was expected to be on the development and approval of overall economic development plans for each depressed area and coordination of proposed projects with the approved plans. Much the same concept was incorporated, to a major or minor degree, in the foreign assistance, civil defense, and poverty programs.

The delegate agency approach appeared to have considerable promise and offered an opportunity to move toward "systems managers" for designated program areas. This promise was not realized, however, because of the inability to resolve the novel problems of relationships among federal agencies that are introduced by the delegation process. These relate to selection and direction of personnel, communications, and final project approval.

ARA was unable to exercise effective control over the selection of personnel to administer delegated programs. When responsibility for ARA programs was merely added to an employee's normal duties, first priority was inevitably given to the work for his or her own agency. A study by Sar Levitan indicated that "communications between the ARA and its cooperating agencies were so poor that in some cases field offices were issued conflicting instructions from their parent agencies. Suspicions and resentments were widespread among officials both in Washington and field."[27] Delegate agencies were inordinately slow in processing applica-

26. Sar A. Levitan, *Federal Aid to Depressed Areas,* The Johns Hopkins Press, 1964, p. 42.

27. Ibid., p. 45.

tions for ARA financial assistance, but it was the ARA officials who were blamed for the delays. Convinced that the system was inherently defective, the ARA urged in 1963 that it be modified drastically or abandoned.

If left to its own devices, ARA in time could probably have established a mutually acceptable and workable *modus vivendi* with delegate agencies. The insuperable obstacle was the pressures from the White House and the Congress. These pressures meant that ARA could not divorce itself wholly from decisions on individual applications. Political realities compelled ARA to divert its major efforts from overall economic development plans to projects of interest to the White House and influential members of Congress. Consequently, ARA tended to duplicate the reviews conducted by delegate agencies, thus contributing to the excessive delays in processing applications. Some believe that the delegate agency system was never given a fair test in ARA.

Evaluations of Office of Economic Opportunity experience with delegate agencies are conflicting. OEO contended that it "was the first agency at the Federal level to develop, set up and live by a system of interagency delegation agreements."[28] Delegate agencies included Labor (Neighborhood Youth Corps), Agriculture (rural loan program), Health, Education, and Welfare (work experience and adult basic education), and Small Business Administration (economic loans). Although the system had not "worked perfectly," in OEO's judgment "a significant start" had been made.

The comptroller general did not share OEO's optimism and recommended that the Congress permanently transfer those programs that were administered under delegation from OEO or recommended for delegation by the president. In five instances— work study, lending and loan guarantees, adult basic education, upward bound, and work experience—the Congress had directed transfer of the programs to delegate agencies. The comptroller general held that OEO had "not been in an effective posi-

28. Comptroller General, "Review of Economic Opportunity Programs," p. 22.

tion to exericse oversight and direction for programs which have been delegated to other agencies."[29] He asserted that the appearance of central direction and coordination had been obtained at the expense of further dividing responsibility for closely related programs and blunting OEO's innovative capacity by weighing it down with administrative burdens.

Much the same line of reasoning is to be found in President Nixon's 1969 message outlining a proposed reorganization of the Office of Economic Opportunity.[30] To maintain strict accountability for the way in which work was performed, President Nixon recommended that functions should be assigned to specific agencies whenever possible, thus avoiding the blurring of lines of responsibility resulting from OEO delegations. The reorganized OEO's mission would be concerned principally with innovating new domestic programs. When an experiment proved successful, the program would be transferred "to other agencies or other levels of government or even the private sector if that seems desirable." OEO would retain certain proven programs, however, which were national in scope, particularly in those cases in which OEO's "special identification with the problems of the poor" made this desirable.[31]

The Congress has been willing to experiment with almost every conceivable type of coordinating formula, but it has drawn the line at proposals for "super coordinators" or "super Cabinet" officers. Except in wartime, the Congress objects to changes that transfer power from the heads of the established agencies to "czars" who are answerable to the president only.

For this reason, John Gardner's proposal for a home-front executive officer or executive vice president attracted little serious attention outside the press.[32] Gardner told *The New York Times*

29. Ibid., p. 168.

30. *Weekly Compilation of Presidential Documents,* August 18, 1969, pp. 1132–36.

31. President Nixon recommended in his 1975 Budget Message that OEO be abolished.

32. *The New York Times,* July 18, 1968.

that the federal government "cannot go on much longer with its present organization" of overlapping and conflicting agencies on domestic problems, and so the president should appoint an "executive officer" to mobilize and coordinate talent and resources in various departments for the home front. The president cannot do the job because he is "too busy" and "he doesn't really like to get in and deal with fights" between Cabinet members. The Budget Bureau and White House staff have only "partial and limited coordinating functions" and "have proven wholly inadequate to the task of coordination."

Gardner's plan was by no means new. In 1955 Herbert Hoover had suggested creating two appointive vice presidents, one responsible for foreign and the other for domestic affairs. President Eisenhower had recommended the establishment of a "first secretary" of the government who would function, in effect, as prime minister with respect to national security and international affairs. From time to time it has been suggested seriously that the vice president be made "coordinator-in-chief," although it is doubtful that any president would be willing to delegate this kind of power to a person whom he did not appoint and cannot remove. Paul David has observed, "The functions, duties and prerogatives of the Vice President, as a member of the Executive Branch are not likely to be expanded except with the formal or informal concurrence of the President; but once such functions, duties and prerogatives are in place, withdrawal through action by the President becomes more difficult than their initial establishment."[33]

As we have seen, President Nixon's "experiment" with the equivalent of assistant presidents for domestic affairs, foreign affairs, economic affairs, and executive management and with counselors for Human Resources, Natural Resources, and Community Development was short-lived. In unveiling the plan in January 1973, President Nixon stated that its purpose was "to integrate and unify policies and operations throughout the ex-

33. Paul T. David, "The Vice-Presidency: Its Institutional Evolution and Contemporary Status," *The Journal of Politics*, November 1967.

cutive branch of the Government" and "to bring about better operational coordination and more unified policy development."[34] On May 10, 1973, Press Secretary Ronald L. Ziegler announced that the president "intended to have more direct lines of communication with members of the Cabinet." Consequently, "the Counsellor role, as originally announced and conceived would be moved aside at this time."[35]

The problems of the modern presidency clearly cannot be resolved by converting the White House into a corporate headquarters with several appointed subexecutives authorized to speak for the corporation. Within the executive branch the president alone has the constitutional duty to exercise leadership in establishing national goals and priorities. The setting of these goals and priorities in terms that can be understood and communicated in actionable form to the operating agencies is the first prerequisite for coordination.

Under existing law the president can delegate coordinating responsibilities to officers appointed by and with the advice and consent of the Senate and agency heads (White House staff are excluded), but he cannot delegate those powers necessary to carry out the responsibility.[36] The president's political powers as our one nationally elected official other than the vice president, and as the leader of his political party, and his constitutional powers to approve legislation and to hire and fire the heads of executive agencies are nondelegable. An assistant president or "super Cabinet" officer without political influence or statutory powers would have nothing going for him but the majesty of his title, unless he were accepted as the president's alter ego. It is doubtful that our constitutional system can accommodate both an elected president and appointed presidential alter egos without impairing the unity of executive power.

If statutory functions were transferred from the departments to a counselor or super Cabinet officer, or if the performance of functions were made subject to his control, he would cease to

34. White House press release, January 5, 1973.
35. *Weekly Compilation of Presidential Documents*, May 11, 1973, pp. 662–63.
36. McCormack Act, 3 U.S.C. 302.

be a coordinator and become a superdepartment head. Arguments can be made for superdepartments, but no one contends that superdepartments will improve the coordination of programs that cut across superdepartmental jurisdictions.

The Jackson Subcommittee was of the view that super Cabinet officers would not ease the president's problems but "would make his burdens heavier." The committee concluded as follows:

> Reforms, to be effective, must be made in terms of the real requirements and possibilities of the American governmental system.
>
> That system provides no alternative to relying upon the President as the judge and arbiter of the forward course of policy for his administration. It provides no good alternative to reliance upon the great departments for the conduct of executive operations and for the initiation of most policy proposals relating to those operations.[37]

Our governmental system has nothing comparable to the ministers without portfolio who perform coordinating functions in many countries with a parliamentary form of government. In Great Britain, for example, ministers without portfolio have been used to coordinate research and development programs and the formulation of coordinated government information policies. Under Chancellors Adenauer and Erhard, a minister without portfolio was responsible for coordinating various matters among members of the German Cabinet who belonged to the chancellor's party and for acting as a liaison with the Cabinet members and leadership of the opposition party.

An American equivalent of a minister without portfolio would increase the options now available to the president. Without such an office, presidents occasionally have utilized Cabinet officers to perform special tasks unrelated to their official duties. A minister without portfolio would be more acceptable to the Congress than a White House coordinator, if he were appointed by the president, by and with the advice and consent of the Senate.

37. Senate Committee on Government Operations, Subcommittee on National Policy Machinery, Vol. 3, pp. 21–22.

He would not be barred by tradition from testifying before congressional committees. Furthermore, as a matter of law, the president could delegate functions to such an officer—something he cannot do to White House staff. As in the case of White House staff, however, a minister's potential effectiveness would be limited by the absence of a constituency and statutory control over federal funds and programs. Nonetheless, a minister without portfolio under some circumstances might afford a desirable alternative to existing coordinating arrangements or the further multiplication of White House staff.

Congress' ambivalence toward coordination is reflected in its discontent with the Bureau of the Budget, an organization that Senator Ribicoff described "as the most mysterious part of the entire Federal Government."[38] Many congressmen saw no contradiction in demanding at one and the same time that executive branch coordination be strengthened but the Budget Bureau's powers to coordinate be curtailed. We suspect that some proposals for new coordinating formulas stemmed more from a desire to cut the Budget Bureau down to size, and thereby undermine the president's authority, than to improve coordination.

The Bureau of the Budget admittedly had its institutional biases. Its style was negative and critical, rather than positive and creative. But this reflected the fact that its assigned role was essentially negative. The development of new programs and advocacy of increased spending were viewed as inconsistent with the bureau's basic mission. This "negativism" inevitably caused conflicts with activists on the White House staff mainly concerned with promoting the president's political interests.[39]

38. Senate Committee on Government Operations, Subcommittee on Executive Reorganization, "Modernizing the Federal Government," January–May 1968, p. 42.

39. Allen Schick, "The Budget Bureau That Was: Thoughts on the Rise, Decline and Future of a Presidential Agency," *Law and Contemporary Problems,* Vol. 25, Summer 1970; Hugh Heclo, "OMB and the Presidency: The Problems of 'Neutral' Competence," *The Public Interest,* Vol. 38, Winter 1975; Larry Berman, "OMB and the Hazards of Presidential Staff Work," *Public Administration Review,* Vol. 38, No. 6, November–December 1978.

Whatever the Bureau of the Budget's limitations may have been, it has yet to be demonstrated that its work can be done better by the Office of Management and Budget, Office of Planning and Evaluation, Office of Policy Development, and presidential assistants with specific program responsibilities. The latter tend to be special pleaders. The important distinction between agencies in the Executive Office of the President, such as the Bureau of the Budget, serving the presidency as an institution and those serving the president in a personal, political capacity has been lost. OMB, OPE, and OPD are regarded not as professional agencies but as extensions of the White House apparatus. None is capable of duplicating the Bureau of the Budget's institutional memory, professionalism, knowledge of the government as a whole, general perspective, critical outlook, and dedication to the interests of the presidency as an institution.

By holding out the promise of a perfect coordinating formula, we have provided a plausible excuse for not facing up to the hard political choices that now confront us. Layers of coordinating machinery can conceal but not cure the defects and contradictions in our governmental system.

If we want coordination, we must first be able to identify and agree on our national goals and priorities and to design programs to accomplish them. Our present mechanisms for national planning and goal-setting work very imperfectly and are in a highly rudimentary stage of development. Solution of the urgent problems confronting America in the 1980s demands something more than skills in political tactics and public relations. We no longer can afford indiscriminately to fritter away our human and material resources on poorly conceived and often contradictory programs whose major purpose is to pacify competing and conflicting group interests.

II

THE POLITICS OF INSTITUTIONAL TYPE

II

Administrative Agencies

The interplay of competing and often contradictory political, economic, social, and regional forces within our constitutional system and pluralistic society has produced a smorgasbord of institutional types. There is something to suit almost every taste, no matter how exotic. Choices from among this rich assortment are seldom determined by strict application of established organizational "principles." Choices are influenced by a complex of tangible and intangible factors reflecting divergent views about the proper sphere of government activity, politics, institutional folklore, program importance and status, visibility, political and administrative autonomy, and, most important, who should exercise control. The theoretical arguments frequently have little relevance to the real issues. The president, the Congress, the bureaucracy, and the constituencies each judge institutional types from a somewhat different perspective and favor those arrangements they believe will best serve their interests.

The Constitution itself provides few guides for institutional development. Numerous proposals in the Constitutional Convention of 1787 to spell out the details of executive branch structure were rejected. The intent of the Constitution makers can be inferred only from the provisions vesting executive power in the president, including the power to appoint, by and with the advice and consent of the Senate, all officers of the United States, whose appointments are not otherwise provided for in the Constitution, and authorizing the president to "require the opinion in writing, of the principal officer in each of the executive departments, upon any subject relating to the duties of their respective offices." Under the Constitution the Congress may by law vest the appointment of inferior officers, as they think proper, in the courts of law, or in the heads of departments.

The references to the "principal officer in each of the executive departments" and the "heads of departments" are significant. There appears to have been a clear intention that the departments of administration be headed by a single officer. George Washington was expressing a view widely held at the time when he stated that "Wherever, and whenever one person is found adequate to the discharge of a duty by close application thereto it is worse executed by two persons, and scarcely done at all if three or more are employed therein. . . ."[1] Federalists generally joined with Washington and Hamilton in considering multiheaded administrative agencies to be weak and irresponsible.

In the successive enactments of the Congress establishing executive agencies, there was no departure from the principle of single-headed administration. Some argued that the Treasury Department ought to be administered by a board of commissioners because "the duties of the office of financier were too arduous and too important to be entrusted to one man," but the proposal was rejected.[2]

Although the Constitution is almost wholly silent on the subject of executive branch organization, there seems to be little doubt that the framers intended that all executive functions be grouped under a limited number of single-headed executive departments. James Monroe, as secretary of state, reflected the prevailing concept of executive branch organization when he said:

1. Quoted in Leonard White, *The Federalists,* The Macmillan Co., 1948, p. 91.
2. Lloyd M. Short, *The Development of National Administrative Organization in the United States,* The Johns Hopkins Press, 1923, p. 92.

> I have always thought that every institution, of whatever nature soever it might be, ought to be comprised within some one of the Departments of Government, the chief of which only should be responsible to the Chief Executive Magistrate of the Nation. The establishment of inferior independent departments, the heads of which are not, and ought not to be members of the administration, appears to me to be liable to many serious objections. . . . I will mention only, first that the concerns of such inferior departments cannot be investigated and discussed with the same advantage in the meetings and deliberations of the administration, as they might be if the person charged with them was present. The second is that, to remedy this inconvenience, the President would, necessarily, become the head of that department himself. . . .[3]

Until 1913, it was most unusual for agencies to be created outside of the principal departments. A considerable number of commissions were established from time to time to perform special tasks, but these were always a temporary nature. The one notable exception is the incorporation of the Smithsonian Institution provided in the 1846 act, but the Smithsonian was funded initially by the Smithson bequest and, consequently, was looked on as a quasi-public institution rather than as a government agency. The first major departures from the accepted pattern of organization came with the establishment of the Civil Service Commission in 1883 and the Interstate Commerce Commission in 1887. In the case of the ICC the Congress did not break completely with tradition. The secretary of the interior was given authority to approve the number and compensation of all commission personnel, except the secretary to the commission. A link between the ICC and the executive department was maintained by requiring that the Commission's annual reports be submitted to the secretary. Independent status was not accorded to the ICC until 1889, when the Congress granted the secretary of the interior's request to be relieved of his supervisory responsibilities. Although the concept of an integrated executive branch struc-

3. *Ibid.*, footnote, pp. 417–18.

ture is accepted in principle, it has encountered strong opposition from those seeking independence and autonomy for programs benefitting their interests. Ronald C. Moe has observed that "the opposition to an integrated executive branch tends to be pluralistic in approach, narrow in its interests, and generally seeks an exception to a general rule instead of promoting its own rule."[4]

Hubert Humphrey described our constitutional system as "a Government of pressures, outside pressures, working on inside people."[5] Outside pressures began to mold and shape executive branch structure as early as the 1860s. The United States Agricultural Society sought the establishment of a Department of Agriculture to place "agriculture upon a plane of equality with the other executive departments."[6] The National Association of School Superintendents lobbied for a Department of Education, and the Knights of Labor for a Department of Labor. In response to these constituency pressures, the Congress created three departments of less than Cabinet rank headed by commissioners: Agriculture (1862), Education (1867), and Labor (1888). The Department of Agriculture was given Cabinet rank in 1889 and the Department of Labor was made a constituent of the Department of Commerce and Labor in 1903. The Department of Commerce and Labor was divided into two separate executive departments in 1913.

Restraints on the organization of agencies independent of the executive departments began to crumble with the establishment of the Federal Reserve Board and Board of Mediation and Conciliation in 1913 and practically disappeared during World War I. World War I also witnessed the first significant use of the cor-

4. Ronald C. Moe, "The Federal Executive Establishment Evaluation and Trends," prepared for the Senate Committee on Governmental Affairs by the Congressional Research Service, Committee Print, 96th Congress, 2nd Session, May 1980, p. 11. An excellent study of U.S. administrative development and the typology of federal organizations.

5. Senate Committee on Government Operations, hearings on S.1571 to establish a Department of Consumers, June 23 and 24, 1960, p. 34.

6. Short, *The Development of National Administrative Organization*, p. 383.

porate form of organization. Except for the War Finance Corporation, which was created by the Congress, World War I corporations such as the Shipping Board, Food Administration, and War Trade Board were chartered under the general incorporation laws of either the states or the District of Columbia. Federal control was maintained over the corporations mainly through the power to appoint directors and such supervision as might be exercised by the Cabinet officer who organized the corporation. The corporate form of organization did not achieve legitimacy until the 1940s, although it was widely employed during the Depression of the 1930s, when such alphabet agencies as the RFC, HOLC, TVA, CCC, FDIC, USHA, and RACC achieved considerable notoriety.[7] Many believed that only war or depression could justify resort to the corporate device.

By 1937 the President's Committee on Administrative Management was able to identify over a hundred separately organized establishments and agencies presumably reporting to the president. President Franklin Roosevelt endorsed the committee's recommendation that the country return to first principles and organize the government's activities within twelve major executive departments. Roosevelt contended that this reorganization was necessary to "bring many little bureaucracies under broad coordinated democratic authority."[8]

We have made some progress since 1937 in reducing the number of independent agencies, but the 1984–85 Government Manual shows that there are still at least fifty-eight agencies organized outside the twelve executive departments. If there were added to the fifty-eight mixed-ownership government corporations, government-sponsored enterprises, private corporations organized and financed by the government to furnish contractual services

7. Reconstruction Finance Corporation, Home Owners Loan Corporation, Tennessee Valley Authority, Commodity Credit Corporation, Federal Deposit Insurance Corporation, U.S. Housing Authority, Regional Agricultural Credit Corporation.

8. Franklin D. Roosevelt, Message to the Congress on Administrative Reorganization, January 12, 1937.

to federal agencies, and intergovernmental bodies, the decrease in the number of independent agencies since 1937 would be even smaller.

The number and variety of institutional arrangements presently utilized by the federal government almost defy classification. Each major grouping contains important subcategories, and significant differences may be identified within any of the subcategories. The following classification makes no claim to scientific exactness; it is intended merely to identify significant organizational types. The word *independent* means only independence from an executive department, and does not imply independence from the president or the executive branch. In popular usage the word has come to have the latter meaning, particularly when applied to the independent regulatory commissions. The listings under each of the headings are not necessarily complete.

EXECUTIVE DEPARTMENTS

State, Treasury, Defense, Justice, Interior, Agriculture, Commerce, Labor, Health and Human Services, Housing and Urban Development, Transportation, Energy, Education.

EXECUTIVE OFFICE OF THE PRESIDENT

White House Office, Council of Economic Advisers, Council on Environmental Quality, Office of Policy Development, National Security Council, Office of Science and Technology Policy, Office of Administration, Office of Management and Budget, Special Representative for Trade Negotiations.

INDEPENDENT AGENCIES

Single-headed: ACTION, Central Intelligence Agency, Environmental Protection Agency, Federal Emergency Management Agency, General Services Administration, National Aeronautics and Space Administration, National

Credit Union Administration, Office of Personnel Management, Peace Corps, Selective Service System, Small Business Administration, U.S. Arms Control and Disarmament Agency, U.S. Information Agency, Veterans Administration.

Multiheaded: American Battle Monuments Commission, Appalachian Regional Commission, Board for International Broadcasting, Commission on Civil Rights, Commission on Fine Arts, Farm Credit Administration, Federal Labor Relations Authority, Federal Maritime Commission, Federal Mediation and Conciliation Service, Merit Systems Protection Board, National Capital Planning Commission, National Mediation Board, National Transportation Safety Board, Panama Canal Commission, Postal Rate Commission, U.S. International Trade Commission, U.S. Postal Service.

FOUNDATIONS

National Science Foundation, National Foundation on Arts and Humanities.

INSTITUTIONS AND INSTITUTES

Smithsonian Institution.

HEW: National Institutes of Health, National Cancer Institute, National Heart Institute, National Institute of Allergy and Infectious Diseases, National Institute of Arthritis and Metabolic Diseases, National Institute of Dental Research, National Institute of Neurological Diseases, National Institute of General Medical Sciences, National Institute of Child Health and Human Development, National Eye Institute, National Institute on Aging.

Commerce: Institutes for Environmental Research, Institute for Basic Standards, Institute for Materials Research, Institute for Applied Technology.

State: Foreign Service Institute.

Justice: National Institute for Law Enforcement and Criminal Justice.

REGULATORY COMMISSIONS

Federal Communications Commission, Federal Home Loan Bank Board, Federal Maritime Commission, Federal Reserve Board, Federal Trade Commission, Interstate Commerce Commission, National Labor Relations Board, Securities and Exchange Commission, Consumer Product Safety Commission, Commodity Futures Trading Commission, Nuclear Regulatory Commission, Federal Energy Regulatory Commission, Federal Election Commission, Equal Opportunity Commission, Occupational Health and Safety Review Commission.

CONFERENCES

Administrative Conference of the United States.

GOVERNMENT CORPORATIONS

Wholly Owned Corporations Under Executive Department Single-headed: St. Lawrence Seaway Development Corporation, Government National Mortgage Association.

Multiheaded: Commodity Credit Corporation, Federal Crop Insurance Corporation, Federal Financing Bank, Federal Prison Industries, Inc., Federal Savings and Loan Insurance Corporation, Pension Benefit Guaranty Corporation, Neighborhood Reinvestment Corporation, Pennsylvania Avenue Development Corporation, Solar Energy and Energy Conservation Bank.

Wholly Owned Independent Corporations Multiheaded: Federal Deposit Insurance Corporation,[9] Export-Import Bank of Washington, Tennessee Valley Authority, Inter-American Foundation, Overseas Private Investment Corporation.

9. Classified as mixed-ownership in Government Corporation Control Act, but in fact wholly owned since the retirement of capital stock in 1948.

Mixed-Ownership Government Corporations

Multiheaded: Central Bank for Cooperatives, Regional Banks for Cooperatives (12), Federal Intermediate Credit Banks (12), Rural Telephone Bank, U.S. Railway Association.

INTERGOVERNMENTAL ORGANIZATIONS

National: Advisory Commission on Intergovernmental Relations.

Regional: Appalachian Regional Commission, Delaware River Basin Commission.

TWILIGHT ZONE

Federal Reserve Banks, Federal Land Banks, Federal Home Loan Banks, Federal National Mortgage Association, National Home Ownership Foundation, National Housing Partnership, Corporation for Public Broadcasting, National Parks Foundation, National Railroad Passenger Corporation, Securities Investor Protection Corporation, Student Loan Marketing Association, U.S. Railway Association, Legal Services Corporation, National Consumer Cooperative Bank.

PRIVATE INSTITUTIONS ORGANIZED AND FINANCED BY THE FEDERAL GOVERNMENT TO PROVIDE CONTRACTUAL SERVICES

Independent Nonprofit Corporations: Aerospace Corporation, Institute for Defense Analyses, Logistics Management Institute, Institute for Urban Studies, Rand Corporation, Research Analysis Corporation, Youthwork, Public/Private Ventures, etc.

University-Affiliated Research Centers: Applied Physics Laboratory, Human Relations Research Organization, Brookhaven Laboratory, MITRE, Lincoln Laboratory, Los Alamos National Laboratory, etc.

Research Center Operated by Private Industry: Oak Ridge National Laboratory.

No general federal laws define the form of organization, powers, and immunities of the various institutional types. Each possesses only those power enumerated in its enabling act or, in the case of organizations created by executive action, set forth by executive order in a contract. Whatever special attributes may have been acquired by the various organizational classes are entirely a product of precedent, as reflected in successive enactments by the Congress, judicial interpretations, and public, agency, and congressional attitudes. For some of the organizations, public attitudes tend to be based more on folklore than on fact.

Few of these institutional types emerged full-blown in their present form. There is very little evidence of conscious thought and planning in the development of new institutions. The approach generally has been highly pragmatic and eclectic. The process has been more derivative than creative. The Interstate Commerce Commission was established in the image of the regulatory organizations then existing in a number of states. The search for an agency with sufficient operating and financial flexibility to conduct the business enterprises undertaken in World War I was ended by borrowing the corporate form of organization from private enterprise. As we have indicated previously, most of the World War I corporations were chartered under the general incorporation laws of states or the District of Columbia. These laws often prescribed forms of organization and financing not particularly well adapted to a public body, and subterfuges were sometimes required to provide pro forma compliance. Until the Panama Railroad Company was reincorporated under federal charter in 1948, it was necessary to issue each director one share of stock to comply with the provisions of the corporation's New York charter. The foundation represents the culmination of efforts by scientists to duplicate within the federal government an organization structure devised for institutions of higher learning. The "captive" corporation was born of improvisations by the Office of Scientific Research and Development in World War II to meet its unique requirements. The Defense Department and

the National Institutes of Health inherited certain contractual arrangements when the OSRD was liquidated after the war. The Judicial Conference provided the model for the Administrative Conference of the United States. Inherited factors have been of considerable significance in influencing relationships within the executive branch, internal organization, mode of operations, method of financing, and public and congressional responses.

Some institutional types are more acceptable than others because they have been borrowed from and are identified in the public mind with nongovernment institutions. This has proved to be of critical importance when the federal government has entered into new and controversial areas of activity. Harold Laski has noted that "most Americans have a sense of deep discomfort when they are asked to support the positive state. . . . They tend to feel that what is done by a government institution is bound to be less well done than if it were undertaken by individuals, whether alone or in the form of private corporations."[10] If a service cannot be performed by private enterprise, then obviously the next best thing is an organization that appears to be insulated against "politics" and that looks as nearly as possible like a private institution. This feeling is evident in the argument raised by the chairman of the Federal Deposit Insurance Corporation against legislation proposed in 1960 to subject the corporation to budget control. Chairman Wolcott contended that "an agency having responsibility for protection of the Nation's money supply should be independent while remaining in the framework of Government. It must be part of the Government in order to escape private pressures; yet, within the Government it must be free of political pressures."[11] The Neighborhood Reinvestment Corporation is described in its enabling act as a "nonbureaucratic approach," an approach that Congressman Stewart B. McKinney argued, freed the corporation from things that make government programs "almost incomprehensible to the

10. Harold J. Laski, *The American Democracy,* The Viking Press, 1948, p. 167.

11. Committee on Government Operations, hearings on H.R. 12092 to make the FDIC subject to budget review, June 21, 1960, p. 34.

average, ordinary citizen."[12] Public distrust of government is somewhat alleviated when programs are administered by corporations or foundations and these agencies are organized in such a way that they are of, but not in, the government. The same distrust underlies arguments for the use of nonprofit intermediaries and reprivatization.

Analysis of statutory provisions reveals that the Congress has followed a reasonably consistent pattern with respect to the organization structure, powers, and immunities of each of the major institutional types. Critical differences among the types are to be found in the provisions of law relating to composition of the directing authority (single-headed or multiheaded), qualifications for appointment, procedures for the appointment and removal of principal officers, method of financing, budget and audit controls, personnel regulations, and advisory councils and committees. These provisions determine the degree of organizational and operating autonomy and in large measure control an agency's relationship to the president, the Congress, and its clientele.

The one official guide to the relative status and protocol ranking of executive agencies is to be found in the Executive Schedule Pay Rates. Agencies are by no means equal in terms of their prestige within the executive establishment or standing in the Congress and the community. The significance of their heads being included in Level II rather than in Level III goes beyond the mere $5000 difference in salary. The infighting can be bitter when amendments to the Executive Schedule are being considered, and some congressional favorites, such as the director of the Federal Bureau of Investigation, have been rewarded with higher rankings than their position would seem to warrant.

The following pecking order is established by the Executive Schedule:

Level I: Executive departments.
Level II: Major agencies of the executive office of the President,

12. *Congressional Record,* July 21, 1978, p. H7136.

such as the Office of Management and Budget; major independent agencies, such as the National Aeronautics and Space Administration, Central Intelligence Agency, Veterans Administration, International Communications Agency; Federal Reserve; Military departments, Agency for International Development.

Level III: Independent agencies, such as the General Services Administration, Small Business Administration; major regulatory agencies, such as the Interstate Commerce Commission and Federal Communication Commission; government corporations, such as the Federal Deposit Insurance Corporation, Export-Import Bank, Tennessee Valley Authority; foundations; major administrations or bureaus within executive departments, such as the Federal Bureau of Investigation, Comptroller of the Currency, and Highway Administration.

Level IV: Independent agencies, such as the Selective Service System, Equal Employment Opportunity Commission, National Transportation Safety Board, St. Lawrence Seaway Development Corporation; bureau heads within executive departments.

Level V: Minor agencies, such as Foreign Claims Settlement Commission; heads and deputy heads of principal constituent units within executive departments and agencies.

Next to the top pay levels, heavy sedans are the most eagerly sought-after status symbols. Under OMB regulations, heavy sedans are reserved for heads of executive departments, the ambassador to the United Nations, and chiefs of Class I diplomatic missions. All others must ride in medium or light sedans.

Executive Departments. The executive departments' position at the apex of the organizational hierarchy remains unchallenged, although the principal assistants to the president now rank above Cabinet officers in public prestige and influence. Major independent agencies such as the Veterans Administration and the General Services Administration may employ more people and spend

more money than some of the executive departments, but both the White House and the Congress make subtle distinctions between the heads of these agencies and Cabinet secretaries. Although there is no statutory basis for the distinctions, other than the Executive Schedule Pay Rates, those who have served in both capacities can testify that the distinctions are real and important.

No exact criteria have ever been prescribed for establishing executive departments. The Congress generally has applied certain pragmatic tests relating to permanence, size, scope, complexity, and, above all, national significance of the programs to be administered by the department. According to the Bureau of the Budget, "departmental status is reserved for those agencies which (1) administer a wide range of programs directed toward a common purpose of national importance; and (2) are concerned with policies and programs requiring frequent and positive Presidential direction and representation at the highest levels of the Government."[13]

Executive departments do symbolize basic national commitments and values, and for this reason the Congress has responded slowly to demands for new departments. Creation of a new department is always regarded as an historic occasion. The reorganization establishing the Department of Defense in 1949 marked the first change in the top executive branch structure since 1913, although this represented more of a merger of the previously existing War and Navy departments than the birth of a new department. The first genuinely new executive department was Health, Education, and Welfare, established in 1953. This was followed by the Department of Housing and Urban Development in 1965, the Department of Transportation in 1966, the Department of Energy in 1977, and the Department of Education in 1979.

Each of the executive departments created since the Civil War, except Energy, Commerce, and Transportation, was required to

13. Statement of David E. Bell, director of the Bureau of the Budget, on S. 1633 to establish a Department of Urban Affairs and Housing, June 21, 1961.

serve an apprenticeship as a non-Cabinet department or agency before being elevated to executive department status. Proposals to convert the Federal Security Agency, the predecessor of HEW, and the Housing and Home Finance Agency, the predecessor of HUD, to executive departments were flatly turned down by the Congress on more than one occasion before they were adopted. The first bill to establish a Department of Transportation was introduced in the Congress in 1890.[14] Seventy-six years were to go by before the department became a reality.

Except for such aberrations as the Tenure of Office Act, the Congress has observed faithfully the organizational precepts laid down by the framers of the Constitution in creating executive departments. Congress has not felt bound by these precepts in dealing with agencies below the executive department level.

Each executive department has a single head. No restrictions are placed on the president's authority to appoint or remove department heads. The statutes differ in specifying presidential authority to direct and supervise a Cabinet officer. The secretary of defense is "subject to direction by the President," and the secretary of state "shall conduct the business of the Department in such manner as the President shall direct." Other acts are silent on the subject of presidential direction. Regardless of the statutory language, Congress recognizes that the heads of executive departments are the "President's men."

Except for a few prerogatives, such as the right to request a formal opinion of the attorney general, there is little that a Cabinet officer can do as a matter of law that cannot also be done by an independent agency head. Budget Bureau witnesses were hard pressed to explain the legal differences between a Housing and Home Finance Agency and a Department of Housing and Urban Development. The differences have their roots in custom and tradition and cannot be discovered in law books.

The Cabinet itself is a creature of custom and tradition without a constitutional or statutory basis. The Cabinet has always

14. S. 4106 introduced by Congressman John J. Ingalls (Kansas) in the 51st Congress, 1st Session.

functioned at the pleasure of the president and in the manner of his choosing. Whatever the role assigned to the Cabinet as a collective entity—and this has varied greatly from one president to another—membership in the Cabinet is of tremendous importance as a symbol of status and rank. Appointment as head of an executive department has always been assumed to confer Cabinet membership without further presidential designation. Of the original Cabinet, all except the attorney general were department heads. The attorney general was included as the government's legal adviser. The Department of Justice became an executive department in 1870.

Others may be invited by the president to attend Cabinet meetings or accorded Cabinet rank. These have included the vice president, the speaker of the House of Representatives, the ambassador to the United Nations, the chairman of the Atomic Energy Commission, the director of OMB, as well as from time to time various special assistants to the president. There are shades of difference between those who are invited to attend Cabinet meetings and those who are present because of the office they hold. Under Eisenhower, only the vice president and the heads of executive departments had high-backed chairs, with their names on engraved plaques, at the Cabinet table.

Invitees are reluctant to volunteer opinions unless the president specifically calls on them. In 1956 the Housing and Home Finance administrator was invited to discuss a subject of vital concern to his agency. But he was seated in the back row against the wall, and President Eisenhower appeared to be wholly unaware of his presence.

Changes in attitude resulting from elevation to departmental status translate into easier access to the White House staff and the chairmen of congressional committees, an improved bargaining position in dealing with other federal agencies and organized constituencies, and better coverage by the communications media. Rufus Miles, assistant secretary for administration of the Department of Health, Education, and Welfare, observed from his experience in both HEW and the Federal Security Agency that there was a "very rapid change in public attitude which came about from the elevation of the status of the then Federal Security Agency to a departmental status. The amount of increased attention that was given to the total organization and its problems was very marked."[15]

The gradations that exist within the executive hierarchy also may be found among the executive departments. Executive departments are by no means equal in power, prestige, or closeness to the president. The presidential inner circle is generally composed of Cabinet members without strong constituency ties, the secretaries of state, defense, and treasury, and the attorney general, to whom the president looks for expert advice, rather than for political support. President Nixon formalized the "inner Cabinet" by his designation of the secretaries of state and treasury and the director of OMB as assistants to the president, and the secretaries of agriculture, HEW, and HUD as presidential counselors. As we have seen, departments differ significantly in personality and outlook, administrative habits, and relationships to the president, the Congress, and the outside community.

Executive Office of the President. Relatively youthful upstarts in the Executive Office of the President have stolen some of the glamour from the Cabinet secretaries. Such Level II luminaries as the director of OMB wield more power and receive a greater press coverage than the heads of most executive departments. In arguing for Senate confirmation of the director of OMB, the House Committee on Government Operations emphasized "the reality" that the director "with his vast power and importance, holds an office of superior rank."[16] As these executive office institutions have approached middle age, their "passion for anonymity" has waned noticeably. But, contrary to popular belief, there is no special magic associated with location in the Executive Office of the President. Heads of executive departments are vested with a certain status by reason of the office they hold; this is not

15. Senate Committee on Government Operations, hearings on "Modernizing the Federal Government," January–May 1968, p. 115.

16. House Report No. 93–109.

true of those in the Executive Office. The directors of some Executive Office units would like to give the impression that they are the powers behind the throne, but they are often so far behind the throne as to be almost invisible.

Classic concepts of organization have not been observed as rigorously by the Congress in establishing the constituent elements of the Executive Office of the President as they have been in the case of executive departments. When the Executive Office of the President was created in 1939, it contained one multi-headed unit, the National Resources Planning Board. Today the Executive Office includes one agency headed by an interagency committee: the National Security Council. The Council of Economic Advisers and the Council on Environmental Quality are also collegiate bodies, but Reorganization Plan No. 9 of 1953 transferred to the CEA chairman the function of reporting to the president with respect to the Council's work.

The Budget and Accounting Act of 1921 recognized that the relationship between a president and his budget director must necessarily be one of intimacy and trust. Consequently, the president was given the power to appoint the director and assistant director without Senate confirmation. Congressman Good pointed out during the floor debate on the act that "these offices would be so peculiarly the President's staff, the President's force, the President, without being questioned with his regard to his appointment, should appoint the men whom he could trust to do his will in the preparation of the budget. . . ."[17] This special status was revoked in 1974, a casualty of Watergate and resentment toward President Nixon's use of impoundment to curtail or discontinue programs authorized by the Congress. Except for White House staff, the heads of the principal Executive Office agencies are now all subject to Senate confirmation. The Congress has refrained from establishing terms of office, or, except for members of the Council of Economic Advisers and the Council on Environmental Quality, specifying qualifications for appointment.

17. Bureau of the Budget, Staff Orientation Manual, April 1958, p. 7.

Congress has been unwilling to give the president a free hand with respect to the organization of the Executive Office of the President. Most department heads now have authority to organize and reorganize their agencies without formal congressional approval, but the president lacks comparable power. President Eisenhower recommended in his 1961 Budget Message that the President be authorized to reorganize the Executive Office so as to "insure that future Presidents will possess the latitude to design the working structure of the Presidential Office as they deem necessary for the effective conduct of their duties under the Constitution and the laws." A bill was introduced for this purpose, but no further action was taken, partly because of a conspicuous absence of enthusiasm on the part of some of the more important people in the Bureau of the Budget who wanted to preserve the bureau's unique position as *primus inter pares*.

The present structure of the Executive Office of the President does not reflect the Committee on Administrative Management's intention that no institutional resources be provided within the office other than those the president found essential to advise and assist him in carrying out functions that he could not delegate. Congressional pressure to provide visibility and enhanced status for favored programs diverted the Executive Office of the President from its exclusive concern with *presidential* business by establishing within it the Office of Economic Opportunity, the National Council on Marine Resources and Engineering Development, and the Council on Environmental Quality. The president was similarly motivated in recommending the establishment of the Special Action Office for Drug Abuse. As a consequence, recent presidents have tended to look to the White House office, not to the institutional agencies within the Executive Office of the President, for necessary staff support.[18]

President Nixon called for "a sharp reduction in the overall size of the Executive Office of the President and a reorientation

18. The Office of Economic Opportunity, National Council on Marine Resources and Engineering Development, and the Special Action Office for Drug Abuse have been abolished.

of that office back to its original mission as a staff for top-level policy formation and monitoring of policy execution in broad functional areas. The Executive Office of the President should no longer be encumbered with the task of managing or administering programs which can be run more effectively by the departments and agencies."[19] Reorganization Plan No. 1 of 1973 streamlined the Executive Office by abolishing the Office of Emergency Preparedness, the Office of Science and Technology, and the National Aeronautics and Space Council.

While concern was expressed that abolition of OST signified "a downgrading of our science apparatus," the House Committee on Government Operations interposed no objection to the reorganization. The committee concluded that, "As a practical proposition, the President cannot be compelled to utilize a policy making and advisory apparatus in the Executive Office against his own preferences. Furthermore, the President should have considerable latitude in determining the composition of the Executive Office."[20] There were those who suspected that abolition of the Office of Science and Technology was motivated more by a desire to punish the scientific community for its opposition to the Vietnam war than by zeal for streamlining the Executive Office.[21] Scientists were unhappy with their eviction from the Executive Office and succeeded in persuading President Ford and the Congress to authorize reestablishment of the office in 1976 as the Office of Science and Technology Policy.

The Executive Office of the President was again reorganized by President Carter "based on the premise that the EOP exists to serve the President and should be structured to meet his needs."[22] Reorganization Plan No. 1 of 1977 either discontinued or transferred the functions of the Offices of Drug Abuse Policy and Telecommunications Policy and the International Economic Pol-

---

19. House Document No. 93–43.

20. House Report No. 93–106, p. 18.

21. *The New York Times,* October 6, 1973.

22. House Document No. 95–185, July 15, 1977.

icy, Federal Property, Energy Resources, Economic Opportunity, and Domestic Councils. The Domestic Council was redesignated the Domestic Policy staff. The plan established an Office of Administration to provide centralized administrative services for components of the EOP.

Under Reagan the Domestic Policy staff was succeeded by an Office of Policy Development. The Council on Wage and Price Stability and the Special Action Office for Drug Abuse Prevention were terminated.

The implications of Executive Office organization for the effective functioning of our constitutional system and the distribution of power among the three coequal branches of government are as yet insufficiently recognized. Given the present involvement of White House staff in functions formerly performed by career personnel within the Executive Office, the exodus of senior staff upon the inauguration of a new president could threaten the continuity of government. The president ought to have the capability to adapt the Executive Office to his perceived needs, but he should not be permitted, in the process, to ignore the needs of future presidents, the Congress, and the people.

Independent Agencies. Columnist David Lawrence was reflecting a common misconception when he wrote, "Basically the RFC is supposed to be an 'independent agency' and not part of the executive department or the White House, but a creature of Congress, *as are all other independent Boards and Agencies*" (italics supplied).[23] The Constitution makes no provision for a fourth branch of government, independent of the president, or for limitations on the president's exercise of executive powers. Whether or not the president can exercise his powers effectively is another matter. Some of the independent agencies have been so structured as to blunt the president's powers and provide de facto independence.

Independent agencies come in all shapes, sizes, and forms. Both the Small Business Administration and the Federal Avia-

23. *Washington Star*, February 27, 1951.

tion Agency, prior to its incorporation in the Department of Transportation, were spun off from the Department of Commerce in an effort to escape an unsympathetic operating environment. None of the independent agencies at present is an embryo executive department comparable to the Housing and Home Finance Agency. As we have indicated, the General Services Administration and the Veterans Administration do exceed smaller executive departments in size, measured in personnel and budget. Some, such as the Veterans Administration and the General Services Administration, are expressly subject to presidential direction or regulations, whereas others, such as the Farm Credit Administration, are almost outside the government altogether.

As far as independent agencies are concerned, the Congress does not believe that the injunctions against multiheaded agencies and limitations on the president's powers of appointment and removal apply. Several have been given all the trappings of a regulatory commission, including multimember boards selected on a bipartisan basis with fixed, overlapping terms of office. Qualifications for appointment may be spelled out in detail, as for the Small Business Administrator and members of the Farm Credit Board.

The Central Intelligence Agency, the U.S. Information Agency, the National Aeronautics and Space Administration, the U.S. Postal Service, and the Veterans Administration Department of Medicine and Surgery are excepted, either in whole or in part, from Civil Service regulations. The ICA, CIA, TVA, Postal Service, and VA have their own personnel systems. Special personnel systems also exist within executive departments, notably the Foreign Service, Public Health Service, and ESSA Corps.

These restrictions and exemptions in and of themselves weaken, but do not eliminate, presidential power. For those who demand sovereignty, not merely autonomy, within the federal structure, the priceless ingredient is financial self-sufficiency. The Farm Credit Administration and U.S. Postal Service are the classic illustrations.

During the 1952 campaign, General Eisenhower was persuaded

by the farm organizations to include in an Omaha speech a pledge "to remove the Federal domination now imposed on the farm credit system. . . . A Federal Farm Credit Board, elected by farmer members, should be established to form credit policies, select executive officers, and to see that sound credit operations will not be endangered by partisan political influence."[24] Farmer ownership and control of the credit institutions somehow became translated into farm organization control of the federal agency responsible for regulating the credit institutions.

When advised that election of members of the Federal Farm Credit Board would be unconstitutional, the farm organizations agreed reluctantly to accept a compromise bill providing for a thirteen-member, part-time board consisting of one member designated by the secretary of agriculture and twelve members appointed by the president, by and with the consent of the Senate, after considering nominations submitted by the national farm loan associations, the production credit associations, and the cooperatives who are stockholders of or subscribers to the guaranty fund of the bank for cooperatives. The Board, in turn, appoints the governor of the Farm Credit Administration, subject to the president's approval. The governor had been a presidential appointee. To ensure that any ties with the president were severed, the law makes it the governor's duty to comply with all board orders and directions.

For all practical purposes, the farm organizations have accomplished their objectives. In practice, the nomination of directors has become the equivalent of election. President Eisenhower held up the appointment of directors for several months in 1957 when confronted with a direct challenge to his authority, but ultimately he went along with the nominations. The governor and the board openly lobbied against the president's proposal to subject the farm credit institutions to budget control. The president could not use his budget powers to bring the Farm Credit Administration into line because, except for appropriations to finance the Cooperative Research and Service

24. Speech at Omaha, Nebraska, September 18, 1952.

Division, all FCA funds are obtained from assessments against the supervised institutions. Without this self-financing provision, open defiance of the president would have been far more hazardous.

The U.S. Postal Service is the most independent of the independent agencies and is practically a law unto itself. The Postal Service is defined by law as "an independent establishment of the executive branch of the United States," but in all other respects it is endowed with the powers and characteristics of a wholly owned government corporation. The service is headed by an eleven-member part-time board of governors, appointed by the president with Senate confirmation. Governors serve for nine-year overlapping terms. The service's chief executive officer, the postmaster general, is appointed by and serves at the pleasure of the board.

The U.S. Postal Service is not subject to the Government Corporation Control Act or the controls normally applied to wholly owned government corporations. The Postal Service Act (Public Law 91–375) includes language comparable to that in Section 102 of the Government Corporation Control Act requiring annual submission of a business-type budget to the Office of Management and Budget but does not authorize OMB to amend or modify the budget. There is no requirement that the budget be transmitted to the Congress. As it is now written, the act creates the impression of control where in fact none exists. Indeed, elsewhere the Postal Service Act provides specifically that "no Federal law dealing with public or Federal contracts, property, works, employees, budgets or funds . . . shall apply to the exercise of the powers of the Postal Service."

The Postal Service is intended to be self-financing, except for reimbursement of any "public service costs" incurred in providing "a maximum degree of effective and regular postal service nationwide." The service is authorized to borrow money and to issue and sell such obligations as it determines necessary in amounts not to exceed $10 billion outstanding at any one time. Avoidance of the "annual battle between the Post Office Department and the Bureau of the Budget, which notoriously results in limitations upon funds available to be appropriated" was cited by the Senate Post Office and Civil Service Committee as "the basic purpose in authorizing the sale of bonds by the Postal Service and exempting it from budget control."[25]

When he proposed that the Post Office Department be reorganized as an autonomous and independent non-Cabinet Postal Service, President Nixon contended that an efficient postal service could not be obtained without insulating the Postal Service "from direct control by the President, the Bureau of the Budget and the Congress" and "partisan political pressure."[26] This argument reflects distrust of our governmental institutions and loss of faith in the democratic process.

Congress is beginning to have second thoughts about the degree of autonomy granted to the U.S. Postal Service. Congressman Morris K. Udall, an original proponent of postal reform, complained that the legislation passed by a vote of 370 to 70 or so, but "I cannot find a single member who voted for it or who will admit voting for it. . . . I am constantly referred to as one of the fathers. I have been thinking of denying paternity."[27] The House of Representatives passed a bill in 1978 to abolish the board of governors and transfer its functions to a presidentially appointed postmaster general. The bill died in the Senate.

Institutions, Foundations, and Institutes. It seems somehow fitting that the Smithsonian Institution should have an organization charter worthy of display with other museum pieces. The Smithsonian Institution remains *sui generis,* and does so for reasons that shall become evident. Purists would find it difficult to reconcile the organizational arrangements established for the Smithsonian with the constitutional doctrine of separation of powers. Appointing authority is vested in the speaker of the

25. Senate Report No. 91–912, p. 9.

26. House Document No. 91–313.

27. Hearings before a Subcommittee of the House Committee on Governmental Operations on Reorganization Plan No. 2 of 1978, June 13, 1978, p. 107.

House of Representatives and the president of the Senate, seemingly in direct violation of Article II, Section 2 of the Constitution.

The Smithsonian has an "establishment" composed of the president, the vice president, the chief justice, and the heads of executive departments, but with no known functions, other than as the institution's "incorporators." The business of the institution is conducted by a Board of Regents consisting of the vice president, the chief justice, three members of the Senate appointed by the president of the Senate, three members of the House of Representatives appointed by the speaker, and six other persons appointed by joint resolution of the Senate and the House. Presumably the president could veto the joint resolution, but this is the extent of his powers over appointments to the Board of Regents. The Institution's principal executive officer, the secretary, is selected by the board.

Congress has appropriated to the institution the annual interest on the $541,379.63 Smithson bequest, but this income constitutes an infinitesimal part of the institution's budget. Today, approximately 90 percent of the Smithsonian's funds come from either direct appropriations by the Congress or grants by federal agencies. Private financing has a symbolic value, and civil service restrictions applicable to most Smithsonian employees do not apply to the secretary and others who are paid from private funds.

In holding that the Smithsonian Institution was not subject to the Freedom of Information Act and the Privacy Act, the Department of Justice concluded that while not "free of doubt," the Smithsonian was not an agency of the United States of the type the Congress intended to be covered. The Department of Justice found that the Smithsonian was "so uniquely distinctive a fusion of public and private cooperation and of joint action by all three traditional branches of government that it seems fairly evident that the Congress could not have meant it to be treated as a traditional agency covered by the three statutes."[28]

28. Moe, "The Federal Executive Establishment Evaluation and Trends," p. 64.

Although problems of relationships within the executive branch have been minimal, the Smithsonian's ambiguous status has stood in the way of its being assigned responsibility for the National Archives and other federal programs related to the arts and humanities. The mixing of private and federal funds has led to practices that have been criticized by the General Accounting Office and the Congress.[29] The Smithsonian has utilized its private funds to launch programs without congressional approval.

Foundations and institutes have become the preferred form of organization for institutions making grants to local governments, universities, nonprofit organizations, and individuals for research in the natural and social sciences, or artistic endeavors. The unique characteristic of these organizations is an elaborate superstructure of advisory arrangements designed to give representatives of grantee groups maximum influence over the allocation of funds. In Chapter 1 we described the structure of the National Science Foundation. The National Foundation on the Arts and Humanities creates the appearance of a single organization, although, in fact, it consists of two independent entities—the National Endowment for the Arts and the National Endowment for the Humanities. Each endowment is headed by a chairman appointed by the president, subject to Senate confirmation, for a four-year term. The chairmen, however, cannot approve or disapprove grant applications without first obtaining the recommendations of a council. The National Council on the Arts is composed of the secretary of the Smithsonian Institution and twenty-four members appointed by the president for six-year terms. In making appointments, the president is requested to give consideration to the recommendations of leading national organizations in each branch of the arts. The National Council on the Humanities has twenty-six members, also appointed for six-year terms. Recommendations for appointments are to be submitted by the leading national organizations concerned with the humanities.

29. Ibid., p. 65.

A National Advisory Council is attached to each of the Institutes under the National Institutes of Health. The councils consist of twelve members, appointed for four-year terms by the surgeon general, with the approval of the secretary of health and Human Services. Members must be leaders in fundamental sciences, medical sciences, and public affairs, and six must be specialists in the field covered by the institute. No grants may be made without council approval.

The title "institute" has been used for agencies engaged in research and training, but the name has had no significance except to provide a better academic standing.

Regulatory and Claims Commissions, Administrative Conference. The independent regulatory commissions and claims commissions have evolved into what the President's Committee on Administrative Management termed "a headless 'fourth branch' of the Government." From what were intended originally to be somewhat differently structured executive agencies, these commissions have been transformed into "arms of the Congress" by constituency pressures, custom, and Supreme Court decisions.

When the Interstate Commerce Commission was established in 1887, the Congress did not believe it was violating sacred writ by giving the secretary of the interior powers over the commission's personnel. In 1902 there was strong sentiment in the Congress for transferring the ICC to the new Department of Commerce and Labor.[30] No conflict was seen in designating the secretary of the treasury as chairman of the Federal Reserve Board in 1913. The secretaries of agriculture, interior, and war constituted the Federal Power Commission when it was established in 1920. By deliberate congressional choice, regulatory functions under the Packers and Stockyards Act of 1921 were assigned to the secretary of agriculture rather than to the Federal Trade Commission. Concepts drawing sharp distinctions between regulatory and executive functions are of relatively recent origin and, to some extent, are an historical accident.

30. Short, *The Development of National Administrative Organization*, p. 422.

Marver Bernstein has defined *independence,* as the term is applied to the regulatory commissions, as relating to one or more of the following conditions: "location outside an executive department; some measure of independence from supervision by the president or a cabinet secretary; immunity from the president's discretionary power to remove members of independent commissions from office."[31] The last condition listed by Bernstein has been of key importance.

The ICC has been the model for the regulatory commissions. The number of commission members varies from three on the Home Loan Bank Board to eleven on the ICC. All except the National Labor Relations Board are bipartisan, and members serve for fixed, overlapping terms of office. At one time it was common for commissions to elect their own chairmen, but all commission chairmen are now designated by the president.

The ICC Act authorizes the president to remove any commissioner "for inefficiency, neglect of duty, or malfeasance in office." Similar language is found in almost all of the statutes creating regulatory commissions, although it has been omitted for some performing exclusively judicial functions. There is indisputable evidence, however, that the language that the Supreme Court has construed to be a limitation on the president's powers was intended by the Congress to be just the opposite. The Tenure of Office Act of 1867 was still in effect when Congress enacted the ICC Act. By including a provision authorizing the president to remove commissioners, even though only for specified causes, the Congress conferred on the president considerably more latitude than he had with respect to other executive officers appointed with the consent of the Senate.

The Supreme Court decisions in the case of *Humphrey's Executor* v. *United States* [295 U.S. 602 (1935)] and *Wiener* v. *United States* [357 U.S. 349 (1958)] have provided the legal foundation for the theory of commission independence. In the *Humphrey* case, the Court drew a distinction between an agency

31. Marver H. Bernstein, *Regulating Business by Independent Commission,* Princeton University Press, 1955, p. 130.

that performs quasi-legislative and quasi-judicial functions, such as the Federal Trade Commission, and an agency primarily concerned with administrative or executive duties. Justice Sutherland held that the Federal Trade Commission "to the extent that it exercises any executive function, as distinguished from executive power in the constitutional sense, it does so in the discharge of its quasi-judicial and quasi-legislative powers, or as an agency of the legislative or judicial branches of government." It was the Court's unanimous view that the president could remove an FTC commissioner for the causes enumerated in the statute and for no other reasons. The Court went beyond the *Humphrey* case when it ruled in the *Wiener* case that President Eisenhower could not remove a member of a claims commission, even though the Congress had not specifically limited the president's removal powers.

Regardless of the Supreme Court decisions, until 1973 the regulatory commissions in some areas enjoyed less independence than some executive agencies. The president, through OMB review of budgets, legislation, and data questionnaires, and Department of Justice control of litigation, was able significantly to influence commission policies, administration, and operations. The Congress in 1973 overrode White House objections and amended the Alaska pipeline bill (1) to authorize the Federal Trade Commission to represent itself in civil court proceedings and (2) to transfer authority for review of independent regulatory commission data requests under the Federal Reporting Services Act from OMB to the General Accounting Office.

The current congressional emphasis on independence is reflected in the exclusion of regulatory commissions from the president's reorganization authority. Until 1977 such a limitation was not contained in the Reorganization Statute. To protect further the independence of regulatory programs, the Senate Committee on Governmental Affairs has recommended the following: (1) independent regulatory commissions should conduct and control their own substantive litigation, except for litigation taking place in the Supreme Court; (2) independent regula-

Indirect means may be employed, however, to convey the president's views to the commission on an individual case. President Eisenhower sent a letter to the chairman of the Senate Foreign Relations Committee urging that "the United States should promptly take whatever action might be necessary to clear the way for commencement of the project [St. Lawrence Seaway]," and forwarded a copy of his letter to the chairman of the Federal Power Commission.[34] The project could not proceed until the commission approved a pending New York–Ontario power application. The Commission got the message and acted favorably.

Evidence has yet to be produced which demonstrates that an autonomous commission most effectively ensures protection of the public interest. On the contrary, the evidence would indicate that "independence" makes the commissions more susceptible to industry influence and congressional intervention. Roger Noll concludes that "independence serves primarily to insulate the agency from the general public."[35]

Many researchers have isolated and confirmed the regulatory commission syndrome. The symptoms of this geriatric malady are disorientation and growing inability to distinguish between the public interest and the interests of those subject to regulation. Noll brands the agencies "as a form of legal cartel for regulated firms."[36]

Similar problems arise from a commission's intimate involvement with the legal profession and the practitioners appearing before it. The domination of the commissions by lawyers can be seen in the case-by-case approach to regulation, emphasis on adversary proceedings, and complex judicialized processes and procedures. It can also be seen in the structure of the organization created to simplify, speed up, and ensure fairness in regulatory processes—the Administrative Conference of the United States.

34. *Congressional Record,* April 25, 1953, p. 40009.

35. Roger G. Noll, *Reforming Regulation: An Evaluation of the Ash Council Proposals,* The Brookings Institution, 1971, p. 35.

36. Ibid., p. 38.

tory commissions should transmit any budget request to the Congress at the same time such messages are submitted to the Office of Management and Budget, as now provided for the Commodity Futures Trading Commission, Consumer Product Safety Commission, and the Interstate Commerce Commission; (3) legislative communications from an independent commission to the Congress should not be subject to prior clearance by the Office of Management and Budget; and (4) top staff officials at the independent regulatory commissions should be selected wholly on the basis of merit, and the selection decision by the agency should not be subject to clearance by officials outside the agency.

To increase political accountability, the Senate committee proposed that the heads of other executive departments be accorded powers comparable to those now vested in the secretary of energy. The secretary of energy is authorized to intervene in proceedings before the Federal Energy Regulatory Commission that have a significant policy impact and to initiate proposed rulemaking.[32]

Presidents are willing to concede a degree of, but not total independence to the regulatory commissions. President Kennedy stressed the continuing responsibilities of the president with respect to the operations of these agencies in his message on "Regulatory Agencies of Our Government."[33] He asserted that "the President's responsibilities require him to know and evaluate how efficiently these agencies dispatch their business, including any lack of prompt decision of the thousands of cases which they are called upon to decide, any failure to evolve policy in areas where they have been charged by the Congress to do so, or any other difficulties that militate against the performance of their statutory duties."

President Kennedy did agree that intervention in individual cases would be improper, unless the executive departments appeared formally as an intervenor in a particular proceeding.

32. Senate Document No. 95–91, 95th Congress, 2nd Session, December 1977, p. xiii.

33. Message to the Congress, April 13, 1961.

The Bureau of the Budget favored a conference limited in membership to responsible federal officials—the chairmen of the major regulatory commissions and the heads of the agencies performing regulatory functions. Although the bureau could and did argue that it was conforming strictly to the Judicial Conference model in excluding the practicing bar from voting membership, its views did not prevail. As constituted by law, the Administrative Conference more nearly resembles the House of Delegates of the American Bar Association than either the Judicial Conference or an executive branch agency. The conference's chief executive officer is a chairman appointed by the president, with the consent of the Senate, for a five-year term. A ten-member council appointed by the president for three-year terms is responsible for approving the agenda, budget, and appointments made by the chairman of conference members from outside the government. Not more than half the council members may be employees of federal regulatory agencies or executive departments.

Plenary powers are vested in an Assembly consisting of not more than ninety-one or less than seventy-five members. At least one third of the Assembly members are to be selected to give broad representation of the views of the practicing bar, scholars in the field of administrative law or government, or others specially informed by knowledge and experience with respect to federal administrative procedure. Appointments of nonlawyers so far represent little more than tokenism. The Assembly conducts its business with all the formality and elaborate procedures of a legislative body. There are committee reports, resolutions, debates, and roll-call votes. Among federal agencies, the Administrative Conference is unique.

Government Corporations. Institutional types are seldom loved or hated for themselves alone. Partisan heat may be aroused by the substance of a program or the personality of the administrator, but rarely by the institutional type. The one notable exception is the government corporation. Although emotions are not as strong as they once were, there are still those who regard the corporate device as good or evil, regardless of how it is used or the purpose it serves.[37]

No responsible person or organization has ever demanded that all departments, bureaus, boards, or commissions be abolished. But the Congress from time to time is flooded with mail demanding that all government corporations be abolished, and bills have been introduced with this objective. At the other extreme are a number of businesspersons and scholars who attribute almost mystic qualities to the corporation and find in it a panacea for most of the ills that beset the government.

The government corporation has become a symbol, and symbols stir strong, and often ambivalent, emotions. At one and the same time the corporation represents the evils of government in business and the virtues of business efficiency and organization in government. The latter view was embraced by the President's Commission on Postal Organization, chaired by Frederick R. Kappel, retired chairman of the board of directors of American Telephone and Telegraph Company, which advocated conversion of the Post Office from an executive department to a government corporation as a means of solving the postal "crisis" and ensuring that the postal service would be run as a "business."[38] Differences of opinion about the value and uses of government corporations are not necessarily a reflection of differences in economic and political ideologies.

Preconceptions have so colored most discussions of government corporations that folklore is often mistaken for fact. Among the most commonly accepted myths are the following: (1) incorporation by itself gives a government corporation certain basic authorities not possessed by other government agencies; (2) a government corporation is not a part of the executive branch but an agency of the Congress; (3) a government corporation is by definition autonomous; and (4) a board of directors is an

37. For history, see Harold Seldman, "Public Enterprise in the United States," *Annals of Public Cooperative Economy,* January–March 1983.

38. President's Commission on Postal Organization, *Towards Postal Excellence,* a report to the President, June 1968.

indispensable attribute of a government corporation. None of these is true.

States have enacted general incorporation laws, but the federal government has not. The distinguishing attributes of a U.S. government corporation are not inherent in the corporate form but stem solely from specific grants of power that have been customarily included in corporate charters enacted by the Congress. The Government Corporation Control Act is, as its name implies, a control act and confers no authority on a corporation.

The government corporation is essentially an empirical response to problems posed by increasing reliance on government-created business enterprises and business-type operations to accomplish public purposes. The United States acquired the Panama Railroad Company when it purchased the assets of the French Canal Company in 1904, but it was not until World War I that the U.S. government became a business entrepreneur on a large scale and established the first wholly owned government corporations.

To accomplish its wartime objectives, the government found it necessary to construct and operate a merchant fleet, to build, rent, and sell houses, to buy and sell sugar and grain, to lend money, and to engage in other commercial enterprises. All these activities had certain unique characteristics that clearly set them apart from what up to then had been construed as "normal" and acceptable government functions: (1) the government was dealing with the public as a businessman rather than a sovereign; (2) users, rather than the general taxpayer, were expected to bear a major share of the cost for goods and services; (3) expenditures necessarily fluctuated with consumer demand and could not be predicted accurately or realistically financed by annual appropriations; (4) additional expenditures to meet increased demand did not necessarily increase the net outlay from the Treasury in the long run; and (5) operations were being conducted within areas in which there were well-established commercial trade practices. Experience demonstrated that enterprises with such characteristics could not be managed effectively under an administrative and financial system designed to control totally different types of government activities.

The keystone of financial control was then, and to a large extent still is, the requirement that Congress provide funds through annual appropriation acts. For this reason, most agencies are not permitted to retain and utilize incidental revenues or to carry over unexpended balances at the end of the fiscal year. Governmental accounting and auditing had the limited purposes of preventing the overobligation of appropriated funds and unlawful expenditures. Furthermore, the Congress was unwilling to permit administrative discretion in those areas of most vital concern to a business—procurement, contracts, sales of goods and property, and personnel. Administrators often found the myriad of regulatory and prohibitory statutes a serious inconvenience, however, loss of flexibility was considered a small sacrifice to place on the altar of public honesty and accountability. But it became evident that any attempt to operate a business enterprise within such a framework would entail not mere inconvenience but certain failure.

The first solution was to charter government corporations under the general incorporation laws of the states and the District of Columbia. Although this device provided necessary flexibility, it created new and equally difficult problems. Considerable doubt existed concerning the propriety of subjecting a federal instrumentality to the provisions of state law. Furthermore, most existing controls to ensure public accountability were abandoned without satisfactory substitutes being provided. Sporadic attempt were made by the Congress and the comptroller general to apply traditional budget and audit controls to government corporations, but the results were such as to discourage further efforts along these lines.

The Government Corporation Control Act of 1945 represents the first official recognition by the Congress of the need for a new type of government institution tailored to the requirements of business programs and for new types of controls over such institutions that would ensure accountability without impairing essential flexibility. The Congress expressly recognized that "the corporate form loses much of its peculiar value without reasonable autonomy and flexibility in its day-to-day decisions and operations. The budget and financial controls imposed upon Government corporations should not deprive them of this freedom and flexibility in carrying out authorized programs. . . ."[39]

The Government Corporation Control Act prohibited the creation of government corporations except by or pursuant to an act of Congress and required that all corporations chartered by the states or the District of Columbia be reincorporated by act of Congress or liquidated by June 30, 1948. The Control Act did not significantly alter or impair the distinguishing characteristics and special powers that had been acquired by government corporations.

Of the thirty corporations created by the Congress since the mid-1960s, seventeen are not subject to the Government Corporation Control Act. For example, there is no reference to the act in statutes enacted during 1970 to establish a Federal Home Loan Mortgage Corporation and a Community Development Corporation.

Whether the omission reflected a conscious attempt to escape ceilings on net corporate outlays (not a requirement of the Control Act)—as was the case when the Congress placed programs of the Export-Import Bank, Rural Telephone Bank, and Rural Electrification Administration outside the budget—or merely sloppy legislative drafting is difficult to determine.

As a body corporate, a government corporation has a separate legal personality distinct from that of the United States. A corporation, therefore, does not enjoy the traditional immunity of the United States from being sued without its consent. A corporation can also be authorized to borrow money in its own name without directly pledging the credit of the United States, although the financial community recognizes that the govern-

39. Senate Report No. 694, 79th Congress.

ment would be most unlikely to refuse to make good in the event of default. The principal advantage is that such unguaranteed corporate obligations are not included under the public debt ceiling.

A corporation is usually given power "to determine the character and the necessity for its expenditures, and the manner in which they shall be incurred, allowed and paid." A corporation is thus exempted from most of the regulatory and prohibitory statutes applicable to the expenditure of public funds, except those specifically applicable to government corporations. Although subject to audit, their expenditures cannot be "disallowed" by the General Accounting Office, which is limited to reporting questionable transactions to the Congress. Some in the General Accounting Office have never become fully reconciled to the loss of disallowance authority, and this has been reflected from time to time in hostility to the conversion to corporations of such agencies as the Washington Airports and the Alaska Railroad.

A very great part of the difference between a corporation and an agency arises from the method of financing its operations. A corporation's funds are generally derived from such sources as capital appropriations, which are not subject to fiscal year limitations, revenues, and borrowings from the Treasury or public. With a few exceptions, such as the Federal Crop Insurance Corporation (administrative expenses) and the TVA (nonrevenue programs), corporations rarely depend on annual appropriations for their funds.

The Congress and the public now generally accept the principle that a government corporation should endeavor to operate, as far as practicable, on a self-sustaining basis and recover through user charges all costs of its operations, including interest, depreciation, and the cost of services furnished by other government agencies. Some fall short of this goal, notably the Commodity Credit Corporation's price support program, which incurs substantial annual losses; but, for most, a break-even operation remains the ultimate objective. Attempts to recover the costs of noncorporate programs from user charges have met with considerable resistance on the grounds that these are no different from traditional government services properly chargeable, in whole or in part, to the general taxpayer.

Mixed-ownership government corporations are not subject to any form of budget control, although within recent years the budgets of the Federal Intermediate Credit Banks and the Banks for Cooperatives have been included in the Budget Appendix. The budgets of the Federal Land Banks and the Federal Home Loan Banks, which have retired the government-owned capital stock, are published in a Budget "annex." Stronger measures advocated by President Eisenhower in his 1961 Budget Message to apply the budget provisions of the Control Act to mixed-ownership corporations were rejected by the Congress.

Wholly owned government corporations are generally required by law to present "business-type" budgets, which the Corporation Control Act provides shall be plans of operations "with due allowance for flexibility." Unlike an agency, which requests specific appropriations, a corporation seeks congressional approval of its budget program as a whole. Congress is authorized to limit the use of corporate funds for any purpose, but it has seldom chosen to do so, except for administrative expenses. In essence, the business-type budget provides for a qualitative rather than a quantitative review of proposed corporate expenditures.

The comptroller general is directed by the Control Act to make an audit of all government corporations "in accordance with principles and procedures applicable to commercial corporate transactions." The comptroller general may make a "comprehensive audit" of noncorporate government enterprises. A comprehensive audit in many respects resembles a commercial audit, but it may also include an examination of the legality of individual items of expenditure.

Employees of government corporations are considered to be employees of the United States,[40] subject to the general laws

40. Sidney D. Goldberg and Harold Seidman, *The Government Corporation: Elements of a Model Charter,* Public Administration Service, 1953, pp. 23–29.

and regulations applicable to government employees. Exceptions have been granted when a need has been established for special flexibility in hiring and dismissing employees and establishing wage scales, as in the case of the Panama Canal Company, Tennessee Valley Authority, Banks for Cooperatives, and Federal Intermediate Credit Banks. Other exceptions are the U.S. Railway Association and the Neighborhood Reinvestment Corporation, whose officers and employees "shall not be considered to be officers and employees of the United States."

A board of directors was once considered to be the hallmark of a government corporation, largely because state incorporation laws generally require the establishment of boards of directors elected by the stockholders. Boards of directors persist in many varieties and forms, even though the need for and usefulness of most boards are highly debatable. David Lilienthal began to entertain serious reservations about the usefulness of the Tennessee Valley Authority board when he served as its chairman. He wrote in his diary that "the board has come to mean me."[41] The Congress replaced the board of directors of the Reconstruction Finance Corporation with a single administrator because the board arrangement had resulted in "diffusion of responsibility." It was noted that existence of a five-man board of directors had made it possible "for individual members to avoid, obscure, or dilute their responsibilities by passing the buck from one to another."[42] Existing corporations or quasi-corporations with single heads are the St. Lawrence Seaway Development Corporation, the Federal Housing Administration, and the Government National Mortgage Association.

The Tennessee Valley Authority, Export-Import Bank, and Federal Deposit Insurance Corporation have full-time boards of directors. The Home Loan Bank Board also serves as the board of directors of the Federal Savings and Loan Insurance Corporation and the Federal Home Loan Mortgage Corpora-

---

41. David E. Lilienthal, *The Journals of David E. Lilienthal: The TVA Years, 1939–1945*, Vol. 1, Harper & Row, 1964, pp. 280–81.

42. Senate Report No. 76, 82nd Congress.

tion. The Community Development Corporation, Federal Crop Insurance Corporation, and Federal Prison Industries have part-time boards composed of both public officials and private individuals. The Commodity Credit Corporation, Pension Benefit Guaranty Corporation, Neighborhood Reinvestment Corporation, and Federal Financing Bank have "in-house" boards made up exclusively of federal officials. The Banks for Cooperatives, Federal Intermediate Credit Banks, and Rural Telephone Bank are managed by part-time boards consisting of directors appointed by the government and directors elected by borrower associations.

The procedures permitted under the Budget and Accounting Procedures Act of 1950, together with the increased use of revolving funds, have considerably narrowed the differences between agencies and corporations. There is nothing to prevent the Congress from conferring on a noncorporate agency some or all of the powers normally granted to a government corporation, except separate corporate status, but the burden of proof shifts to those arguing for special treatment.

The secretary of housing and urban development, in effect, has been constituted as a "corporation sole" for the purpose of administering the college housing, urban renewal, and other public enterprise funds. These funds have not been organized as corporations, but, nonetheless, the secretary in carrying out his duties under the laws creating the funds may sue and be sued, borrow money, and exercise comparable powers and is subject to the budget and audit provisions of the Government Corporation Control Act applicable to wholly owned government corporations. This approach was developed initially to shore up the position of a weak Housing and Home Finance administrator by vesting powers in him rather than in one of the highly autonomous agency constituents subject only to his "coordination." Other agencies, such as the Bonneville Power Administration, have gradually over the years acquired some but not all of the attributes of a government corporation.

Government corporations are organized to achieve a public

purpose authorized by law. As far as purpose is concerned, a wholly owned government corporation cannot be distinguished from any other government agency.[43] This view was vigorously stated by the U.S. Supreme Court in the case of *Cherry Cotton Mills* v. *U.S.* [327 U.S. 536 (1945)] when it held that the fact "that the Congress chose to call it a corporation [Reconstruction Finance Corporation] does not alter its characteristics so as to make it something other than what it actually is, an agency selected by the government to accomplish purely governmental purposes." The functions of a corporation are the same as those of any administrative agency; the differences between the two are to be found in the *methods* employed to perform the functions and in the techniques utilized by the president and the Congress to fulfill their constitutional responsibilities.

Not since Arthur E. Morgan, the first chairman of the Tennessee Valley Authority, has a director of a wholly owned corporation attempted to challenge the president's overriding authority. Morgan insisted that he was responsible solely to the Congress, not the president, and refused to answer questions asked by President Franklin D. Roosevelt.[44] When President Roosevelt removed Morgan for "contumacy," his action was sustained by the courts.[45]

As a general rule, the president looks to the heads of executive departments and agencies for immediate direction and supervision of government corporations. Corporations are generally made subject to supervision by the department head responsible for the functional area in which the corporation is operating. Only three wholly owned corporations—the Tennessee Valley Authority, Export-Import Bank, and Federal De-

43. Harold Seidman, "The Theory of the Autonomous Government Corporation: A Critical Appraisal," *Public Administration Review*, Vol. 12, No. 2, 1952; Harold Seidman, "Public Enterprise Autonomy: Need for a New Theory," *International Review of Administrative Sciences*, Vol. XLIX, No. 1, 1983.

44. Senate Document No. 155, 75th Congress, 3rd Session, p. 105.

45. *Morgan* v. *Tennessee Valley Authority*, 115 F 2d. 900, certiorari denied, 312 U.S. 701.

posit Insurance Corporation[46]—report directly to the president. In some instances, independence has been the equivalent of "isolation" from those with ultimate authority for making national policy. As a regional agency without a national constituency, the Tennessee Valley Authority is especially vulnerable if it does not have strong presidential backing, because no Cabinet officer is responsible for defending its interests and some have looked on it as a competitor. Not until the Congress authorized the TVA to market its own revenue bonds was the authority able to obtain funds necessary to finance major expansion of its power-producing facilities.

Mixed-ownership corporations present a distinct class of supervisory problems. These corporations have at times demanded all of the privileges of a public agency without being willing to accept the responsibilities. Mixed-ownership corporations have been successful in maintaining at least a degree of independence from both the president and the Congress, particularly those that are self-financing and have a majority of directors nominated or elected by private stockholders. For this reason the Eisenhower administration decided in 1956 to oppose the establishment of additional mixed-ownership corporations, even though the second Hoover Commission had endorsed the principle of "mutualization."[47]

The very fact that government corporations are "different" causes them to be viewed with some suspicion by the General Accounting Office and the Appropriations Committees. Bureaucracies, whether in the legislative or executive branches, have an innate distaste for institutions that do not fit neatly into the existing system and upset established routines. Nonetheless, the legitimacy of the government corporation as a member of the fed-

46. The Federal Deposit Insurance Corporation is classified in the Government Corporation Control Act as a "mixed-ownership" corporation, but the stock held by the Federal Reserve Banks has been retired. FDIC is presently a "no-stock" corporation, as are most wholly owned government corporations.

47. Commission on Organization of the Executive Branch of the Government, "Lending, Guaranteeing and Insurance Activities," a report to the Congress, March 1955, pp. 11–13.

eral institutional family is no longer open to question. The corporation gained full respectability when President Truman laid down criteria for the use of government corporations in his 1948 Budget Message.[48] President Truman stated the following:

> Experience indicates that the corporate form of organization is peculiarly adapted to the Administration of governmental programs which are predominantly of a commercial character— those which are revenue producing, are at least potentially self-sustaining, and involve a large number of business-type transactions with the public. In their business operations such programs require greater flexibility than the customary type of appropriation budget ordinarily permits. As a rule the usefulness of a corporation lies in its ability to deal with the public in the manner employed by private enterprise for similar work.

48. House Document No. 19, 80th Congress, pp. M57–M62.

12

Advisory and Intergovernmental Bodies: Twilight Zone

Advisory Bodies. Alexander Hamilton in Federalist Paper No. 70 argued that the unity of executive power could be destroyed "either by vesting the power in two or more magistrates of equal dignity and authority, or by vesting it ostensibly in one man, subject in whole or in part to the control and cooperation of others, in the capacity of counselors to him."[1] No executive can disregard with impunity "advice" by his counselors, particularly when they represent powerful elements in the community and their advice is not offered privately. Advice becomes limiting when an executive's discretion in the choice of his advisers is restricted by law or executive order and advisory bodies assume an independent status.

As with interagency committees, a distinction needs to be maintained between ad hoc, task-oriented advisory groups and continuing advisory bodies with a right to review, question, and be consulted about program policies and execution. It is the latter category that is of concern to us here.

For several so-called advisory bodies the title "advisory" is a misnomer. Advice ceases to be advice when a grant cannot be

1. Clinton Rossiter, ed., *The Federalist Papers,* The New American Library, Inc., 1961, p. 424.

made without first obtaining the approval or recommendations of an advisory council. In the previous chapter, we cited the powers vested in advisory councils to the National Foundation on Arts and Humanities and the various institutes under the National Institutes of Health. Other advisory committees have coveted such authorities and some have succeeded in obtaining them without express statutory sanction.

Congress customarily has established fixed, overlapping terms of office for committee members. Qualifications for committee membership are normally couched in quite broad language. For example, the twelve public members of the Advisory Committee on Vocational Education are to be persons "familiar with the vocational education needs of management and labor (in equal numbers), persons familiar with the administration of state and local vocational educational programs, other persons with special knowledge, experience or qualifications with respect to vocational education, and persons representative of the general public." Exceptions are statutory provisions, such as those authorizing the Council of the American Historical Association to appoint two members of the National Historical Publications Commission or permitting designated organizations or groups to nominate or recommend committee members.

While the statutes may appear to allow considerable executive latitude in selecting "advisers," the president or other appointing officer is seldom in a position to ignore suggestions from the constituencies they represent. Self-designated elites in some professional groups have monopolized appointments to advisory committees. The House Committee on Government Operations noted with concern that a majority of the advisers to the National Institutes of Health were drawn from the relatively small number of institutions that receive the bulk of NIH grant funds.[2] Few nonmembers of the National Academy of Sciences were named to serve on the prestigious and influential Presi-

2. House Committee on Government Operations, "The Administration of Research Grants in the Public Health Service," House Report No. 800, 90th Congress, 1st Session, p. 61.

dent's Science Advisory Committee.[3] The peer review system of the National Endowment for the Arts was criticized in a report initiated by the House Appropriations Committee for relying "too heavily on a 'closed circle' of advisors" from the arts community.[4] If members of advisory committees are supposed to reflect the views of broad sectional, professional, economic, or social interests, obviously they must have a standing with and be acceptable to the organizations that represent those interests.

Advisory committees are by no means essential to ensure that affected individuals or groups have a voice with respect to federal programs or policies. Consultation is considered to be a prerequisite for democratic administration. Indeed, Section 4 of the Administrative Procedures Act requires, with some exceptions, public notice of proposed agency rulemaking and an opportunity for interested persons to express their views before a final decision is taken. In some instances, advisory committees merely formalize and legitimatize consultative arrangements established by custom and practice.

David Truman correctly points out that for groups with effective access to the president, department heads, and congressional committees, "the advisory committee and similar devices of consultation may be more a handicap than an advantage."[5] It is no accident that the veterans organizations have made no efforts to institutionalize their role as advisers to the Veterans Administration. Whatever the intentions of the government or interest group, formalization of consultative arrangements is likely to result in mutual "co-optation"—to borrow a word from the social psychologists. Each may find its freedom of action significantly reduced. The outside organization may be identified with government policies that are unpopular among some elements of its constituency, but that for one reason or another it is unable or

3. Daniel S. Greenberg, *The Politics of Pure Science*, The New American Library, Inc., 1967, p. 15.

4. *Washington Post*, May 4, 1979.

5. David B. Truman, *The Governmental Process*, Alfred A. Knopf, 1964, p. 461.

unwilling to oppose publicly. An organization quickly loses influence when it becomes known that its advice on major issues has been rejected. Consequently, it must be highly selective in choosing the issues on which it is willing to risk a public rebuke. Furthermore, once arrangements are formalized, privileged access may be jeopardized by the admission into the club of others with competing or contrary interests.

What the government basically wants from advisory committees is not "expert" advice, although occasionally this is a factor, but support. Advisory boards may be utilized to lend respectability to new or controversial programs such as poverty and foreign assistance. It is hoped that board members will act as program missionaries and assist in mobilizing support for the program both in their home communities and in the Congress. Many have been extremely effective in this role, although their zeal does not always reflect selfless dedication to the public interest. The House Committee on Government Operations observed that "when some of the same individuals who have served on advisory councils for many years receive substantial NIH grants, and also testify before the Congress in support of the Agency's appropriations, the appearance of favoritism is unavoidable."[6] Testimony by these expert witnesses, coupled with skillful behind-the-scenes lobbying, certainly played a part in persuading the Appropriations Committees to recommend more money for NIH programs than was requested in the president's budget.

Missionary ardor can boomerang and be turned against the president or department head. Zealots are predisposed to be willing accomplices of agency dissidents in covert and overt campaigns not only to overcome budgetary limits but also to thwart proposed policies and reorganizations that are not to their liking. Advisers are not subject to the restraints applicable to public employees and cannot be disciplined for insubordination. The Advisory Council to the National Institute of Mental Health worked closely with the institute director in organizing opposition to a 1960 proposal to reorganize the Public Health

6. House Committee on Government Operations, p. 62.

Service. The plan called for transfer of important elements of the NIMH to a new Division of Mental Health. The surgeon general was reluctant to alienate the council by going forward with the plan and it was abandoned.[7]

Attempts to use advisory bodies as "window-dressing" can also boomerang. President Kennedy created a Consumer Advisory Council under the aegis of the Council of Economic Advisers as what he hoped would be an innocuous alternative to a White House Office of Consumer Counsel promised during the campaign. Unfortunately, council activists took the executive order rhetoric seriously and were very aggressive in pressing demands for an elaborate program and budgetary resources. Wearied from his efforts to control this fractious group, a CEA staff man wrote a plaintive memorandum titled "Who left this bastard on our doorstep?" recommending that the Council of Economic Advisers be relieved of its onerous responsibilities. No agency was willing to volunteer for the assignment, so the council was reorganized and given independent status.

Individuals are attracted to service on advisory groups for a variety of reasons—honor, prestige, influence, curiosity, and opportunity for public service. The last is by no means the least important. Many people do accept a moral obligation to serve their country, but would prefer to do so in a way that does not compel them to give up their private interests.

Individuals may be motivated by dedication to the public interest, but this is seldom true of organizations concerned with promoting the economic interests of their members. Like the government, these organizations may try to utilize advisory groups for their own benefit. This poses a threat when advisory committees are allowed to develop into an invisible government responsible neither to the president, the Congress, nor the people. The danger is very real when public officials confuse advice with direction.

7. Edith T. Carper, "The Reorganization of the Public Health Service," in *Governmental Reorganization: Cases and Commentary,* Frederick C. Mosher, ed., The Bobbs-Merrill Co., Inc., 1967.

Secretary of Commerce Sinclair Weeks was criticized severely by the Anti-Trust Subcommittee of the House Judiciary Committee in 1956 for creating advisory arrangements that "effected a virtual abdication of administrative responsibility on the part of Government officials in that their actions in many instances are but the automatic approval of decisions already made outside the Government in business and industry. The Secretary of Commerce, in BDSA, has created an organization which in the name of the Government has been used to advance throughout the Government the cause of private interests. Failing to control its activities, he has allowed an agency of the Government to become an instrument for inside influence and advancement of special interests." The committee concluded the following: "In such circumstances the Government agency becomes a spokesman for private interests, and because it speaks in the guise of presumably disinterested Government, it is all the more disarming."[8]

The situation that existed in the Department of Commerce in the mid-1950s was unique only because Secretary Weeks saw nothing wrong with this kind of incestuous relationship between a government department and its advisory committees. Today, major defense contractors are able to exercise considerable influence through membership on Department of Defense Advisory Committees. Boeing has twenty-three committee memberships, Lockheed twenty, United Technologies thirteen, McDonnell Douglas eleven, Northrop ten, Rockwell International seven, General Dynamics seven, and Grumman seven.[9]

With the proliferation of advisory bodies (928, a net increase of 44, reported by the president in 1984, with an annual cost of $71 million) and the growing dependence of diverse groups on the federal government for survival, the potential for conflicts of interest inherent in advisory arrangements could no longer be

8. House Committee on Judiciary, Anti-Trust Subcommittee, "Interim Report on WOC's and Advisory Groups," August 24, 1956, pp. 90, 99.

9. Gordon Adams, *The Politics of Defense Contracting*, Transaction Books, 1982, p. 171.

ignored.[10] In February 1962, President Kennedy issued a memorandum on "Preventing Conflicts of Interest on the Part of Advisers and Consultants to the Government" and promulgated Executive Order No. 11007, prescribing regulations for the formation and use of advisory committees.

President Kennedy instructed agency heads to "oversee the activities of such consultants to ensure that the public interest is protected from improper conduct and that consultants will not, through ignorance or inadvertence, embarrass the Government or themselves in their activities." The memorandum called attention to the conflict-of-interest statutes, defined ethical standards of conduct, and required advisers to disclose their financial interests. The conflict-of-interest laws were found to be unduly restrictive when applied to temporary and intermittent employees, and the Congress liberalized the restrictions in 1963. Public Law 87–849 established a category of persons designated "special Government employees" and exempted them from some but not all of the restrictions imposed on the private activities of full-time employees. A special employee is defined as an individual appointed or employed to serve, with or without compensation, for not more than 130 days during any period of 365 consecutive days.

Executive Order No. 11007 directed that "no committee shall be utilized for functions not solely advisory, and determinations of actions to be taken with respect to matters upon which an advisory committee advises or recommends shall be made solely by officers or employees of the Government." The order sets forth the following rules: (1) meetings shall not be held without government approval; (2) the government should formulate or approve the agenda; (3) all meetings must be conducted in the presence of a full-time government employee who may adjourn the meeting when he considers adjournment to be in the public interest; (4) minutes must be kept of each meeting and, for Industry Advisory Committees, a verbatim transcript; and (5) un-

10. *Federal Advisory Committees,* Thirteenth Annual Report of the President, fiscal year 1984.

less otherwise provided by law, committees shall terminate not later than two years from the date of formation, except when the department head makes a finding that continuance is in the public interest. The Business Advisory Council severed its ties with the Department of Commerce rather than comply with these rules.

The force and effect of the Kennedy executive order were somewhat weakened by the necessity to exclude committees "for which Congress by statute has specified the purpose, composition and conduct." Such important committees as the advisory councils of the National Institutes of Health are not subject to the order.

Congress judged the guidelines established by Executive Order No. 11007 to be inadequate because (1) no provision is made for executive oversight of the formation, management, and use of advisory committees; (2) funding of advisory bodies is not covered; (3) most requirements can be waived by the agency head, if he declares it to be in the public interest; and (4) balanced representation of varying social and economic interests is not required.[11]

The Federal Advisory Committee Act of 1972 (Public Law 92–463) declares that "new advisory committees should be established only when they are determined to be essential and their number should be kept to the minimum necessary." Committee meetings shall be open to the public and "fairly balanced in terms of points of view represented and the functions to be performed." The act directs that a Committee Management Secretariat be established within the Office of Management and Budget with responsibility for reviewing committee performance, recommending the abolition of unnecessary or obsolete committees, and prescribing administrative guidelines and management controls.[12]

11. House Report No. 91–1731.

12. Office of Management and Budget regulations are set forth in Circular No. A–63 Revised. Secretariat functions have been transferred to the General Services Administration.

Joint Congressional–Executive Agencies. The Supreme Court's ruling in *Springer* v. *Philippine Islands* [277 U.S. 189 (1928)] that it is unconstitutional for legislators to serve on executive bodies has been violated in both spirit and practice. Joint executive–legislative study commissions have been common since the first Hoover Commission. Membership on these commissions generally is weighted in favor of the congressional representatives. Congressional appointees outnumbered executive appointees on the Hoover Commission two to one. Furthermore, executive and legislative representatives do not serve in comparable capacities. Members appointed by the president, particularly from the executive branch, are construed to be administration spokespersons and can make commitments on the president's behalf. Congressional members obviously cannot commit the Congress and speak only for themselves. Any compromises are likely to be entirely one-sided.

While congressional membership on ad hoc study commissions can be defended as not constituting an overt violation of the separation-of-powers doctrine, congressional membership on permanent executive bodies does raise serious constitutional questions. Six of the fifteen members of the Smithsonian Institution's governing body, the Board of Regents, come from the Senate and House (three each). The Migratory Bird Conservation Commission consists of the secretary of the interior as chairman, the secretary of agriculture, two members of the House of Representatives selected by the speaker, and two senators selected by the president of the Senate. The commission has various administrative duties, including approval of land purchases or rentals and the fixing of prices at which bird sanctuaries may be purchased or rented. Three senators and three congressmen are members of the Advisory Commission on Intergovernmental Relations. Two senators and two congressmen constitute a majority of the seven-member National Forest Reservation Commission, which passes on lands recommended by the secretary of agriculture for acquisition as national forests by purchases or exchange. In administering the Agricultural Trade Development and Assistance

Act, the president must obtain the advice of a committee consisting of the secretary of agriculture, the AID administrator, the director of management and budget, and chairmen and ranking minority members of the Agriculture Committees. The committee is required "to review from time to time the status and usage of foreign currencies . . . and shall make recommendations to the President as to ways and means of ensuring to the United States (1) the maximum benefit from the use of such currencies . . . and (2) the maximum return from sales."

Intergovernmental Organizations. Our Constitution makers anticipated that the several states might be confronted by problems that cut across state boundaries and would have to devise suitable arrangements to facilitate interstate cooperation in dealing with them. Article I, Section 10 of the Constitution permits states, with the consent of the Congress, to enter into compacts and agreements with each other, although the authority is stated negatively. There is no evidence that the Constitution drafters envisaged circumstances that would warrant comparable agreements or compacts between the federal government and one or more sovereign states.

Until recently the constitutional, legal, financial, and organizational obstacles to the development of workable intergovernmental institutions were considered to be nearly insuperable. When the Tennessee Valley Authority was created, it was assumed generally that there was no feasible alternative to a strictly federal approach to regional development. But the TVA proved not to be the answer. Moves to duplicate the successful TVA experiment in the Columbia and Missouri river basins failed to generate enthusiasm either in the regions or within the federal establishment. The TVA seems destined to be the first and the last wholly federal regional development agency.

Halting steps were taken in the 1950s to provide for state participation in river basin planning. States were invited to propose individuals for appointment to the Arkansas-White-Red and New England–New York River Basin Committees chaired by the Army Corps of Engineers. In 1958, the Congress established a

U.S. Study Commission for the Southeast River Basins and a similar study commission for Texas. These commissions consisted of federal and state representatives, with an unaffiliated chairman appointed by the president. There was no departure, however, from the concept that these commissions were federal agencies, and to conform with constitutional provisions it was believed necessary to give the state representatives federal appointments.

The same pattern was adopted when the Advisory Commission on Intergovernmental Relations was created in 1959. Panels of names are submitted by the Governors' Conference, Council of State Governments, American Municipal Association and U.S. Conference of Mayors, and the National Association of County Officials, but appointments to the Commission are made by the president. The president has some leeway, since a panel must include two names for each vacancy. For example, the president selects four governors from a panel of eight proposed by the Governors' Conference.

Except for the somewhat unusual procedures for selecting commissioners, there appears to have been no congressional intention to create anything other than a permanent bipartisan federal commission. Commission employees are by law "federal employees" and, until 1966, the ACIR was not authorized to receive funds from state and local governments or nonprofit organizations. In accepting appointments to the commission, governors, mayors, and other local officials are placed in the anomalous position of being federal officials for some purposes. This has been a source of embarrassment, because local officials may be debarred by local law from accepting an appointment to a federal position, or if they are permitted to serve, they may be prohibited from accepting compensation or reimbursement for their expenses.

For linkages to be forged among the sovereign but increasingly interdependent partners in the federal system, the organizational dilemma had to be resolved. The 1961 Governors' Conference urged federal–state collaboration to devise "a more comprehensive approach to joint Federal–State planning, and to closer Federal–State coordination in the development of plans and programs."[13] The emphasis was on *joint* federal–state planning within an appropriate institutional framework.

The proposed Water Resources Planning Act of 1961 became a target for those demanding a new approach. States objected strongly to presidential appointment of the states' representatives on the river basin commissions because this would make them mere instruments of the federal government. The bill was not enacted.

Different but no less vexing constitutional doubts had to be satisfied before the Congress approved the Delaware River Compact in 1961. The Delaware River Basin Advisory Committee—consisting of representatives of the governors of Delaware, Pennsylvania, New Jersey, and New York and the mayors of New York and Philadelphia—developed a legislative proposal for creation by interstate–federal compact of a unified water resources agency for the Delaware River Basin. Inclusion of the federal government as a party to an interstate compact was without precedent. Even though the plan called for the federal government to become a signatory, a federal representative was not invited to participate in negotiating the compact.

Apart from the general question of whether a federal–state compact was permissible under the Constitution or desirable as a matter of public policy, specific objections were registered against provisions that had the effect of limiting federal power in such critical areas as control of navigable waters, interstate and foreign commerce, and project authorizations. The Congress approved the compact with reservations protecting federal powers in these areas, authorizing the president to modify any provision of the comprehensive plan adopted by the Delaware River Basin Commission insofar as it affects the powers and functions of federal agencies, and preserving the president's freedom to act in national emergencies.

Although fears that a federal–state compact would make it

13. Resolution adopted by the Governors' Conference, June 28, 1961.

possible for the signatory states to exert undue political pressure on federal agencies have not materialized, many remain uneasy about the compact approach. The Delaware River Commission's accomplishments to date are modest. Potential controversy was avoided when the Commission accepted as its own the comprehensive plan for the Delaware River Basin developed by the Army Corps of Engineers.

The troublesome issue of federal appointment of state members of joint bodies was again raised in 1962 by the governor of Alaska's request for establishment of a Federal–State Development Planning Commission for Alaska. This time the Bureau of the Budget proposed to bypass the constitutional issue by having the President create a Federal Development Planning Commission for Alaska and the governor a state planning commission, and then marrying the two commissions by a memorandum of understanding signed by the president and the governor. The action documents were drafted by a team representing the Bureau of the Budget and the governor.

Executive Order No. 1150, April 2, 1964, notes that "the Governor of Alaska has declared his intention to establish a State Commission for reconstruction and development planning" and directs the Federal Commission created by the order to work with its state counterpart in developing coordinated plans and preparing recommendations for the president and the governor with respect to both short-range and long-range development programs. President Johnson did not sign the memorandum of understanding, but both parties accepted the memorandum as the agreed-upon terms of reference for the commissions.

Enactment in 1965 of the Water Resources Planning Act, the Appalachian Regional Development Act, and the Public Works and Economic Development Act marks a watershed in federal–state cooperation. The Water Resources Planning Act made significant changes in intergovernmental relations and the machinery for coordination among federal agencies. River basin commissions authorized under the act are composed of a chairman appointed by the president, and representatives of interested federal agencies and the participating states, designated by federal agency heads and governors, respectively. The commissions are to prepare joint, coordinated, and comprehensive plans for federal, state, interstate, local, and private development of water and related land resources and to recommend priorities for action.

Disputes about veto authority, the number of federal agencies to be represented on a commission, and voting procedures were resolved by providing that in the work of a commission "every reasonable endeavor shall be made to arrive at a consensus of all members on all issues." If a consensus cannot be obtained, then each member is to be afforded an opportunity to present and report his or her individual views. This approach was feasible because a commission's functions are exclusively advisory.

The Appalachian Regional Development Act was even more explicit in spelling out the terms of the new partnership between the states and the federal government. Federal membership of the Appalachian Regional Commission is limited to the "Federal co-chairman" appointed by the president. Each participating state in the Appalachian region is also entitled to one member, who shall be the governor or his designee. Decisions by the Commission require the affirmative vote of the federal cochairman and of a majority of state members. The federal government agreed to pay administrative expenses for the first two years, but after that each state is to pay its pro rata share of the costs, as determined by the commission. No one employed by the commission "shall be deemed a Federal employee for any purpose."

Although the Appalachian Regional Commission is generally judged to be a "political success," it is regarded by some critics as "simply an unnecessary complication, a useless additional level of government."[14] The Advisory Commission on Intergovernmental Relations found that the commission "has not functioned as an overall coordinator and planner of Federal assistance to the region it serves. It lacks authority over the programs

14. Advisory Commission in Intergovernmental Relations, *Improving Federal Grants Management,* 1977, p. 44.

of other departments, and it has had little success in influencing their efforts."[15] The commission has been somewhat more effective in coordinating and targeting activities for which it has received direct funding and in fostering a "spirit of regionalism" among the members.

Twilight Zone. Once institutional types are assimilated into the family of government institutions, they lose much of their charm for those who prefer public services to be packaged in the trappings of private enterprise. Many advocates of the government corporation have now shifted their affections to what they describe as a "COMSAT-type corporation," although it is by no means certain what they mean by the term. COMSAT was used as the model for the National Housing Partnerships authorized by the Housing and Urban Development Act of 1968.

Confusion about the status of the Communications Satellite Corporation is understandable. It is not a covert government corporation, and the Congress, after prolonged and often bitter debate, rejected proposals for government ownership and operation of the communications satellite system. The Communications Satellite Act of 1962, however, does raise questions about the private character of the venture by providing for presidential appointment, with Senate confirmation, of the corporation's incorporators and three members of the board of directors.

Senator Javits was not alone in expressing the view that "the U.S. Government will sit in on management through three of fifteen directors."[16] Javits conceived of the presidential directors as the defenders of the public interest. But there is nothing in the legislative history to support this interpretation of the directors' role. Indeed, all the evidence runs to the contrary.

Under the Communications Satellite Act, up to 50 percent of the corporation's stock may be held by communications common

15. Ibid. For an evaluation of regional organizations, see Martha Derthick and Gary Bombardier, *Between State and Nation,* The Brookings Institution, 1974.

16. Lloyd D. Musolf, ed., *Communications Satellites in Political Orbit,* Chandler Publishing Company, 1968, p. 143.

carriers. If half the stock were to be held by the carriers and half by the general public, obviously there would be a need for a "neutral" director or directors to resolve potential deadlocks. The Kennedy administration intended that the presidential directors perform this function. There was some concern that if the president named only one director, it would be difficult to avoid the implication that he was a government spokesperson. It was suggested, therefore, that the president be authorized to designate three directors.

Attorney General Robert Kennedy emphasized that "neither the incorporators nor the Presidentially appointed directors are to be classified as officers of the United States." His opinion was backed by Senator Kefauver, who stated that the three directors would owe a fiduciary obligation to the corporation but not to the government.[17]

Of all the means available to exert government influence and safeguard the public interest, presidential appointment of directors is probably the least effective and may have undesirable side effects. According to Herman Schwartz, "their presence may reinforce the belief that the Government assures the profitability of the Corporation" and "may dampen the zeal of the regulatory agencies."[18] As Senator Edmund Muskie stated with respect to the Securities Investor Protection Corporation:

> What I am fearful of is with industry representatives and public representatives on the board, that a request or application for a Treasury backup, use of the Treasury line of credit, could be interpreted as a public decision whereas actually the corporation is a private corporation, and it is a private request. . . . It seems to me the public membership on the private corporation, although it is a minority in fact, would be leaned upon as a crutch by the SEC and the Secretary of the Treasury for use of the Treasury backup.[19]

17. Ibid., pp. 136, 137.

18. Ibid.

19. Senate Committee on Bank and Currency, Subcommittee on Securities, hearings on S.2348, S.3978, 91st Congress, 2nd Session, p. 248.

Presidentially appointed directors are committed to and must support board decisions, even when they vote against them.

Early experiments with mixed boards demonstrated that the arrangement had serious drawbacks. The government was represented on the board of the second Bank of the United States, established in 1816, by five directors. President Jackson complained in a message to the Congress on December 1, 1834, of "exclusion of the public directors from a knowledge of its most important proceedings."[20] The two government directors of the Union Pacific Railroad were treated as spies and antagonists and in 1887 recommended that the appointment of public directors be discontinued.[21] Protection of the public interest can be better ensured from the outside than from within a corporation.

COMSAT's status may be somewhat ambiguous, but it is crystal clear compared with that of several organizations that float suspended in a twilight zone between the public and private sectors. Among the oldest are the twelve Federal Reserve Banks. The capital stock of the Reserve Banks is held by the banks that are members of the Federal Reserve System. The board of directors of each bank is composed of six directors elected by the stockholders, three of whom must be engaged actively in agriculture, industry, or commerce, and three public directors appointed by the board of governors of the Federal Reserve System. Bank presidents are appointed for five-year terms by the board of directors, subject to approval by the board of governors. Among other functions, the banks have been given the privilege of issuing currency and they act as depositories and fiscal agents of the United States. Although privately owned and controlled, the banks are public institutions performing public functions. This fact is recognized by the requirement that net earnings be paid into the U.S. Treasury and that, in the event of liquidation, any surplus remaining after payment of all debts, dividends, and the par values of capital stock shall become the property of the U.S. government.

20. Lloyd D. Musolf, *Mixed Enterprise*, Lexington Books, 1972, p. 55.
21. Ibid.

The board of governors has resisted successfully periodic attempts by a few members of the Congress to apply budget and audit control to Federal Reserve operations. Any move along these lines, no matter how modest, is construed to be an attack on the system's integrity and independence. Chairman William Martin, for example, warned that ". . . budgetary control of our operations, of our budget, is fundamental in our concept of the independent status of the System. If you want to nationalize the System, why the surest way to do it is through control of the budget."[22]

In his 1969 Economic Report, President Johnson proposed that (1) the term of the chairman of the Federal Reserve Board be appropriately geared to that of the president to ensure "harmonious policy coordination"; and (2) Congress review procedures for selecting Reserve bank presidents "to determine whether these positions should be subject to the same appointive process that applies to other posts with similar important responsibilities for national policy."

Institutions such as the Federal Land banks and Federal Home Loan banks have been allowed to drift into the twilight zone without surrendering important privileges that they possessed as government instrumentalities, including access, either directly or indirectly, to the federal Treasury. Retirement of government-owned stock, however, has meant a relaxation of government controls and exemption from the comptroller general's audit authority.

If one applied the traditional tests—private stock ownership, election of a majority of directors by private stockholders, and predominantly non-Treasury financing—a logical argument can be made that the Federal Reserve banks, Federal Land banks, and Federal Home Loan banks belong in a class apart from other government institutions. A logical rationale cannot be developed for the host of government-sponsored corporations, presumably created in the image of COMSAT, but without pro-

22. Joint Committee on Economic Report, Subcommittee on General Credit Control and Debt Management, hearings, March 11, 1952, p 121.

vision for private ownership. All they have in common with COMSAT is that they are declared by congressional fiat not to be agencies or instrumentalities of the U.S. government.

It is difficult to identify any unique attributes that are shared by such government-sponsored enterprises as the Corporation for Public Broadcasting, Federal National Mortgage Association, National Home Ownership Foundation, National Railroad Passenger Corporation, National Park Foundation, Securities Investor Protection Corporation, Student Loan Marketing Association, Legal Services Corporation, and U.S. Railway Association that warrant the nongovernment classification. Directors of the Corporation for Public Broadcasting, National Home Ownership Foundation, National Park Foundation, Securities Investor Protection Corporation, Legal Services Corporation, Student Loan Marketing Association, and U.S. Railway Association are appointed by either the president or a Cabinet member, or public officials designated to act ex officio. The National Home Ownership Foundation, for example, has an eighteen-member board of directors consisting of fifteen appointed by the president and the secretaries of housing and urban development and agriculture, and the director of the Office of Economic Opportunity. The board of the Securities Investor Protection Corporation is composed of five directors appointed by the president and two named by the secretary of the treasury and the Federal Reserve Board. Except for the Federal National Mortgage Association, National Railroad Passenger Corporation, and Student Loan Marketing Association, there is no provision for private equity investment in the enterprises. Few are financially self-sufficient, and all are supported directly or indirectly from the U.S. Treasury. Funds are obtained either by direct appropriations, as with the Corporation for Public Broadcasting, Legal Services Corporation, National Home Ownership Foundation, and U.S. Railway Association, or by grants and government-guaranteed or Treasury-backed loans.[23]

23. For a discussion of government-sponsored enterprise, see Harold "Government-Sponsored Enterprise in the United States," in *The*

Government-sponsored enterprises cannot be differentiated from their counterpart government agencies in terms of function, organization, and financing. The distinguishing characteristics of the enterprises are to be found exclusively in exemptions from the Government Corporation Control Act and laws applicable to federal personnel, funds, and contracts. Whatever the reasons advanced publicly, the objective has been to exclude expenditures from the budget and avoid controls.

According to the House Budget Committee, "the Congressional Budget Act has had the effect of significantly enhancing the value of off-budget status. Off-budget agencies are not covered by the new Congressional process and they are not included in the aggregate or functional amounts set forth in the Congressional budget resolutions."[24] Outlays of the so-called off-budget federal agencies and programs (Federal Financing Bank, Pension Benefit Guaranty Corporation, Postal Service, Synthetic Fuels Corporation, Rural Telephone Bank, and U.S. Railway Association) are estimated at $12.5 billion for 1985. The excluded outlays of government-sponsored enterprises have jumped from relatively small amounts in the 1960s to an estimated $44.3 billion for 1985.[25]

There are those who argue that exemptions from controls are necessary and desirable to safeguard corporate "independence" and avoid partisan political pressures.[26] But exemptions from the civil service laws are not designed to and have not prevented political appointments. Difficulties occur when an enterprise is controlled by directors and staff at odds with the incumbent ad-

---

litical Economy, Bruce L. R. Smith, ed., Macmillan & Co. (London), 1975. Also see Lloyd Musolf and Harold Seidman, "The Blurred Boundaries of Public Administration," *Public Administration Review*, Vol. 40, March–April 1980.

24. House Committee on Budget, "Congressional Control of Expenditures," January 1977, p. 77.

25. The United States Budget for fiscal year 1986, 6–15.

26. See testimony of Dr. James Killian on Corporation for Public Broadcasting in hearings before Senate Commerce Committee on S. 1160, 90th Congress, 1st Session, pp. 140–41.

ministration. President Nixon vetoed the bill providing for two-year increased funding for the Corporation for Public Broadcasting because of "fundamental disagreements concerning the direction which public broadcasting has taken and should pursue in the future."[27] The veto was followed by John W. Macy, Jr.'s, resignation as the corporation's president. Macy had been chairman of the Civil Service Commission under President Johnson.

The Carnegie Commission on the Future of Public Broadcasting confirmed that "appointments to the CPB board have become highly politicized." The Commission concluded that the Corporation had not succeeded in providing "insulation from federal pressure."[28]

Labeling as "private" what is in reality "public" for cosmetic reasons or to obtain fictitious budget reductions can contribute to loss of faith in our democratic institutions. Misbranding is no less heinous because it is practiced by the government. The most flagrant example is the Energy Security Corporation proposed by President Carter.[29] Distinctions between what is public and what is private are becoming increasingly blurred, but we cannot abandon these distinctions altogether without fundamental alterations in our constitutional system. The maintenance of this distinction has been considered essential both to protect private rights from intrusion by the government and to prevent usurpation of government power.

If the Congress can turn public agencies into nongovernment institutions merely by waving its legislative wand, presumably there would be no legal bar to declaring that such agencies as the Tennessee Valley Authority and Federal Housing Administration are no longer agencies or instrumentalities of the United States. This device could be employed not only to exclude ex-

27. House Document No. 92–320.

28. Carnegie Commission on the Future of Public Broadcasting, *A Public Trust*, Bantam Books, 1979, pp. 70, 75.

29. Ronald C. Moe, "Government Corporations and the Erosion of Accountability: The Case of the Proposed Energy Security Corporation," *Public Administration Review*, Vol. 39, November–December 1979.

penditures from the budget, but also to circumvent the civil service laws and regulations, conflict-of-interest statutes, and other laws that control the conduct and activities of officers and employees of the United States.

Intermingling of public and private duties places public officials in an ambiguous position. There are many unanswered questions. Do the secretaries of housing and urban development and agriculture serve as directors of the National Home Ownership Foundation in their official capacity, or as private citizens? To whom are federal officials accountable for their actions as directors? If the foundation is not an agency and instrumentality of the United States, what then are its responsibilities to the president, the Congress, and, ultimately through them, the people?

The ambiguous status of government-sponsored enterprises inevitably generates conflicts with the government sponsors. The Federal National Mortgage Association insisted that HUD Secretary Patricia Harris exceeded her authority in directing that 30 percent of FNMA's mortgage purchases be made in inner city areas.[30] The secretary is authorized by law to require that "a reasonable portion of the corporation's mortgage purchases be related to the national goal of providing adequate housing for low- and moderate-income families, but with reasonable economic return to the corporation."

The laws creating COMSAT, Corporation for Public Broadcasting, National Home Ownership Foundation, National Park Foundation, National Railroad Passenger Corporation, Securities Investor Protection Corporation, and U.S. Railway Association contain significant gaps. No express authority is conferred on the president to remove directors whom he appoints. Is the power to remove implied in the power to appoint, or will the Supreme Court follow the doctrine laid down in the *Humphrey* and *Wiener* cases?

Other options are available to the Congress, which can minimize or eliminate these problems. Federally chartered or organized private corporations are by no means uncommon. These

30. *The New York Times,* February 22, 1978.

include national banks, federal savings and loan associations, small business investment companies, the Aerospace Corporation, and the Rand Corporation. But controls to protect the public interest have been provided by regulation, authority to give or withhold financial support, and contractual agreements without directly involving the government or government officials in the management of private organizations.

The New Federalism: Government by Contract. Why Congress favored the organizational approach typified by such government-sponsored enterprises as the Corporation for Public Broadcasting is a matter for speculation. It may reflect congressional disenchantment with the "think tanks" and other nonprofit corporations that have symbolized what Don K. Price calls "the new Federalism."[31] These institutions are creatures of the executive, not the Congress. Most of them were organized at the initiative of executive departments and financed under contracts that the Congress had no opportunity to review or approve. President Johnson launched the Urban Institute by press release. The pioneer nonprofit, the Rand Corporation, was sponsored by the Air Force in 1948, but it is doubtful that many members of the Congress were even aware of its existence until several years later.

The emergence of the nonprofit corporation is cited as "one of the most striking features of America's postwar organization."[32] As is characteristic of organization innovation in the United States, the nonprofit corporation evolved almost by accident and without conscious planning out of the need to devise institutional arrangements adapted to changing government requirements. Organization theories normally follow rather than precede organizational innovation. By the time the theoretical justification is developed, an institution is likely to have achieved maturity and may be in its dotage.

31. Don K. Price, *Government and Science—Their Dynamic Relation in American Democracy,* New York University Press, 1954.

32. Bruce L. R. Smith. "The Future of the Not-for-Profit Corporations," *The Public Interest,* No. 8, Summer 1967, a highly perceptive analysis of the growth, use, and potential of not-for-profit corporations.

Each major class of institutions is peculiarly a product of a particular epoch in U.S. history. Regulatory commissions were a response to problems growing out of the Industrial Revolution, notably the threat of monopolistic control of the nation's wealth and resources. Government corporations were born of war and depression. The dramatic developments resulting from the scientific and technological revolution commencing after World War II have had an enormous impact on the institutional structure and role of the federal government, business, and academic organizations.

Prior to World War II, the total federal research and development program is estimated to have cost about $100 million annually. In fiscal year 1950, total federal research and development expenditures were about $1.1 billion. In fiscal year 1986, the total is expected to reach $55 billion. The increase since 1950 demonstrates the extent to which major initiative and responsibility for promoting and financing research and development have shifted from private enterprise and universities to the federal government.

Given the magnitude of its new and rapidly expanding responsibilities, the government had no practical choice other than to enlist the support of outside organizations, which had or could obtain the necessary personnel and institutional resources. The proportion of the research and development budget allocated to direct federal operations has steadily declined. In his report to President Kennedy on "Government Contracting for Research Development," Budget Director David E. Bell saw no alternative to continued government reliance on the private sector "for the major share of the scientific and technical work which it requires."[33]

Today more than 80 percent of federal expenditures for research and development are made through nonfederal institutions. Most of it goes to established business and academic insti-

33. Bureau of the Budget, "Report to the President on Contracting for Research and Development," Senate Document No. 94, 87th Congress, 2nd Session, May 17, 1962, p. 2.

tutions, either in the form of grants or under cost-plus fixed-fee contracts. Cost-plus fixed-fee contracts generally are negotiated on a noncompetitive basis and provide for government reimbursement of all allowable project costs. The formula for calculating the fee is negotiated by parties to a contract. Because the "fee" constitutes a contractor's profit, the Bell report expressed doubts about the appropriateness of paying fees to nonprofit organizations and recommended that "development" or "general support allowances" be substituted.

Employment of contractors to conduct or support operations on behalf of the government is by no means new. "Contracting-out" has an ancient lineage. So convinced an advocate of laissez-faire as Adam Smith drew the line at the prevalent eighteenth-century practice of contracting-out the collection of public revenues to tax farmers. Smith believed that "Government, by establishing an administration under their own immediate inspection of the same kind with that which the farmer establishes, might at least save the profit, which is almost always exorbitant."[34]

What is new are the so-called GOCO contracts providing for private industry or university management and operation of such government-owned facilities as the Oak Ridge and Argonne National Laboratories, and the nonprofit corporations, organized independently or under university sponsorship. The nonprofit corporations fall into four main categories: (1) university-affiliated research institutes or laboratories that perform some applied research or experimental tasks, such as the Applied Physics Laboratory of the Johns Hopkins University; (2) corporations such as Aerospace and MITRE, created to furnish systems engineering and technical management services; (3) think tanks established to provide operations research and analytical services; and (4) social research and demonstrations.

Many figures have been bandied about as to the number of nonprofit corporations that are for all practical purposes government "captives." Bruce L. R. Smith attributes claims about the

34. Adam Smith, *The Wealth of Nations*, The Modern Library, Random House, 1937, p. 384.

proliferation of nonprofits to "idiosyncracies of definition." It is his view that there are about 20 organizations "that fit a reasonable definition of the [nonprofit] corporation as a nongovernmental entity with its own governing structure, dependent on government clients, but independent of the annual authorization and appropriation cycle of government agencies."[35]

All these corporations were organized by the government solely for the purpose of entering into contracts to furnish services to the government. In some instances, the government selected the "incorporators" of the nonuniversity-affiliated institutions. Charters were obtained under the laws of the state where the institution was incorporated. Individuals invited to serve as trustees were either picked by the contracting agency or chosen with its approval. Except for grants made by the Ford Foundation to provide initial working capital to Rand and the Institute for Defense Analyses, financing came entirely from the federal government.

In many respects the nonprofit corporations are indistinguishable from early government corporations chartered under state law. Seemingly, the Government Corporation Control Act provision that "no corporation shall be created, organized, or acquired by any officer or agency of the Federal Government . . . for the purpose of acting as an agency or instrumentality of the United States, except by or pursuant to an Act of Congress specifically authorizing such action" would apply to nonprofit corporations. Committee counsel raised this point during hearings on the Bell report but did not press his question.[36] The comptroller general has been discreetly silent on the subject.

General H. H. Arnold certainly did not intend to "create, organize, or acquire a corporation" when in 1945 he entered into a contract with the Douglas Aircraft Company for Project RAND. His objective was not to innovate, but to preserve the close association between the scientific community and the military that

35. Bruce Smith, "The Future of the Not-for-Profit Corporation."

36. House Committee on Government Operation, hearings on "Systems Development and Management," Part I, June 1962, pp. 57–58.

had been nurtured under Office of Scientific Research and Development auspices during World War II. The working partnership of the military and the scientists had produced significant advances in weaponry and in the deployment and use of weapons systems. This kind of capability could not be built into the formal Air Force organization structure without either bypassing the established chain of command or sacrificing direct access to the chief of staff. The first alternative was wholly unacceptable to the military and the second to the scientists.

By 1948 RAND had proved itself and there was every indication that the program would be continued and expanded. But the association with the Douglas Aircraft Company was a source of increasing uneasiness because of the potential for conflicts of interest. University affiliation was considered and rejected. With the concurrence of the Air Force and the Douglas Company, Rand was organized as an independent nonprofit corporation under the laws of the state of California.

Few realized at the time that Rand was the precursor of a new generation of federal instrumentalities. Rand itself fathered the System Development Corporation and Analytic Services, Inc. The Operations Research Organization established by the Army in 1947 as a Johns Hopkins University affiliate was converted in 1961 to the independent Research Analysis Corporation. In 1956 the Department of Defense asked a number of leading universities to sponsor the Institute for Defense Analyses. The Department of Defense organized the Logistics Management Institute in 1961. Use was confined to the military until 1968, when the Urban Institute was created.

Imposition of personnel "freezes" and inflexible personnel ceilings has spawned a new generation of nonprofit corporations to manage social demonstrations. Howard Rosen, director of Research and Development, Department of Labor, explained that the department had no choice but to organize the Manpower Demonstration Research Corporation, Corporation for Public/Private Ventures and Youthwork, to design and implement a complex $212.5 million youth employment and demonstration program. Speaking as one of the midwives of the Manpower Demonstration Research Corporation, Rosen stated: ". . . and you are told, don't hire anybody, but come in with these facts and information. Realistically, there is no alternative but a non-profit organization."[37]

Few of the copies captured fully the unique qualities that constituted the inner essence of Rand. The distinct characteristics that made Rand "different" were (1) its extremely broad terms of reference; (2) a high degree of autonomy in the choice of research projects and in setting deadlines; (3) acceptance as part of the Air Force team; (4) independence of the established hierarchy and military chain of command; (5) access to top decision makers; and (6) a research "atmosphere" conducive to original and nonconformist thinking.

Nonprofit "intermediaries" such as the Manpower Demonstration Research Corporation are performing tasks that government agencies would do themselves if they could hire the people. These are not advisory "think tanks," but program administrators. MDRC was designated to plan, design, and implement the Youth Incentive Entitlement project. It functions as a staff arm of the Labor Department, and its scope of operations is not left to the discretion of the corporation's directors.

Contract arrangements offer something far more tangible than an opportunity to create institutions with a suitable research environment. Nonprofit corporations, together with university-affiliated research centers and other types of contract organizations, provide a means for escaping irksome government controls and regulations. Salary limitations do not apply to contract personnel, nor do the ceilings on the number of civilian employees. The Armed Services find it easier to obtain money than to secure allocations of civilian "spaces," so there is a ready market for an organizational device that permits hiring outside the ceiling. Contract operations are funded under "contractual services,"

---

37. National Academy of Public Administration, *Government-Sponsored Nonprofits,* November 1978, p. 15. See this report for a general discussion of nonprofits.

which ordinarily would receive far less intensive OMB and congressional scrutiny than the object classifications for personnel services. To some extent, the nonprofit corporation fills the void left by the taming and assimilation of the government corporation.

As an added fillip, contracting may broaden the base of public support by fostering alliances with politically influential organizations and groups in the private community. This was a major factor motivating the Agency for International Development to contract out its operations wherever possible. Links of gold can be stronger than links of steel. Don Price has observed that "this new system is breaking down the political opposition to federal programs even more effectively than did the system of grants to the states."[38] Debates about improper government competition with private enterprise generate considerably less heat when public programs are administered by private agencies.

This immunity from political opposition does not necessarily extend to independent nonprofit corporations. Institutions like Rand have no constituency other than their own employees and government sponsor. More and more they are being looked on as the illegitimate offspring of the miscegenous mating of the public and private sectors. Profit-making companies resent the intrusion of nonprofit contractors into such fields as systems engineering and technical direction, which traditionally have been reserved for competitive industry. Universities are also fearful about competition from the nonprofits. Viewed as a device for broadening the base of public support, independent nonprofit corporations are considerably less effective than other types of contractual arrangements.

Rather modest steps to develop a new set of ground rules were taken with the issuance of Bureau of the Budget Circular No. A-49 in February 1958. The circular directed agencies to develop criteria for the use of management and operating contracts. Several functions were ruled "off-limits" for contracting, including direction, supervision, and control of government personnel, and

38. Don K. Price, *The Scientific Estate*, Oxford University Press, 1968, p. 73.

determination of basic government policies. Agencies were requested to consider other alternatives before contracting with an institution of higher learning to administer a large-scale applied research and development facility. The circular attracted little attention in the Department of Defense or the Congress, and efforts to obtain compliance were minimal.

In the same year, the Bureau of the Budget raised with the secretary of defense the possibility of creating a new type of organization, to be called a Research Institute, which would provide a means for reproducing within the government structure some of the more positive attributes of the nonprofit corporation. The suggestion was ignored at the time but revived in the Bell report, again with no results. The comptroller general in 1969 urged that the proposal be reconsidered.[39]

By 1961 contracting had grown to the point that, in the judgment of the House Appropriations Committee, "the Government is moving toward a chaotic condition in its personnel management because of this practice."[40] The committee stated the following in its report on the 1962 Defense Department appropriation bill:

> Some bold decisions must be made in regard to this mushrooming phenomenon before tremendous injury results to vital Defense programs and programs of other departments and agencies of the Federal Government.
>
> The employees of such organizations are paid indirectly by the taxpayer to the same extent as employees under civil service are paid directly by the taxpayer. The pertinent major difference is that their pay is higher. . . . To a considerable extent the use of contracts is merely a subterfuge to avoid the restrictions on civil service salary scales.

39. Comptroller General of the United States, report to the Congress on "Need for Improved Guidelines in Contracting for Research and Development with Government-Sponsored Non-profit Contractors," February 10, 1969, p. 59.

40. House Committee on Appropriations, Department of Defense Appropriation Bill 1962, House Report No. 574, 87th Congress, 1st Session, June 23, 1961, pp. 53–54.

The committee recommended a $5 million reduction in the Aerospace Corporation budget because its salaries and overhead were too high.

Deep concerns were also expressed in the Bell report, although it concluded "many kinds of arrangements—both direct federal operations and various patterns of contracting now in use—can and should be used to mobilize the talent and facilities needed to carry out the Federal research and development effort."[41] The need was emphasized for "discriminating" choices based on "getting the job done effectively and efficiently" and "avoiding assignments of work which would create inherent conflicts of interest."

The Bell report did recognize that affirmative measures were required both to arrest the progressive erosion of the government's in-house capability and to prevent nonprofit corporations from abusing their exemption from government controls and regulations. Salaries and related benefits and the use of fees to acquire capital facilities were singled out for special attention. When the contracting system itself did not provide built-in controls, such as by competitive bidding, it was recommended that the basic standard for approving salaries and related benefits should be comparability with compensation paid to persons doing similar work in the private economy. It was proposed also that upon dissolution of a nonprofit corporation the government should have first claim on its assets. Contractors were successful in blunting the full force and effect of these recommendations, but the recommendations foreshadowed clearly the trend of government policies. The nonprofit corporation has ceased to be a sanctuary from government controls and congressional scrutiny.

Rather than be assimilated into the system, organizations such as Rand have sought to reduce their dependence on the federal government. Rand was aggressively seeking to develop outside business even before the involvement of two Rand employees in the disclosure of the "Pentagon Papers" threatened federal support.

41. Bureau of the Budget, p. 8.

The comptroller general views with considerable concern the efforts by Rand and other government-sponsored nonprofits to solicit outside business. He foresees that "there would be problems if these organizations that have operated on Government funds and acquired their capabilities with Government support were to be allowed to move freely into the private economy" where they would have an "unfair" competitive advantage.[42]

The Bell report saw in a variety of clients a means for enhancing the objectivity and independence of organizations engaged in operations and policy research. But these anticipated benefits, which may well be illusory, are more than offset by the loss of mutual confidence and trust. There is a great deal of difference between being *the* client and being *a* client. Those advisers who are most influential have common goals and values and no divided loyalties.

Herbert Roback, counsel to the Military Operations Subcommittee of the House Committee on Government Operations, graphically pictured a scene with an "Air Force general pacing up and down the room" and "a Rand fellow lying on the couch listening to him."[43] This kind of relationship was jeopardized seriously when Rand began serving the Office of the Secretary of Defense and is bound to be eroded further as Rand becomes increasingly committed to clients other than the Air Force.

Government-sponsored nonprofit corporations are another manifestation of the prevailing antibureaucratic bias. The question is whether the nonprofits provide a cure or are merely symptomatic of basic but remediable deficiencies within the federal system.

The alternative of employing nonprofit intermediaries such as the Manpower Demonstration Research Corporation and think tanks on the Rand model should not be excluded when their superiority to government organizations can be demonstrated, but the decision should not be dictated by arbitrary and obsolete regulations. There is no bar to developing within the govern-

42. Comptroller General of the United States, p. 50.
43. House Committee on Government Operations, p. 64.

ment institutions that can function with speed, flexibility, and independence. Organizational innovation should not be confined to the nongovernmental sector. The time has come to recognize the need for diversity in government institutions and in the application of government controls.

Proliferation of twilight-zone agencies is likely to continue as long as the president and the Congress insist on playing a political shell game with employment statistics and off-budget expenditures. Personnel ceilings control not the number of those working for the federal government, but the number of those reported as working for the federal government. The *Washington Post* has estimated that the number of people paid by the federal government is well over double the number listed on the official civilian payroll.[44] Use of extragovernmental devices has enabled the president and the Congress to avoid facing up to the fact that they have created the conditions that now make it difficult for the bureaucracy to get things done.

44. *Washington Post,* July 10, 1978, also see Barbara Blumenthal, "Uncle Sam's Army of Invisible Employees," *National Journal,* May 5, 1979.

III

CONCLUDING OBSERVATIONS

13

Concluding Observations

If any thesis emerges from the previous chapters, it is that in the choice of institutional types and structural and procedural arrangements we are making decisions with significant political implications. In saying this, we do not imply that the administrative consequences of those decisions can be safely ignored. By allowing political expediency to dictate the design of administrative systems, a president can create major obstacles to the accomplishment of his basic political goals and the effective functioning of the democratic process. If present trends are not reversed, we run the risk that the federal structure will become, not a reflection, but a caricature of our pluralistic society.

At the very time when the solution of urgent national problems demands diversity in government institutions, flexibility, and effective cooperation among executive agencies, the federal government is moving in the opposite direction.

An organization structure that provides access for particular groups within the community is not necessarily flawed, unless it prejudicies policy outcomes, prevents teamwork, and permits private groups to exploit public institutions for their own benefit. The question is one of balance. One does not combat parochialism in the departments by bringing the interest group brokers into the White House. Neither is parochialism fought by inviting specialized interest associations and "public interest" lawyers to mold public policy in court. In designing any political structure, whether it be the Congress, the executive branch, or the judiciary, it is important to build arrangements that weigh the scale in favor of those advocating the national interest.

Structural arrangements and administrative systems can significantly affect the political balance and program results. But to prescribe reorganization as the cure-all for current frustrations reflects either a mistaken diagnosis or an inability to identify and come to grips with the real problems. Too often reorganization and procedural reform are employed to create the illusion of progress where none exists.

The federal government is well equipped to perform its traditional functions with reasonable effectiveness—to disburse money, administer grants and contracts, build dams, highways, and other public works, and collect taxes. The government has not yet developed the capability to deal with the highly complex social and economic problems confronting the nation, the solutions to which demand radically new approaches.

Failure to devise new institutions and to modify control systems in the light of the varied needs of modern government is reflected in the increasing reliance on extragovernmental institutions "to get the job done." William J. Grinker, president of Manpower Research Development Corporation, and others accept it as "simply a fact of life that many restrictions under which bureaucracies work impede their ability to hire quickly or reassign personnel to a new and complex undertaking." According to Grinker, there is no realistic alternative to the use of government-sponsored nonprofits and comparable twilight-zone agencies because "the government can, when necessary, spend money quickly, but it is less able to launch quickly a social program with a major, sophisticated research component."[1]

The nonprofits and government-sponsored enterprises are a means of avoiding, not solving, the critical problems confronting

1. National Academy of Public Administration, *Government-Sponsored Non-Profits*, November 1978, pp. 73, 90.

the government in the 1980s. It is more expedient to go outside the system altogether than to attempt the difficult and politically sensitive task of creating new institutional forms and reforming the central control systems. Often the central budget, personnel, procurement, and audit agencies would prefer to be bypassed rather than alter their uniform rules to accommodate diversity or depart from traditional ways of doing business.

Federal bureaucrats today are as much the victims as the cause of red tape. All too frequently the congressional, judicial, and White House response to complex substantive issues is the imposition of additional procedural constraints. As a result, limited personnel resources must be diverted to activities that contribute little, if anything, to the delivery of services.

One of the most respected and experienced public administrators, Dwight Ink, has warned that the present system discourages initiative and risk taking and "tends to confine thousands upon thousands of federal managers to a world in which processes, procedures, audits and investigations overshadow public service. Process also overwhelms substance in our system of rewards and punishment for federal employees." Ink concludes that "the way to improve government is not in further centralization of administrative procedures, or the addition of more debilitating checks and balances."[2]

Reorganizing the executive branch structure and the addition of judicial procedures will not produce the necessary new approaches or responsible and accountable public institutions capable of effectively performing *public* functions. If competence in government and improved service delivery are the objectives, then the place to start is with a cost-benefit analysis of existing controls and regulations.

Even before the Reagan administration effort on behalf of "regulatory relief," President Carter strongly advocated "deregulation" of private industry. In his 1978 State of the Union address, Carter emphasized that the government was "vigorously

2. Statement before the Senate Subcommittee on Post Office and General Services, September 19, 1984.

pursuing the effort begun last year to reduce the burden of out-dated, ineffective and nit-picking regulations." As persuasive a case can be made for "deregulating" the government. Efforts to eliminate either purely symbolic or counterproductive regula-tions and mandated procedures should be undertaken by the president, the Congress, and the central control agencies.

Deregulation cannot succeed without the support and coop-eration of the Congress. Support will not be forthcoming as long as efforts to reorganize and improve executive branch manage-ment are viewed as potential threats to committee and subcom-mittee jurisdictions and congressional prerogatives. Proponents of the legislative veto, dual reporting requirements, and com-parable arrangements that inject the Congress or its committees into the executive chain of command need to be persuaded that you do not strengthen the Congress as an institution by weaken-ing the president and the department heads. These arrangements enable the bureaucracy to play off one branch of the government against another and make it more difficult to maintain account-ability for executive actions. The Congress has found that it is incapable of satisfactorily controlling the U.S. Postal Service, reg-ulatory commissions, and government-sponsored enterprises that it has exempted in whole or in part from presidential oversight and direction.

Atomization of political power will not make government more responsive. The notion that our governmental institutions can be reformed by emasculating them persists. When political power is fractionalized, the capability to obtain positive action is seri-ously impaired. All that is left is the power to veto—a situation conducive to stalemate.

Administration of federal services will not be brought closer to the consumers by so diffusing authority that effective delega-tion is impossible. Centralization of authority must precede de-centralization. Whenever the exercise of executive authority is made contingent on agreement by the Congress or others at the headquarters level, delegation outside of Washington presents difficult problems and is sometimes impossible. A department head can only delegate the powers vested in him. Paradoxically, the centralization of procedural controls—regulatory review, budgetary mandating, and personnel constraints—is no more likely to promote agency responsiveness than the diffusion of authority. Such instruments are not only blunt and insensitive to local conditions, they are also difficult to delegate.

Proposals to break up the present constituencies by moving from a functional to a regional or geographic executive branch structure would merely substitute one form of particularism for another. National purposes will not be strengthened by reorganizing to give primary emphasis to sectional interests. These are even more difficult to deal with than conflicts among program areas. A member of Congress can defend politically measures that favor one program area over another but may feel constrained to demand "equal treatment" for the represented state or district. The pressure on the Congress to "log-roll" and to spread the money around on a geographic basis without regard to peculiar local needs or national priorities would be increased rather than abated.

To revive the ancient debate about the relative merits of departmentalization according to major purpose, major process, clientele, materiel, or geography would be profitless and divert attention from the real issues. The doctrine of organization according major purposes advanced by the President's Committee on Administrative Management and the first Hoover Commission has brought about a more logical and consistent grouping of government activities within the executive departments and eliminated such organizational anomalies as the assignment of health functions to Treasury and education functions to Interior—anomalies by no means uncommon in the period prior to 1939. Changes in our national values, goals, and priorities may well argue for some restructuring of the executive branch. But it should be recognized that structural change by itself cannot be expected to curb appreciably the power of the centrifugal forces within our governmental system or to get at the roots of our current difficulties.

The benefits that are supposed to flow from departmentalization are by no means automatic. The influence exercised by departmental headquarters is often negative and control oriented. Many departments remain "holding companies" composed of a collection of autonomous units each speaking for its own limited constituency. The walls between bureaus within a department may be as impermeable as those between departments, sometimes more so.

Reorganization studies have concentrated primarily on the organization of the executive branch with only relatively brief reference to internal departmental organization. Yet, as a determinant of organizational behavior, the latter is the most important. As a result of the recommendations of the first Hoover Commission, the Congress has removed some of the legal impediments to the exercise of secretarial authority. But it has shown no disposition to relax the extralegal restraints against internal reorganizations that upset committee jurisdictions or threaten to alter the balance of power among constituencies or between the constituencies and the secretary.

Cabinet secretaries rarely bring to their jobs the unique combination of political insight, administrative skill, leadership, intelligence, and creativity required for the successful management of heterogeneous institutions with multiple and sometimes conflicting purposes. Most are content to be a "mediator-initiator" or a reactor to initiatives coming from the White House, the Congress, the bureaucracy, and the several constituencies represented by the department. Anything other than a passive approach is likely to encounter opposition from the Congress, which believes that major bureaus should be allowed to run themselves without undue secretarial interference. This is especially true of the so-called professional bureaus. We accept the principle of civilian control of the military profession but not of the nonmilitary professions such as medicine, education, science, and engineering.

The Hoover Commission task force on departmental management recognized that "the external demands on a Secretary are such" that he or she cannot "give continuing attention to internal problems."[3] It assumed that the undersecretary, or, in the case of the Department of Defense, the deputy secretary, would become the "top internal point of departmental direction." Deputy secretaries of defense have been used in this way, as have such undersecretaries as Charles Murphy, who served under Secretary of Agriculture Orville Freeman, but these are the exceptions. An undersecretary suffers from much the same disabilities as the vice president and is subject to the same frustrations. Only under unusual circumstances is he able to establish the personal rapport and relationship of mutual trust with the secretary that are essential if he is to act as an "alter ego." He can exercise authority in his own right only when the secretary is absent or the secretarial post is vacant. Because anything he says is construed to represent departmental policy, he must be highly circumspect if he is to avoid the appearance of usurping secretarial prerogatives.

The failure of undersecretaries generally to evolve into general managers or executive vice presidents has left a vacuum within the departmental management systems that has never been satisfactorily filled. This vacuum cannot be filled merely by multiplying the number of staff advisers to the secretary. Attempts to use budget, planning, management, and analytical staffs to compensate for the deficiencies of line management are seldom successful and represent a misuse of staff talents. As one secretary expressed it, what he needed were "people to do the job," not more people to tell him how someone else should do the job.[4] Former HEW Secretary Folsom was making the same point when he said that we had made considerable progress in strengthening the staff resources available to a secretary and now his "chief concern was the need for more line officers."[5]

As departments are presently organized, a secretary is con-

3. Commission on Organization of the Executive Branch of the Government, task force report on "Department Management," January 1949, p. 11.

4. Based on notes of personal conversation.

5. Senate Committee on Government Operations, Subcommittee on Executive Reorganization, hearings on "Modernizing the Federal Government," January–May 1968, p. 221.

fronted with a dilemma. If he utilizes his assistant secretaries as line officers, then he has no one at the top political level with departmentwide perspective whom he can use for assignments that cut across program jurisdictions. If he uses his assistant secretaries as staff, then he has no one between him and the bureau chiefs on whom he can rely to get jobs done. We find no consistent pattern within the executive departments, but the trend is toward using assistant secretaries in the line, with the notable exception of the Department of Transportation.

There is probably no pat solution to this dilemma. No two departments have identical managerial requirements. Each must have a system adapted to its own environment. It seems clear, however, that present restrictions on establishing executive positions at the undersecretary and assistant secretary level, limiting the transfer or pooling of appropriations among organizational units to achieve common program objectives, and specifying the details of departmental organization and administrative procedures inhibit managerial innovation and experimentation. As James E. Webb points out, "if the organizational framework in which executives are fitted is rigid, the executive cannot be flexible."[6]

Departments are structured to administer national programs in accordance with uniform national standards. Solutions to many of our current problems require programs that are tailored to the special needs of a particular region or community. These types of programs by their very nature cut horizontally across established departmental jurisdictions at all levels of government. It is with respect to horizontal organization that the conventional wisdom of the orthodox doxology is least helpful. Hierarchical concepts of management cannot be applied to many of the newer social programs, which require the collaboration of a number of coequal government organizations on a single project, without any one having final authority.

The rigidities in our departmental systems are major deter-

6. James E. Webb, *Space-Age Management*, McGraw-Hill Book Co., 1969, p. 141.

rents to lateral communications and cooperative efforts. Agencies find it difficult to work together when they have incompatible administrative systems. It is as if we had designed one system to operate on 25-cycle current and another on 60-cycle. Converters are expensive and inefficient.

Up to now, insufficient attention has been given within either the executive branch or the Congress to the need for standardizing administrative provisions. Differences often reflect nothing more than historical accident or the predilections of a particular agency lawyer or congressional committee. Congress has no procedures for central review of proposed legislation or regulations to eliminate inconsistencies and conflicts in nonsubstantive administrative provisions. Administrative requirements in closely related programs may differ with respect to rulemaking, documentation to establish eligibility, control of property and funds, personnel standards, reporting procedures, geographic boundaries, auditing, planning, and definitions of common items such as "facilities."

For the horizontal programs, we need the "adaptive, rapidly changing temporary systems" advocated by Warren Bennis. Flexibility is essential so that the resources and people to solve specific problems can be drawn on regardless of organizational boundaries. In designating project managers, there is a need for discretion to ignore traditional hierarchical distinctions among departments and agencies, secretaries, administrators, and directors.

Needed changes in the present system are not likely to be produced by management improvement spectaculars launched from time to time by the Office of Management and Budget. The most recent example is President Reagan's much publicized "Reform 88." White House interest in such programs rarely extends beyond the press release announcing its creation.

Centrally directed and controlled management improvement programs can well be counterproductive. Comptroller General Charles A. Bowsher criticizes the centrally directed approach as causing "unavoidable confusion between the issues of program policy and program implementation" and allowing "those responsible for day-to-day management of government programs and agencies to escape accountability for the results of their actions." He warns that[7]

> The centrally directed approach diverts energy and attention from the operating agencies, where the problems really are and where effective solutions must be found and implemented. OMB, GSA, and OPM cannot create, operate, and maintain effective management systems and procedures on their own; only the operating agencies can do that.

In the Reagan administration there is an additional tendency to confuse effective management with managerial controls. Great emphasis has been placed on ideological loyalty and central clearance of communications as well as budgets, regulations, and personnel decisions and far less on managerial competence and experience. Ultimately, competent government, however well organized and controlled from above, cannot be obtained without managerial skills. Whether the government succeeds or fails will depend on its ability to recruit, develop, and effectively use career managers.

The president's primary task is leadership: setting national goals and priorities and mobilizing public support for his programs. Once he has established his goals, then he needs to consider carefully the means to be employed in reaching them. His decisions on program design, institutional type, organizational jurisdiction, and management system may well determine who will control and benefit from a program and, ultimately, whether national objectives are achieved. These decisions should not be governed solely by application of traditional organization doctrines. In evaluating the design and organization of new programs or proposed reorganizations of existing programs, the basic questions to be asked are the following

7. Charles A. Bowsher, "Building Effective Public Management," *The Bureaucrat*, Vol. 13, Winter 1984–85.

1. What is the nature of the constituency that is being created, or acquired, and to what extent will it be able to influence policies and program administration?
2. Is the constituency broadly based or does it represent narrow interests antithetical to some of the public purposes to be accomplished by the program?
3. What committees of the Congress will exercise jurisdiction and to what extent do they reflect the interests of the constituencies to be served by the program or those of groups hostile to program objectives?
4. What is the culture and tradition of the administering department or agency? Will it provide an environment favorable to program growth, stunt development, or produce a hybrid?
5. What are the constituencies to whom the administering agency responds? Would there be any obvious conflicts of interest?
6. Where are the loci of power with respect to program administration: the president, the agency head, the bureaus, congressional committees, professional guilds, interest groups, and so on? Are provisions made to ensure an appropriate balance of power and to prevent domination by any single group? Are the ultimate powers of the president protected and supported?
7. To what extent and in what way is access to those with decision-making power limited?
8. Does the program design foster dominance by a particular professional perspective and will this result in distortion of program goals?
9. Is provision made for an "open" system engineered in such a way that there are no built-in obstacles to joint administration with related government programs and cooperative efforts?
10. What safeguards are provided to ensure that no group or class of people is excluded from participation in the program and an equitable share in program benefits?

11. Do the type of institution and proposed organization provide the status, visibility, public support, and administrative system appropriate to the function to be performed?

12. Do the organizational and procedural arrangements simplify or complicate the problems of defining responsibility and maintaining accountability for program results? To what extent do they encourage "buck passing"?

Whether or not meaningful improvements in executive branch organization and in the management of the federal system can be obtained will depend in part on reorganization of the congressional committee structure. The particularistic elements in our society will always triumph over the general interest as long as they are nourished and supported by committees and subcommittees that share their limited concerns. At a minimum, committee and subcommittee jurisdictions should be compatible with current assignments of responsibilities within the executive branch and take into account interrelationships among programs so as to permit unified consideration of closely related and interdependent programs and evaluation of program objectives. Even modest reforms are unlikely, however, unless an informed and aroused electorate demands that the Congress modernize its organization and procedures. The assumption that only members of Congress are affected by congressional organization is no longer tenable.

Improved organizational effectiveness will also depend on the treatment of regulatory and management issues by the Judiciary. The much enlarged role of the courts as administrative overseers and a parallel increase in demands for more formalized procedures at all levels not only have increased organizational rigidity and complexity, they have further blurred the lines of responsibility and accountability. Because judicial toleration of administrative discretion is now far less than in the past, the procedural demands of statutory mandates to administrators must be determined in advance by Congress and the president. Otherwise they will be discovered by the courts.

The Hoover Commission doctrines were somewhat dated when they were first published. They have served their purpose, and most of the basic recommendations have been implemented. Our government has undergone revolutionary changes in the thirty-five years that have elapsed since the Hoover reports. The principles of organization advanced by the Hoover Commission have not lost their validity, but read by themselves they do not contribute materially to our understanding of current problems of government organization and management. It is fruitless to look to them for solutions.

We will compound the problems if we demand simple answers. The growing interdependence of the federal government, state and local governments, and many private institutions; increasing reliance on administration by grant, contract, and regulation; and the greater utilization of multijurisdictional programs have added new dimensions to public administration. Whatever strategy is devised must be as sophisticated as the problems it seeks to solve and retain sufficient flexibility to permit rapid adjustments to changing circumstances. It cannot deal with the executive branch as if it existed in isolation and must take into account the linkages between congressional and executive organization, and the Judiciary. If we persist in thinking of organization in terms of lines and boxes on an organization chart, our efforts to discover viable approaches to our current dilemma will certainly fail.

Select Bibliography

General

Appleby, Paul H. *Policy and Administration*. University of Alabama Press, 1949.

Bennis, Warren G. *Changing Organizations: Essays on the Development and Evaluation of Human Organization*. McGraw-Hill Book Co., 1966.

Committee on Governmental Affairs, U.S. Senate. *The Federal Executive Establishment: Evolution and Trends*. Committee Print, 96th Congress, 2nd Session, May 1980.

Comptroller General of the United States. *Implementation: The Missing Link in Planning Reorganization*. March 20, 1981.

Emmerich, Herbert. *Federal Reorganization and Administrative Management*. University of Alabama Press, 1971.

Gulick, Luther and L. Urwick, eds. *Papers on the Science of Administration*. Institute of Public Administration, 1937.

Kaufman, Herbert. "Reflections on Administrative Reorganization." In *Setting National Priorities: The 1978 Budget*. The Brookings Institution, 1977.

March, James G. and Johan P. Olson. "Organizing Political Life: What Administrative Reorganization Tells Us About Government." *American Political Science Review*, No. 77, 1983.

McConnell, Grant. *Private Power and American Democracy*. Alfred A. Knopf, 1967.

Moe, Ronald C. *The Hoover Commissions Revisited*. Westview Press, 1982.

Polenberg, Richard. *Reorganizing Roosevelt's Government: The Con-

troversy Over Executive Reorganization 1936–1939. Harvard University Press, 1966.

Short, Lloyd Milton. *The Development of National Administrative Organization in the United States.* The Johns Hopkins Press, 1923.

Skowronek, Stephen. *Building a New American State: The Expansion of National Administrative Capacities 1877–1920.* Cambridge University Press, 1982.

Szanton, Peter, ed. *Federal Reorganization: What Have We Learned?* Chatham House, 1981.

Waldo, Dwight. *The Administrative State.* 2nd ed., Holmes and Meier, 1984.

Congress

Craig, Barbara H. *The Legislative Veto: Congressional Control of Regulation.* Westview Press, 1983.

Davidson, Roger H. and Walter J. Oleszek. *Congress Against Itself.* Indiana University Press, 1977.

Fenno, Richard F., Jr. *Congressmen in Committee.* Little, Brown and Co., 1973.

Fisher, Louis. *The Politics of Shared Power.* Congressional Quarterly Press, 1981.

Gilmour, Robert S. and Barbara H. Craig. "After the Legislative Veto: Assessing Alternatives." *Journal of Policy Analysis and Management,* Vol. 3, No. 3, 1984.

Kirst, Michael W. *Government Without Passing Laws.* University of North Carolina Press, 1969.

Sundquist, James L. *The Decline and Resurgence of the Congress.* The Brookings Institution, 1981.

Wilson, Woodrow. *Congressional Government.* Meridian Books, 1956.

The Presidency

Califano, Joseph A., Jr., *Governing America.* A Touchstone Book, 1981.

Heclo, Hugh A. *A Government of Strangers: Executive Politics in Washington.* The Brookings Institution, 1977.

Heclo, Hugh A. and Lester Salamon. *The Illusion of Presidential Government.* Westview Press, 1981.

Mosher, Frederick L. "The Changing Responsibilities and Tactics of the Federal Government." *Public Administration Review,* November–December 1980.

Mosher, Frederick C. et al. *Watergate: Implications for Responsible Government*. Basic Books, 1974.

Nathan, Richard P. *The Administrative Presidency*. John Wiley & Sons, Inc., 1983.

National Academy of Public Administration. *Revitalizing Federal Management: Managers and Their Overburdened Systems*. November 1983.

Redford, Emmette S. and Marlin Blissett. *Organizing the Executive Branch: The Johnson Presidency*. The University of Chicago Press, 1981.

Salamon, Lester M. "Rethinking Public Management: Third Party Government and the Changing Forms of Government Action." *Public Policy*, Vol. 29, No. 3, Summer 1981.

Salamon, Lester M. and Michael S. Lund, eds. *The Reagan Presidency and Governing America*. The Urban Institute, 1985.

Szanton, Peter, ed. *Federal Reorganization: What Have We Learned?* Chatham House, 1981.

Wayne, Stephen. *The Legislative Presidency*. Harper & Row, 1978.

Judiciary

Advisory Commission on Intergovernmental Relations. *Regulatory Federalism: Policy, Process, Impact and Reform* (A–95). February 1984.

Carter, Lief H. *Contemporary Constitutional Lawmaking: The Supreme Court and the Art of Politics*. Pergamon Press, 1985.

Chayes, Abram. "The Role of the Judge in Public Law Litigation." *Harvard Law Review*, Vol. 89, 1975, p. 129.

Cooper, Phillip J. *Public Law and Public Administration*. Mayfield Publishing Co., 1983.

Cortner, Richard C. *The Bureaucracy in Court*. Kennikat Press, 1982.

Cox, Archibald. *The Role of the Supreme Court in American Government*. Oxford University Press, 1976.

Cramton, Roger C. "Judicial Law Making and Administration." *Public Administration Review*, Vol. 36, September–October 1976, p. 551.

Davis, Kenneth Culp. *Administrative Law Text*, 3rd ed. West Publishing Co., 1972.

———. *Administrative Law Treatise*. Vols. 1–5. K. C. Davis Publishing Co., 1978–84.

Friendly, Henry J. "Some Kind of Hearing." *Pennsylvania Law Review*, Vol. 123, 1973, p. 1267.

Horowitz, Donald L. *The Courts and Social Policy*. The Brookings Institution, 1977.

346   *Bibliography*

Johnson, Frank M. "The Constitution and the Federal District Judge."
     Texas Law Review, Vol. 54, 1976, p. 903.
Neely, Richard. *How Courts Govern America.* Yale University Press,
     1981.
Pederson, William E., Jr. "Formal Records and Informal Rulemaking."
     Yale Law Journal, Vol. 65, 1975, p. 38.
Rabkin, Jeremy. "Captive of the Court: A Federal Agency in Receiver-
     ship," *Regulation,* May–June 1984, p. 16.
Schwartz, Bernard. *Administrative Law,* 2nd ed. Little, Brown and Co.,
     1984.
Stewart, Richard B. "The Reformation of American Administrative
     Law." *Harvard Law Review,* Vol. 88, 1975, p. 1669.
Wood, Robert. "Professionals at Bay: Managing Boston's Public
     Schools." *Journal of Policy Analysis and Management,* Vol. 1,
     Summer 1982, p. 454.

The Executive Establishment

Crozier, Michael. *The Bureaucratic Phenomenon.* University of Chicago
     Press, 1963.
Halperin, Morton H. *Bureaucratic Politics and Foreign Policy.* The
     Brookings Institution, 1974.
Heclo, Hugh A. *A Government of Strangers: Executive Politics in
     Washington.* The Brookings Institution, 1977.
Katzman, Robert A. *Regulatory Bureaucracy.* The MIT Press, 1980.
Kaufman, Herbert. *The Administrative Behavior of Federal Bureau
     Chiefs.* The Brookings Institution, 1981.
Kaufman, Herbert. *The Forest Ranger—A Study of Administrative Be-
     havior.* The Johns Hopkins Press, 1960.
Kiern, Lawrence I. "Changing the Guard." *Naval Institute Proceedings,*
     February 1985.
Lambright, W. Henry. *Governing Science and Technology.* Oxford
     University Press, 1976.
Mosher, Frederick C. *Democracy and the Public Service,* 2nd ed. Ox-
     ford University Press, 1982.
Navasky, Victor S. *Kennedy Justice.* Atheneum, 1971.
Rourke, Francis E. *Bureaucracy, Politics and Public Policy.* Little,
     Brown and Co., 1969.
Webb, James E. *Space-Age Management.* McGraw-Hill Book Co., 1969.

Federal System

Advisory Commission on Intergovernmental Relations. *The Federal Influence on State and Local Roles in the Federal System* (A–89). November 1981.

———. *The Federal Role in the Federal System: Restoring Confidence and Competence* (A–86).

———. *The Future of Federalism in the 1980's* (M–126). July 1981.

Brown, Lawrence D., James W. Fossett, and Kenneth T. Palmer. *The Changing Politics of Federal Grants*. The Brookings Institution, 1984.

Derthick, Martha. *The Influence of Federal Grants*. Harvard University Press, 1970.

Derthick, Martha and Gary Bombardier. *Between State and Nation: Regional Organization of the United States*. The Brookings Institution, 1974.

Grodzins, Morton. *The American System,* Daniel J. Elazar, ed. Rand McNally and Co., 1966.

Hale, George E. and Marian Lief Palley. *The Politics of Federal Grants*. Congressional Quarterly Press, 1981.

Hawkins, Robert B. Jr. ed. *American Federalism a New Partnership for the Republic*. Institute for Contemporary Studies, 1982.

Ruttenberg, Stanley H. and Jocelyn Gutchess. *The Federal State Employment Service: A Critique*. The Johns Hopkins Press, 1970.

Salamon, Lester M. and Michael S. Lund, eds. *The Reagan Presidency and the Governing of America*. The Urban Institute Press, 1985.

Sanford, Terry, *Storm over the States*. McGraw-Hill Book Co., 1967.

Walker, David B. *Toward a Functioning Federalism*. Winthrop Publishers, Inc., 1981.

Typology

Adams, Gordon. *The Politics of Defense Contracting*. Transaction Books, 1982.

Goldberg, Sidney D. and Harold Seidman. *The Government Corporation: Elements of a Model Charter*. Public Administration Service, 1983.

Moe, Ronald C. *Administering Public Functions at the Margins of Government: The Case of Federal Corporations*. HD2755. Congressional Research Service, December 1, 1983.

Moe, Ronald C. *The Federal Executive Establishment: Evolution and Trends*. Prepared for the Senate Committee on Governmental

Affairs by the Congressional Research Service (Committee Print). May 1980.

Musolf, Lloyd. *Uncle Sam's Private Profit Seeking Corporations.* Lexington Books, 1983.

Newland, Chester A. "Executive Office Policy Apparatus: Enforcing the Reagan Agenda." In the *Reagan Presidency and the Governing of America,* Lester M. Salamon and Michael S. Lund, eds. The Urban Institute Press, 1985.

Noll, Roger G. *Reforming Regulation.* The Brookings Institution, 1971.

Orlans, Harold, ed. *Nonprofit Organizations: A Government Management Tool.* Praeger, 1980.

Seidman, Harold. "Government Sponsored Enterprise in the United States." In *The New Political Economy,* Bruce L. R. Smith, ed. Macmillan & Co. (London), 1975.

———. "Public Enterprise Autonomy: Need for a New Theory." *International Review of Administrative Sciences,* Vol. XLIX, No. 1, 1983.

———. "Public Enterprise in the United States." *Annals of Public and Cooperative Economy,* No. 1, March 1983.

———. "A Typology of Government." In *Federal Reorganization: What Have We Learned?* Peter Szanton, ed. Chatham House, 1981.

Index